Foreword

Scientists from four countries cooperated in a research effort aimed at the improvement of operational reliability via innovations in design and testing and systematic maintenance. The scientists had varied backgrounds ranging from mathematics to applied mechanical engineering, and the results of this effort are documented in this book. The research programme involved seminars and workshops open to academia and industry, and the undersigned has had the pleasure of participating in two of these. The level of discussions was generally of a high quality, particularly with regard to the engineering issues; the unique aspect was the comradeship between those with a mathematical orientation and those with an engineering orientation. I am convinced that more such collaborative platforms will be the way of the future, and will help enhance the state of the art of the subject.

By way of a selective overview, and an associated commentary, the following points come to mind.

Sören Andersson emphasizes, and rightly so, the importance of testing, making it an integral part of the product development process. This is in line with Taguchi's call for planned experimentation and testing.

The word 'tribology' refers to the science and technology of interacting surfaces in relative motion. Kenneth Holmberg gives what is to me an excellent overview of tribological accelerated life testing. In this paper, he describes various types of wear and the effects of lubricants on these. Upon reading this work, I am left with the conviction that even though wear can be thought of and described in physical terms, its characterization has to be in terms of probabilistic considerations. The role of factorial designs for accelerated testing is alluded to as a way of getting more information, but the notion of information needs elaboration. Eldar Onsøyen continues with Holmberg's theme on accelerated life testing of tribological components but emphasizes the role of condition monitoring with such tests. For statisticians interested in getting a better feel for the engineer's notion of ageing and wear, the above two papers would be a valuable overview.

Akersten, Bergman and Pörn talk about reliability information from failure data, and in so doing give an exposition of Bayes—Empirical Bayes modelling and its role in reliability analysis. Also, their discussion on various sources of potential information and the utility of such information is *de facto* an advocacy for the use of 'meta analysis' in reliability. The paper by Huseby and Natvig is more mathematical than the other papers in this collection; the emphasis here is on the use of dependent expert opinion in reliability—a topic which is gaining prominence in the practice of the subject. Finally, Simola, Laakso, and Hänninen, Kosonen and Unga talk of the occurrence and analysis of point process data in maintainability studies of nuclear power plants. A Bayesian analysis of their data would be an interesting alternative to the strategy taken by the aforementioned, especially since the nuclear industry has accumulated rich sources of expert opinions and engineering judgments in dealing with its operations.

The papers by Al-Najjar, Kuoppala *et al.* and Radzikowski emphasize the role of condition monitoring in reliability studies. This is one area of research which, though very relevant and promising, has pretty much been overlooked by most theoretical researchers in reliability even though its connection with the Cox model of biostatistics is obvious. I am hopeful that future research in reliability theory will focus on this issue which seems to be gaining much favour with engineers.

The final five papers of this volume take reliability engineering into the high-technology arena by talking about 'expert systems' and the use of computer graphic visual images in monitoring the performance of complex systems. These appear to be attractive possibilities whose impact only time can tell. A natural possibility for advancing the state of the art here is to merge the ideas of Huseby and Natvig with regard to expert opinion into the general schemata of the above five papers.

By way of a closing comment, it is gratifying to note that the theory and practice of reliability is thriving in the Scandinavian countries and in Europe as a whole. This book is a fine testament to the collaborative

OPERATIONAL RELIABILITY AND SYSTEMATIC MAINTENANCE

OPERATIONAL RELIABILITY AND SYSTEMATIC MAINTENANCE

Edited by

K. HOLMBERG & A. FOLKESON

Editorial board
C. AAGE, S. ANDERSSON, B. BERGMAN, A. FOLKESON (Secretary),
K. HOLMBERG (Chairman), R. ØSTVIK

ELSEVIER APPLIED SCIENCE
LONDON and NEW YORK

ELSEVIER SCIENCE PUBLISHERS LTD
Crown House, Linton Road, Barking, Essex IG11 8JU, England

Sole Distributor in the USA and Canada
ELSEVIER SCIENCE PUBLISHING CO., INC.
655 Avenue of the Americas, New York, NY 10010, USA

WITH 8 TABLES AND 133 ILLUSTRATIONS

© 1991 ELSEVIER SCIENCE PUBLISHERS LTD

British Library Cataloguing in Publication Data

Operational reliability and systematic maintenance.
1. Engineering equipment. Testing
I. Holmberg, K. II. Folkeson A.
620.004

ISBN 1-85166-612-5

Library of Congress Cataloging-in-Publication Data

Operational reliability and systematic maintenance / K. Holmberg & A. Folkeson (editors).
    p.   cm.
Includes bibliographical references and index.
ISBN 1-85166-612-5
1. Reliability (Engineering)   2. Maintainability (Engineering)   3. Accelerated life testing.
4. Industrial equipment—Reliability.   I. Holmberg, K. (Kenneth) II. Folkeson, A.
TA169.069   1991   91-11181
620'.00452—dc20   CIP

Photoset by Interprint Ltd (Malta)
Printed in Great Britain at the University Press, Cambridge

efforts between engineers, mathematicians and statisticians working on reliability problems. Hopefully this effort is a precursor to similar future endeavours. I enjoyed my association with the individuals involved, both professionally and personally.

Nozer D. Singpurwalla
Washington, DC, USA

Preface

This book gives a review of the results created by a Nordic research programme, 'Terotechnology—Operational Reliability and Systematic Maintenance', which has been running from 1988 through 1990. It has involved the following research centres and institutes in Denmark, Finland, Norway and Sweden:

— The Technical University of Denmark (DTH), Department of Ocean Engineering and Institute for Production Management and Industrial Engineering
— The Foundation for Scientific and Industrial Research at the Norwegian Institute of Technology (SINTEF), Production Engineering Department
— Linköping University (LiTH), Department of Design and Production
— Risø National Laboratory, Denmark, System Analysis Department and Electronics Department
— The Royal Institute of Technology (KTH), Stockholm, Department of Fluid Technology and Department of Machine Elements
— The Technical Research Centre of Finland (VTT), Electrical Engineering Laboratory and Production Engineering Laboratory
— The University of Oslo (UiO), Institute of Mathematics

Important sources of finance have been:

— The Nordic Industrial Fund
— The Danish Technical Research Council (STVF)
— The Council of Technology (Teknologirådet), Denmark

— The Ministry of Industry and Trade, Finland
— The Federation of Finnish Metal Engineering and Electromechanical Industries (FIMET)
— The Technology Development Centre of Finland (TEKES)
— The Royal Norwegian Council for Scientific and Industrial Reseach (NTNF)
— The Swedish Association of Engineering Industries (Sveriges Mekanförbund)
— The Swedish National Board for Technical Development (STU)
— The Center for Maintenance Research (UTC), Sweden

Industrial companies in all four countries and the participating institutes have taken care of the rest of the financing. The sponsorship from the Nordic Industrial Fund has been absolutely necessary for keeping this multinational undertaking together.

The purpose of the programme was to help achieve better reliability and reduced maintenance cost for industrial equipment by developing methods for testing, condition monitoring and treatment of data, especially in the communication between designers and users. The end objective was to improve industrial competency in the Nordic countries. By publishing this book, we hope to achieve this.

We would like to thank all the people involved, especially two particular persons involved in the early stages of the programme. The late Professor Helge Christensen took part enthusiastically in the planning work until his much too early death put an end to his engagement. Professor Nils Mustelin played an important role by helping to bring people together, structuring the problem area and organizing funding efforts. His engagement ended when his organization, the Nordic Cooperative Organization for Applied Research (Nordforsk), was discontinued. The enthusiasm and inspiration shown by those two remarkable persons has been of great importance in the continuation of our work.

Kenneth Holmberg & Anders Folkeson

Contents

List of Contributors

Numbers in parentheses indicate the chapter(s) with the author's contribution.

CHRISTIAN AAGE (4.5), *The Technical University of Denmark, Department of Ocean Engineering, DK-2800 Lyngby, Denmark*
PER-ANDERS AKERSTEN (2.1), *Akerstens Tillförlitlighetsteknik AB, PO Box 9055, S-650 09 Karlstad, Sweden*
BASIM AL-NAJJAR (3.1), *Linköping University, Department of Mechanical Engineering, Division of Quality Technology, S-581 83 Linköping, Sweden*
SÖREN ANDERSSON (1.1), *Royal Institute of Technology, Department of Machine Elements, S-100 44 Stockholm, Sweden*
BO BERGMAN (1.4, 2.1), *Linköping University, Department of Design and Production, Division of Quality Technology, S-581 83 Linköping, Sweden*
PALLE CHRISTENSEN (4.3), *Risø National Laboratory, DK-4000 Roskilde, Denmark*
PETRI ENWALD (3.2), *Technical Research Centre of Finland, Laboratory of Production Engineering, PO Box 111, SF-02151 Espoo, Finland*
ANDERS FOLKESON (Introduction), *Royal Institute of Technology, Department of Machine Elements, S-100 44 Stockholm, Sweden*
NILS GJERSØE FOG (4.5), *The Technical University of Denmark, Department of Ocean Engineering, DK-2800 Lyngby, Denmark*
CHRISTIAN HAGE (4.4), *The Technical University of Denmark, Institute of Production Management and Industrial Engineering, DK-2800 Lyngby, Denmark*
MOHSEN HAKIM (1.4), *Linköping University, Department of Design and*

Production, Division of Quality Technology, S-581 83 Linköping, Sweden
SEPPO HÄNNINEN (2.3), *Technical Research Centre of Finland, Laboratory of Electrical Engineering and Automation Technology, SF-02150 Espoo, Finland*
KENNETH HOLMBERG (1.2), *Technical Research Centre of Finland, Laboratory of Production Engineering, SF-02150 Espoo, Finland*
A.B. HUSEBY (2.2), *University of Oslo, Institute of Mathematics, PO Box 1053, Blindern, N-0316 Oslo 3, Norway*
ERKKI JANTUNEN (3.2), *Technical Research Centre of Finland, Laboratory of Production Engineering, PO Box 111, SF-02151 Espoo, Finland*
HANS ERIK KONGSØ (4.3), *Risø National Laboratory, DK-4000 Roskilde, Denmark*
MIKKO KOSONEN (2.3), *Teollisuuden Voima Oy, SF-27160 Olkiluoto, Finland*
RAUNO KUOPPALA (3.2), *The Finnish Defence Forces, General Headquarters, Electrotechnical Section, PO Box 919, SF-00101 Helsinki, Finland*
KARI LAAKSO (2.3), *Technical Research Centre of Finland, Laboratory of Electrical Engineering and Automation Technology, SF-02150 Espoo, Finland*
KURT LAURIDSEN (4.2), *Risø National Laboratory, DK-4000 Roskilde, Denmark*
B. NATVIG (2.2), *University of Oslo, Institute of Mathematics, PO Box 1053, Blindern, N-0316 Oslo 3, Norway*
ELDAR ONSØYEN (1.3), *SINTEF, The Foundation for Scientific and Industrial Research at the Norwegian Institute of Technology, N-7034 Trondheim, Norway*
REIDAR ØSTVIK (4.1), *SINTEF, The Foundation for Scientific and Industrial Research at the Norwegian Institute of Technology, N-7034 Trondheim, Norway*
JETTE L. PAULSEN (4.2), *Risø National Laboratory, DK-4000 Roskilde, Denmark*
KURT PÖRN (2.1), *Studsvik Nuclear AB, S-611 82 Nyköping, Sweden*
URHO PULKKINEN (3.4), *Technical Research Centre of Finland, Laboratory of Electrical and Automation Engineering, PO Box 34, SF-02150 Espoo, Finland*
PAWEL RADZIKOWSKI (3.3), *Royal Institute of Technology, Department of Fluid Technology, S-100 44 Stockholm, Sweden*
KAISA SIMOLA (2.3), *Technical Research Centre of Finland, Laboratory of Electrical Engineering and Automation Technology, SF-02150 Espoo, Finland*

NOZER D. SINGPURWALLA (Foreword), *The George Washington University, Institute for Reliability and Risk Analysis, Washington, DC, USA*
UFFE THORSTEINSSON (4.4), *The Technical University of Denmark, Institute of Production Management and Industrial Engineering, DK-2800 Lyngby, Denmark*
ESA UNGA (2.3), *Teollisuuden Voima Oy, SF-27160 Olkiluoto, Finland*

Introduction

Reliability and Maintenance Technology

ANDERS FOLKESON

Royal Institute of Technology, Department of Machine Elements,
S-100 44 Stockholm, Sweden

The problem area dealt with in this volume can be divided into four principal parts:

(1) Accelerated Testing
(2) Failure Data Information
(3) Condition Monitoring
(4) Availability Performance Assurance

Figure 1 shows the structure and interaction between these parts. In order to secure good availability performance, reliability issues have to be considered at the planning and design stages. The information exchange between designers and machine users is very important. Testing is necessary for prediction of the operative performance and life of components or machines. To achieve realistic testing times, the testing is usually performed under accelerated conditions. For machinery used in production, condition monitoring is an important way of controlling maintenance efforts in order to avoid outage. Statistical treatment of failure data from the operation of machinery is another important tool for securing availability performance.

PART 1: ACCELERATED TESTING

In the product development process it is necessary to verify that new designs meet reliability requirements. Identification of weak points or

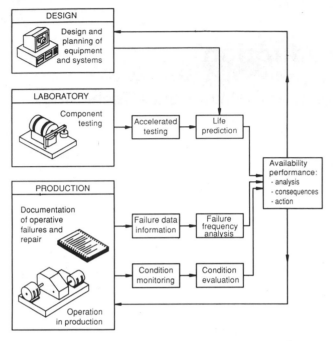

Fig. 1. Methods for improvement of operational reliability.

estimation of the product lifetime is desirable. Testing is therefore usually necessary. Operational life for machines might be in the order of several decades. An investigation of failure modes or times to failure under normal operating conditions may result in unrealistic laboratory times. A solution is to test with one or more stresses increased over the normal operation level; this is known as accelerated testing. The test results are then extrapolated to estimate the reliability under normal conditions. The mathematical tool for doing this is a physical model like the Arrhenius, the Eyring, the power rule or others.

In mechanical equipment operational failures most often have tribological causes such as wear on sliding parts like bearings or seals or surface fatigue in rolling element bearings or gearings. In such cases the power rule is usually the best model.

Typical ways of raising the stress level in mechanical equipment are by increasing mechanical stress, pressure, humidity, temperature, frequency or speed or by contamination of lubricant or environment. It is extremely important in the test design to make sure that the increased stress level will not result in the 'wrong' failure mode, that is a failure mode different from the one to be expected under normal operational conditions. This is very sensitive in the case of tribological failures, for example in machines for process industry. Typical failures are wear leading to backlash in bearings or leakage in seals and surface fatigue leading to pitting in rolling bearings or gearings.

Testing may be performed at different levels: field test of a complete machine, rig test of a complete machine, component test (gears, rolling element bearings), miniature test (gear interaction), contact simulating test (gear material testing in disc machine) or sample test (pin-disc, four-ball, etc.).

Factorial planning of the test design is a powerful tool for short and effective testing. Such testing makes it possible to study the interaction between different parameters.

The different chapters in this volume deal with accelerated testing from different points of view. Accelerated testing in the context of product development is treated by Andersson. The tribological fundamentals for mechanical testing is the theme of Holmberg. Accelerated testing of hydraulic components has been studied by Onsøyen in a forthcoming PhD thesis from The Norwegian Institute of Technology. He has investigated the deterioration of gear pumps for oil platforms, the worst environment possible. The importance of accelerated testing and the use of factorial designs for the improvement of reliability are emphasized by Bergman.

PART 2: FAILURE DATA INFORMATION

The goal of reliability engineering is to improve product and system reliability in a cost-effective way. Both failure occurrence and failure consequences have to be taken into account. To reach this goal, the appropriate data and their correct treatment to obtain reliability information are of the utmost importance.

Different aspects of the transition from failure data to reliability information are treated within the programme. One part is concerned with the combination of reliability information and failure data from different sources. In another part the effect of repair and the treatment of failure data from repairable systems are studied. In a final part of the programme the causes of failures experienced and their effects are studied in order to plan and improve upon the maintenance process.

At Oslo University the combination of expert opinions and failure data is treated. Huseby and Natvig in this volume consider correlations between experts' opinions due to overlap from their respective sources of knowledge. They consider decisions, the consequences of which depend on future failure events, using the Bayesian approach.

The same general approach is taken by Kurt Pörn, of Studsvik Nuclear AB, in his PhD dissertation from Linköping University (see Akersten *et al.* in this volume). However, the sources of information considered are based on failure data from similar components in similar environments. These may be more or less relevant to the reliability performance of a studied component. Thus robustness with respect to the relevance of these other sources is an important issue, which is studied in depth.

The treatment of failure data from repairable systems is the subject of Akersten's forthcoming PhD thesis from Linköping University and is summarized in Chapter 2.1 in this volume. Simple graphical techniques based on the TTT-concept (Total Time on Test) and their theoretical basis are studied.

For the improvement of systems and their maintenance it is important to consider not only times to failure but also causes and consequences. In an applied study performed at VTT (The Technical Research Centre of Finland) on motor operated valves, Simola *et al.* consider these questions using the simple but powerful tools FMECA (Failure Modes and Effects and Criticality Analysis) and MECA (Maintenance Effects and Criticality Analysis). Also quantitative statistical analyses concerning repair and unavailability times and failure trends are demonstrated.

PART 3: CONDITION MONITORING

Improved reliability and availability of industrial production equipment has been achieved by the use of new methods for measuring and analysing the condition of the machinery. By using effective condition monitoring techniques, failures can be predicted well in advance and unexpected production stops avoided. This results in considerable economic savings for the industry.

Vibration measurement is the most used technique for on-line condition monitoring in industry today. Often only the overall vibration level is being measured in order to follow the trends in the condition of the machinery. However the development of measuring, recording and analysing equipment and techniques has made it possible to get more detailed and reliable information about the condition of the machinery. The normal vibration caused by the running machinery does not disturb the measured signal if the measurement is performed at high frequencies using the acoustic emission technique. The periodicity in the vibration spectrum, e.g. families of harmonics and uniformly spaced sidebands, can easily be detected using cepstrum analysis. The huge amount of information from various transducers that has to be gathered in a large production plant can be collected by computers, which can also analyse the data and produce the output in a suitable form for the maintenance personnel.

Wear debris in the lubricating oil of the machinery carries with it valuable information on the condition of the machinery. Wear particle counting is a conventionally used technique for hydraulic oils. More information can be achieved by analysing both the size distribution and the shape of the metallic wear particles by ferromagnetic particle analyser and microscope. In very clean environments, where even small amounts of wear have to be detected, spectrometrical oil analysis (SOAP) is a suitable method. Recently on-line transducers for wear particle analysis have been developed. With these transducers the process of condition monitoring can be automated and the errors caused by sample collecting technique and the time lag involved with laboratory analysis are removed.

The confidence level of condition monitoring can be increased by using a number of different methods simultaneously because they almost always complement one another. Today statistical methodology is available for modelling of condition dependent failure rate functions in mechanical systems and also for selection of condition monitoring technique and strategy. Graphical methods for the estimation of the threshold level of the monitoring parameters have been proposed—see Al-Najjar in this volume—in order to reach better cost efficiency.

Kuoppala et al. review available condition monitoring techniques and present two case studies on their suitability and sensitivity performed at VTT. Radzikowski has studied on-line monitoring of contamination level in hydraulic oils at KTH (The Royal Institute of Technology, Stockholm). The basic criteria for the selection of condition based maintenance strategy for mechanical systems have been studied at Linköping University and a model is presented by Al-Najjar.

PART 4: AVAILABILITY PERFORMANCE ASSURANCE

This part is an attempt to tie all parts together. It consists of development of methodology for treatment, combination and analysis of life data, failure frequency data and condition data in order to use and maintain production resources to achieve minimization of operational and maintenance costs.

The whole context with the connections between different parts is described in Fig. 2.

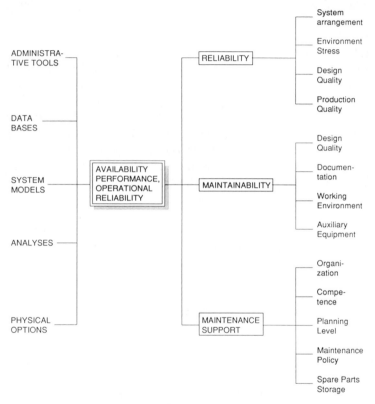

Fig. 2. The concept of Availability Performance (Operational Reliability).

Establishing the optimum maintenance function for a technical system is not an unambiguous task but very much depends on what is understood by the term 'maintenance function' for this particular application. This will vary in different technical cases of actual maintenance. Different companies and different managers will choose different approaches to the same situation.

Maintenance has to encompass a vast spectrum of variations. One can just mention the following cases:

— A company making mechanical components in small series with machine tools, welding and manual work. Here is a minor difference between production and maintenance.
— A larger process production plant, working with automated, continuous 24-hour production. Local failures may stop the total production or seriously influence safety. Production availability and safety are key words.
— A passenger car, made in large series for large variation in use by drivers with variable skills. Maintenance should be built in from the manufacturer.
— A satellite, or a submarine oil pumping platform, where reliability is given very high priority. In such cases there is very limited availability for maintenance. To satisfy reliability, redundancy and very high quality components are used.
— Electronic equipment, where functional capability depends on a large number of electronic circuits or components. Maintenance is a fault-finding and replacement procedure.

Industrial availability performance and its assurance is a vast problem area which has been studied at SINTEF (The Foundation for Scientific and Industrial Research at the Norwegian Institute of Technology) by Østvik. In this volume he presents a top management definition of company objectives, plans and needs. A tool has been developed for PC usage in the assessment and planning of maintenance programmes for production equipment.

At Risø National Laboratory in Denmark a decision support system for maintenance planning for industrial plants has been developed. Paulsen and Lauridsen describe their study of information flow such as exchange of information between designer and user of industrial plants. They have developed a software tool for a decision support system. Christensen and Kongsø go deeper into the interaction between the reliability model and the strategies for operation and maintenance of a plant.

At The Technical University of Denmark, Fog and Aage have studied a computer graphics approach for modelling of complex marine installations, thereby helping maintenance personnel to operate efficiently, also under stressing conditions. A computer-based visual modelling system for this purpose is presented.

At the same university, Thorsteinsson and Hage have developed an analytical tool to be used by companies to give a visual presentation of the managerial efforts concerning maintenance. The tool is used to increase awareness of how a company handles the managerial maintenance tasks and for preliminary analyses before the company designs a new maintenance technology.

PART 1

Accelerated testing

1.1

Testing—An Integrated Part of the Product Development Process

SÖREN ANDERSSON

Royal Institute of Technology, Department of Machine Elements, S-100 44 Stockholm, Sweden

ABSTRACT

Product development is the process of transforming a 'product definition' into a final product under given constraints like cost, time etc. A general trend is a more methodical development process due to increased product complexity, competitiveness and demands on quality. Testing consequently has to become a more integrated part of the process than it is today. A fundamental physical approach on design is an advantage in many respects for most steps within the development process. Relations between systems, sub-assemblies, components and critical points may easily be generated by ordinary dynamic modelling and flow analyses. Failure mechanisms with their models are thus directly related to overall functions. The need for testing and its degree of acceleration may vary depending on the type of product, company, etc., but also on the type of problem and in what stage of the development process it is done. Continuous component and material tests and access to equipment and people who know how to do different types of tests is an important and necessary preparation for modern development.

INTRODUCTION

Prototype test–fix–retest cycles during product development have by tradition had an important role in the product development process of many mechanical products. As a result we may see many successful companies today with high quality products, who have used that technique to a great extent. The test methods used can be characterized mainly as prototype field tests of trial-and-error type with the purpose of identifying weak points of the design but in many cases also of finding out the actual physical demands on the products. Most such tests may not look well planned and thus many useful data have been missed; the fact is, however, that they have in many cases given good products.

An accepted statement followed by many designers is that product quality and reliability must be designed into the product. As a consequence of that and many other demands originating from increased competitiveness, product complexity, standards and other regulations, the interest in and use of a more methodical development process are increasing.

The object of this paper is to show how and when different types of testing are necessary and to show that such testing has to come in as an integrated part of the product development process.

PRODUCT DEVELOPMENT

Product development means development of a new product that satisfies the 'product definition'. The word product is restricted here to a physical product. The development of a product contains many activities of technical, economical and marketing origin. Since product development is surrounded with many constraints of different types, it is not surprising that a number of different development models have been formulated. The so-called 'integrated product development model' has been the main guideline in Swedish industry for some time (Sv. Mekanförbundet, 1987).

The 'product definition' is the specification of the requirements and important features based on customer needs, new technology breakthroughs and/or results of inernal as well as external research. Based on the 'product definition', the product design starts with the clarification of the task resulting in a *detailed product specification*. This plus the conceptual design, embodiment design and detail design are described in detail by Pahl and Beitz (1984).

Another model of interest is the 'two step rocket' model for customer oriented production. By customer orientation is meant production mainly based on the customer's needs. The activities are divided into two phases:

Phase 1: The development phase
Phase 2: The order phase

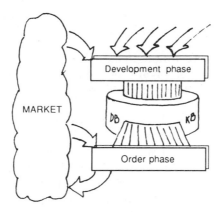

Fig. 1. Customer oriented production. (Modified after Prof. G. Sohlenius.)

with parallel activities within each phase according to Fig. 1.

The development phase contains product and production system development. The main goal is to build up a product system with all the necessary data for the following order phase. The design principles used will roughly follow that outlined above, i.e. conceptual design, embodiment design and detail design. The results of the design and the data generated have to be of such range and quality and structured and stored in such a way that all necessary information and data are available for the second phase, i.e. the order phase.

One advantage with this 'two step rocket' model is that it shows the advantage and need of early systematic analyses and testing of products under development. The time available for development can apparently be extended due to the advance of as much complete data for the order phase as possible, since the important constraint, time to market, is in most cases equal to the time for the order phase. Another important fact that points towards more systematic design is that the costs associated with the final product are mainly determined early in the development process when the development costs are low.

TESTING

The purposes of testing during product development are many, of which the following may be mentioned:

— to produce strength and lifetime data for materials and components,

— to determine loads or stresses on components and systems,
— to validate models.

All this can be achieved with a great number of different tests. Seen from the product development point of view, the different types may be classified according to Holmberg (this book, Chapter 1.2):

Field tests:	Tests in the field with prototypes and products.
Rig tests:	Tests of whole systems or sub-assemblies in rigs with standardized or realistic load spectra.
Component tests:	Tests of individual components or machine elements with standardized or realistic load spectra.
Miniature tests:	Tests of miniaturized and simplified components are run with standardized load or realistic load spectra.
Contact simulating and simple sample tests:	Tests in simplified test machines simulating typical failure mechanisms and physical processes under well controlled conditions.

Testing in general is time consuming and costly and there will always be some need for a reduction of time and cost. The necessary test time to obtain relevant and desired data can be reduced in many ways, of which the following are the most common:

— increasing the stress
— trend observations
— excluding non-damaging sequences (e.g. excluding stress cycles with amplitudes less than a value that will not cause any crack initiation or crack propagation)

The first principle, increasing the stress, i.e. increasing load, pressure, temperature, etc., is normally applied through accelerated testing.

The goal of *field tests* may be to determine the physical parameters that will act on the equipment as a result of the function or to determine the behaviour or the state of the equipment in different situations. The recorded data may be used in design and for test as base data for rig and component loading. It may also be used for validation of models and verification that specified demands are satisfied. Field tests cannot be made before some sort of prototype is available. The possibility of taking advantage of field test data early in the design process therefore depends on whether the design is of original, adaptive or variant type. In order to obtain as much information as possible, field tests in many areas comprise both:

(1) long term tests where data are recorded during a relatively long time but at rather few characteristic points;
(2) short term tests with different independent activities separately tested and recorded at as many characteristic points as possible.

The possibilities of making changes to prototypes other than small modifications are normally rather limited. However, in most cases development of new products will seldom start from scratch. Further developments and/or modifications of known principles and products are usually the normal case. If so, it is possible to test special components and assemblies at realistic running conditions much earlier than in the first case. Sub-assemblies and components may be integrated in old products with well-known properties and tested under realistic conditions in the field.

Rig tests in comparison with field tests are made in order to

— have better control of the test and thus have possibilities of repeating the tests,
— observe different phenomena more accurately,
— reduce the test time and thus improve the possibilities for modifications.

Component tests may be made for different reasons namely:

— to determine the relation between, for example, a stress at a point on the component as a result of an external load on the component;
— to determine the strength of the component at different running conditions;
— to determine the dynamic behaviour of the component.

Design of products includes to a great extent the combination of known components. Therefore, adequate component models with corresponding data are of great value during the whole design process. Component modelling and model validation are therefore an important part of the development process. Tests of components with respect to strength are another important part. In many cases component suppliers can supply adequate data, but if not, it is advisable to continuously run component tests in-house (Onsøyen, this book, Chapter 1.3).

Miniature tests are made when the actual components or assemblies are of such size or cost that miniaturization is a convenient alternative in order to produce test data. The problem with miniature test results is the extrapolation to full scale. A typical miniaturized test rig is the FZG-test rig for gears which also may be characterized as a contact simulating test rig. The loads used may either be of standard type, i.e. constant amplitude, or realistic and thus are determined in analogy with the rig tests mentioned above.

Contact simulating and simple sample tests give data necessary for simulations of system behaviour and in dimensioning of structures as well as interfaces. These tests are mainly of accelerated type. They are easy to perform. The results are obtained quickly and reliability data can be readily produced. However, the data obtained are sometimes difficult to use for other situations than those similar to the test configuration. One general rule is to run the test so that the same failure mechanism is obtained in the material test as in the real situation. That problem is especially pronounced for tribological (see this book, Chapter 1.2) and environmental tests. Nevertheless, this type of test may grow in importance as a result of a combination of better computer design aids and more systematic and physically oriented development procedures.

PHYSICAL APPROACH ON DESIGN

One important and natural basis for design is the fundamental physical principle of continuity. For a spatial region or control volume V, the change of a stored quantity is equal to the difference between the flow of the quantity into and out from the volume and the flow of the quantity generated from sources within the control volume. The quantity may be energy, momentum or material.

Paynter (1961) used this principle for analysis and design of engineering systems based on the continuity of energy. He assumed that the energy transport through the boundary S, Fig. 2, between the environment E and the control volume V is at relatively few areas of restricted extent, so-called ports. If we assume that the internal energy storage and the internal sources are lumped in discrete regions and that the ports are spatially localized such that each port can be evaluated individually, we get

$$\sum_j \mathrm{d}W_{\text{st},j}/\,\mathrm{d}t = \sum_i P_{\text{tr},i} + \sum_k P_{\text{s},k} \tag{1}$$

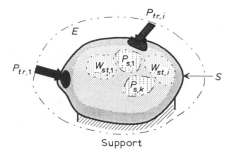

Support

Fig. 2.

where $W_{st,j}$ is the instantaneous energy stored in the jth discrete region, $P_{tr,i}$ is the power transported through the boundary S of the control volume V at the ith port, and $P_{s,k}$ is the power source at the kth discrete region. $W_{st,j}$ for mechanical systems can be set equal to the sum of the potential energy, the kinematic energy and the thermal energy. $P_{tr,i}$ is positive if directed into the control volume. $P_{s,k}$ is positive if it is a power source. Dissipation due to friction, for example, is negative, i.e. a sink in respect to the 'mechanical' power flow but positive in respect to the thermal flow. Energy can neither be created nor destroyed, but it can take many different forms. That means that the sum $P_{s,k}$ must be equal to zero, but contains many terms.

SPECIFICATION

Function is defined according to Pahl and Beitz (1984) as the general input/output relationship of a system whose purpose is to perform a task. Related to the fundamental physical relation above, function is the relationship between ports.

Functions are usually defined by statements consisting of a *verb* and a *noun* as in the following examples: change speed, magnify force, etc. It has been found to be advantageous to distinguish between the *main functions* with related *main ports* and the *auxiliary functions* which are determined by the solutions satisfying the main functions. A typical example of an auxiliary function is to support a shaft which normally is solved by bearings.

A detailed product specification as the result of an analysis of the task is the first step in the design process. This analysis is mostly made with the aid of different praxes and checklists. Based on the physical approach above, a functional specification of a design problem could be limited to the following points:

(1) *Define the main ports*, i.e. the in- and outports directly related to the function.
(2) *Define the boundary S of the control volume*, i.e. the geometry and the properties of the surface. One important part is to specify the 'supports', i.e. where the 'function' may be supported (Prabhu & Taylor, 1990).
(3) *Define the environment E outside S*.

CONCEPTUAL DESIGN

Based on the specification, it is elementary to establish an overall function that shall be fulfilled by a physical solution. It is, however, important that the function is quantified with tolerances as precise as possible. The next step in the design process is to generate different concepts that may satisfy the overall function. It is probably during this step that the basis for a good or bad design is set.

Different possible solutions of the design problem are generated during the conceptual design phase. The solutions correspond to different function structures but with the same overall function.

The different concepts will be analysed from different points of view. The evaluation of concepts is mostly based on experience and different evaluating methods (Pahl & Beitz, 1984). A rather different but nevertheless interesting approach is the axiomatic design principle proposed by Suh (1990).

Independent of which method that will be used, there is a great advantage to model the concepts and simulate their behaviour as early as possible. The fundamental physical approach outlined above is then a very good starting point. The modelling is in most cases fairly simple and requires just ordinary knowledge of dynamic modelling of mechanical systems. Here, predetermined component models may be a good help.

During modelling it may be found that the constitutive relation or transformation function of a process is not known or that actual data are not available. It is then natural to make the necessary search and/or tests as soon as possible in order to evaluate the relation and produce the missing data. These types of tests are mostly of fairly short duration and do not have to be either complicated or expensive. One problem, however, is the relatively large number of parameters that might have an influence on the function. That has to be considered in the test 'design' in order to get the desirable relations and data in reasonable time.

FLOW ANALYSES

Flow analyses are useful in all steps of the design process. However, what will be focused on here is the usefulness of flow analyses in weak point identification, which in service is one of the most difficult parts of the product development. As the design process progresses, more and more detailed data on the whole system, sub-systems and components as well as prototypes will be available for analyses and tests. Important analyses are now the weak point identification followed by FMEA (Failure Mode and Effect Analysis).

Flow analysis of a system is nothing new. Designers have always had different types of flow analyses and simulations in mind. The reason for focusing on it here is to show the connection between the fundamental physical relation above, weak point identification and test planning. An example is the function 'reduce speed' with the specification shown in Fig. 3(a). The function can be satisfied with a gearbox according to Fig 3(b). The weak point identification analyses may now be made according to the following principles:

(1) *Identify all interfaces in the main power flow.* In this example they are at the inport (1) and the outport (2). These two points are thus potential weak points. Furthermore, interfaces may be found between the pinion and the gear (3) and the gear and the shaft (4) which also are potential weak points.

(2) *Identify cross-section and flow direction changes in the structure of the main power flow.* Such points are at (5) but probably also at (1) and (2), and in Fig. 3(d) probably the most critical points are the teeth of the pinion and the gear, (12) and (13) respectively.

(3) *Identify all the supports along the main power flow.* In this case all the bearings (6), (7), (8) and (9) are supports along the main power flow at which conditions influence the function. Sometimes even the shafts at the ports have to serve as supports.

(4) *Identify all interfaces between the supports and the defined boundary S of the control volume V.* In this case the flow from bearing (6) passes to the housing via the interface (10) and further to the ground by the interface (11) which may be a machine foot. Observe that welds are also interfaces.

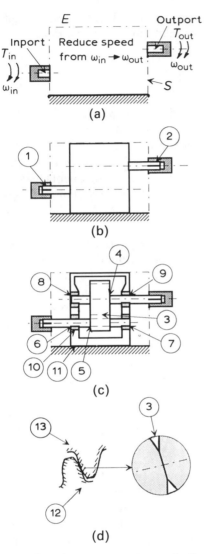

Fig. 3. Potential weak point identification by flow analyses: (a) specification; (b) solution; (c) and (d), see text.

(5) *Identify cross-section and flow direction changes of the structure between the supports and the defined boundary S of the control volume V.* In the example studied this is the region close to the bearings, i.e. the transition from the support of the bearing and the housing wall.

The different potential weak points may now be analysed further with FMEA, giving the most critical points for further studies.

Flow analysis technique is also useful in test 'design' and planning, since the interrelations between the system, the components and the critical points may be easily seen. Continuing the example above, the main power flow, which is determined by the outport, has to pass the interface between the pinion and the gear, i.e. the conformal contact between the tooth flanks. A test setup for this type of contact therefore should be run such that the power density in the test is not too far from the actual case.

The power concentration in this contact is extremely high in comparison with most other critical points in this example. However, due to the importance in mechanical engineering of this type of high power density contact, failure mechanism studies as well as life prediction investigations have long been made within the discipline of tribology. The different types of failure that may occur at the interface between the teeth are scuffing or scoring, mild wear, abrasive wear and surface fatigue, Fig. 4. Each failure mechanism has its own character.

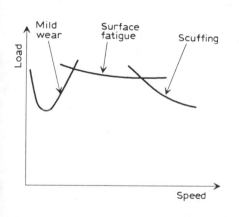

Fig. 4. Failure modes for gear contacts as a function of load and speed.

LIFE AND RELIABILITY ESTIMATION

Life estimations are always made for weak points, which support the importance of the weak point identification analyses. A missed critical point may seriously influence the estimation. Therefore, some tests are just made to verify that this is not the case. Different models, depending on the failure mechanism expected, are used and the models are often power laws.

The life is the time the critical point can withstand the stresses exposed under running. The resistance or strength may for mechanical systems be divided into:

— strength of the structures,
— strength of the interacting surfaces.

The strength is in both cases dependent on:

— the bulk material properties,
— the surface properties.

The intention in this chapter is not to cover the whole subject but instead to focus on some work that may be of interest for life and reliability estimations of structures and interacting surfaces, concentrating on the latter aspects.

Structures

Fatigue is one of the most important failure mechanisms in mechanical engineering. Among the more interesting work in this field is that of Samuelson (1988) who covered the whole chain from field tests via component tests to life predictions in design. Samuelson introduced a parameter known as the duty, D:

$$D = \sum_i n_i \Delta \sigma_i^k \qquad (2)$$

which is one parameter for the stress time history and the capacity, C:

$$C = N_i \Delta \sigma_i^k \qquad (3)$$

which in turn is a corresponding parameter for the fatigue strength of the component and structure material; n_i is the number of cycles at stress level i. The other parameters in eqns (2) and (3) are defined by the S–N curve, Fig. 5.

The prediction of fatigue life is normally based on the Palmgren-Miner linear damage rule, which in this case will give the linear damage d as

$$d = \sum_i n_i / N_i = D/C \qquad (4)$$

The Samuelson approach increases the possibilities of using recorded load time histories from field tests in design of new products at an early stage. The approach may also be used for other failure mechanisms than fatigue. Sliding wear and surface fatigue may be treated in the same way.

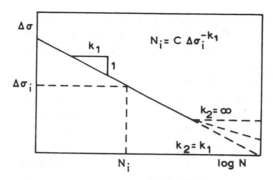

Fig. 5. S–N curve with definition of parameters (Samuelson, 1988).

The main difference in these cases is the value of k which for the sliding wear case is 1 and for the surface fatigue case is about 3.

Interacting surfaces

Interacting surfaces under relative movement may fail due to the following types of failure 'mechanisms':

— severe wear (or seizure, scoring, scuffing)
— mild wear
— abrasive wear
— surface fatigue
— corrosive wear

Details of these failure mechanisms and lubrication theories can be found in any textbook on tribology. One book of special interest, due to its systematic approach, is *Tribology—A Systems Approach to the Science and Technology of Friction, Lubrication and Wear*, by Czichos (1978).

Severe wear can happen at any time if critical parameters exceed a transition limit. The risk of this type of failure happening must be very low due to the potential consequences. The first step in the design of interacting sliding surfaces is therefore to make sure that the conditions are such that the risk of this transition is minimized. However, the possibility of any prediction is rather limited.

The transition from a desired mild sliding situation to a severe situation with catastrophic high friction and wear for lubricated contacts has been studied experimentally by de Gee *et al.* (1978) in a pin-disc type of test equipment. They introduced the concept of the transition diagram, i.e. a kind of lubrication-mechanism map (Holmberg, this book, Chapter 1.2). Salas-Russo (1990) has made further investigations on the transition by studying the influence on the transition load of sliding speed and surface roughness. He also used a pin-disc test machine but in contrast to the stepwise loading de Gee *et al.* used, the load is applied as a ramp and the test is finished within one revolution of the rotating test disc. The test duration is typically 200 ms. Figure 6 shows the results of a test series with different surface finishes on the discs. The pin pressed against the disc is a ball-bearing ball. The results clearly show the importance of *smooth surfaces* which is a detail which always has to be considered in lubricated contacts.

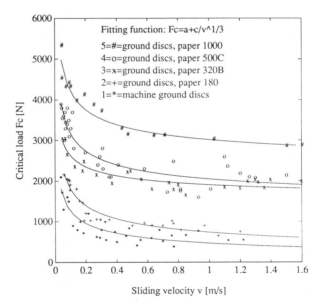

Fig. 6. The transition load as a function of sliding speed v and surface roughness (Salas-Russo, 1990).

Although some work has been done on the transition from a mild to a severe sliding situation, it is not possible to predict the risk for the transition for a real sliding surface yet. Much more research has to be done on this problem before the data obtained can directly be used in prediction and design of lubricated sliding contact surfaces. For comparison and for analyses of reasonable surface modifications that may influence the transition level, however, this type of rather simple and quick material test should be used in the development process.

If the conditions are such that the actual running conditions are sufficiently below the transition limit, the typical wear process under lubricated conditions can be characterized as mild and predictable. A typical such wear curve is shown in Fig. 7.

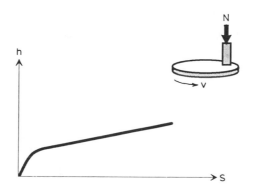

Fig. 7. Mild wear in a sliding contact: $h=$ wear depth, $s=$ sliding distance.

The running-in wear depth h_{r-i} and the wear rate dh/dt after running-in are dependent on the degree of separation of the contact surfaces by the lubricant, which can be characterized by the Sommerfeld number. The dependence is schematically shown in Fig. 8. At low sliding speed or high load or low viscosity the lubricant film cannot separate the surfaces and the asperities will rub against each other. The surfaces will wear and the lubrication type is boundary. However, if the speed or viscosity is increased or the load is decreased the ability to separate the surfaces will increase and thus the wear will decrease. The lubrication type will change from boundary to mixed and possibly also to full film i.e. a separating film may be formed depending on the form and the topography of the surfaces. The wear coefficient k will naturally decrease with the degree of separation.

The wear depth h of a surface is, after a short running-in period, proportional to the contact pressure p and the sliding distance s of the surface against the opposite surface:

$$h = h_{r-i} + kps \qquad (5)$$

where h_{r-i} is the running-in wear depth and k is the wear coefficient (in

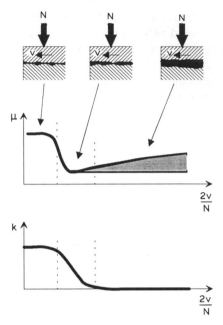

Fig. 8. The wear dependence on the degree of separation of the contact surfaces. N = normal load, v = sliding speed, μ = coefficient of friction, η = lubricant viscosity, k = wear coefficient.

m^2/N). If the sliding speed is v, the wear rate dh/dt is

$$dh/dt = kpv \qquad (6)$$

This expression can be used with advantage in life and reliability predictions. The wear rate is rather low in most practical situations. Failure tests originating from wear may consequently be long. For this type of phenomenon it is therefore necessary to reduce the test time by studying the wear trend and from that make life and reliability estimations. Lydersen (1988) studied these types of tests from a statistical point of view. He named the trend observation deterioration measurements and treated different types of deterministic models of which the wear model, eqn (6), was the simplest.

The determination of the wear coefficient can easily be made with pin-on-disc, type test machines. The relevance of this type of simple test has of course been discussed and there are different opinions of the usefulness of the data obtained. The wear coefficient may, however, also be determined from component, rig and field tests. The author's experience of the use of wear data from different types of tests is very good. Predictions have been used on many different applications and as long as the wear is of a mild type predictions have given fairly good results. It is, however, important to analyse the running conditions very accurately.

In order to check if the linear wear relation above may also be used in the prediction of sliding wear in contacts with simultaneous rolling and sliding, as in gears, a wear study on slow running gears was made by Andersson and Eriksson (1990). The results from that study show that the theoretical calculated wear distribution agrees well with the measured wear distribution. The estimated wear coefficients from the gear tests agree well with corresponding data obtained in other applications and test machines. The gear tests were made with an FZG test rig which is a standardized test machine, see Fig. 9. The results are shown in Fig. 10.

The wear tests of the slow running gears were run with and without filters. The results without filtration of the lubricating oil gave a higher wear rate than with filtered lubricant which indicates that *cleanliness* in lubricated sliding contacts is an important factor. The results should be used with care since only one test was made with filtration. Lack of cleanliness is, however, found to be one of the most important reasons

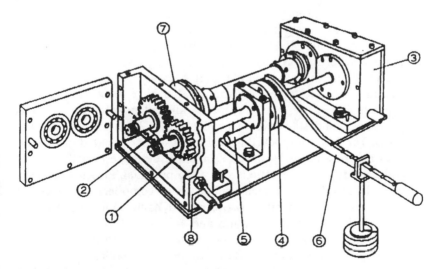

Fig. 9. FZG gear test rig. Key: 1 test pinion, 2 test wheel, 3 drive gear, 4 load clutch, 5 locking pin, 6 load lever and weights, 7 torque measuring clutch, 8 temperature sensor.

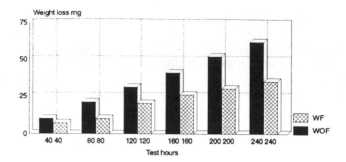

Fig. 10. FZG wear test results. Accumulated weight loss in mg without (WOF) and with (WF) filters.

for life reduction in rolling bearings, and of the same importance as surface finish for the life of rolling bearings according to Jacobson (1990).

DISCUSSION AND SUMMARY

The possibilities of utilizing the potential of different types of testing during product development may vary depending on many factors, such as the long-term development policy of companies, the degree of systematics in design, the technology level, etc. The type of tests that may be used at different stages of the process are field tests, rig tests, component tests, contact simulating tests and simple sample tests.

Time and costs are typical constraints that have to be considered in development. There are, however, many different possibilities to reduce time and costs and still develop products with high performance and reliability. The 'two step rocket' model for customer oriented production indicates one possibility. However, systematic design, especially if based on fundamental physical relations, has a big potential. Relations between the overall function of a system, sub-systems, components and critical points may easily be generated by ordinary dynamic modelling and flow analyses. Critical point identification and analysis is further the base for life and reliability estimations. Failure mechanisms with their models at critical points are thus directly related to overall functions.

The need for testing and its degree at different stages of product development will naturally be related to the different design problems by the systematic physical approach, Testing will be an integrated part of the development process. However, the necessary preparations have to be done, of which the following are important:

— access to equipment and people who know how to do different types of tests;
— continuity of component and material tests.

REFERENCES

Andersson, S. & Eriksson, B. (1990). Prediction of the sliding wear of spur gears. *NORDTRIB'90, 4th Nordic Symposium on Tribology—Lubrication, Friction and Wear*, Hirtshals, Denmark.

Czichos, H. (1978). *Tribology—a Systems Approach to the Science and Technology of Friction Lubrication and Wear*. Elsevier, Amsterdam.

de Gee, A.W.J., Begelinger, A. & Salomon, G. (1978). Failure of thin film lubrication; function-oriented characterization of additives and steels. *ASLE Trans.*, **23**(1), 23.

Jacobson, B. (1990). Good lubricant cleanliness—as important as good finish for the life of bearings. *NORDTRIB'90, 4th Nordic Symposium on Tribology—Lubrication, Friction and Wear*, Hirtshals, Denmark.

Lydersen, S. (1988). *Reliability testing based on deterioration measurements.* Doktor Ingeniöravhandling 1988:32, Institutt for Matematiske Fag, Trondheim.

Pahl, G. & Beitz, W. (1984). *Engineering Design*. The Design Council, London.

Paynter, H.M. (1961). *Analysis and Design of Engineering Systems*. MIT Press, Cambridge, MA.

Prabhu, D.R. & Taylor, D.L. (1990). On deriving supported configurations of mechanical systems from their functions. *Int. Workshop on Formal Methods in Eng. Design*, Colorado Springs.

Salas-Russo, E. (1990). *Failure in lubricated sliding steel contacts.* Licentiate Thesis, TRITA-MAE-1990:8, Department of Machine Elements, Royal Institute of Technology, Stockholm.

Samuelson, J. (1988). *Fatigue design of vehicle components: Methodology and applications.* Report No. 88–23, Department of Aeronautical Structures and Materials, Royal Institute of Technology, Stockholm.

Suh, N. (1990). *The Principles of Design*. Oxford University Press, Oxford, UK.

Sv. Mekanförbundet (1987). *Design Guide* (in Swedish). Sveriges Mekanförbundet 87204.

1.2

Tribological Bases for Accelerated Testing

KENNETH HOLMBERG

Technical Research Centre of Finland, Laboratory of Production Engineering, SF-02150 Espoo, Finland

ABSTRACT

High quality and reliability of machine components is achieved by knowing their tribological behaviour and lifetime. The objective of accelerated testing is to provide this information in a short space of time and at a low cost. In accelerated testing the real contact is simulated under more severe conditions in a simplified mechanical device with controlled parameter variation possibilities. The test is relevant to real component performance only if it is done in a controlled way without changes in the tribological contact conditions. This can be assured by using wear maps, test parameter monitoring and wear track analysis.

INTRODUCTION

The reliability of the mechanical components is essential for the attainment of high quality in machines and apparatus. One of the most common reasons for the unsatisfactory reliability of machines is wear and wear failures in the mechanical components. The tribological behavour of a moving mechanical contact in a machine is very complex and thus difficult to predict.

During the last few decades an increasing amount of work has been done to determine the tribological mechanisms that control the wear and friction in machine components. This understanding gives us today the possibility of performing better and more reliable accelerated tests, providing us with relevant information about the likely behaviour of the machine.

The purpose of this Chapter is to describe the tribological background that has to be taken into account when performing the accelerated testing of machine components, and to show three methods by which the reliability and the applicability of the results to the real components in the machines can be improved.

TRIBOLOGICAL CONTACTS AND FAILURES

Tribological contacts include all contacting surfaces moving in relation to each other. Common tribological contacts in machines are bearings, gears, brakes, cylinders, sliders, wheels and material moving scoops, transporters or grippers.

The physical and chemical actions that take place in a tribological contact, e.g. between two gear teeth, produce a resistance to motion, i.e. friction, and the removal of material from the contacting surfaces, i.e. wear. It is important to note that both the friction and wear are not material parameters but system parameters depending on the whole tribological contact process that takes place. Figure 1 shows how all the input parameters together control the contact process that results in friction and wear.

Wear in the contact is mainly considered in the following discussion because wear is of central importance from a reliability point of view, while friction is important from a performance point of view. The wear process in a contact is normally a combination of several different mechanisms and actions. The material removing process can be divided into the four basic mechanisms of wear shown in Fig. 2. These are adhesive, abrasive, fatigue and chemical wear.

It is useful to study these wear mechanisms separately because each of them has its own characteristic features and obeys certain physical or chemical laws that to some extent can be mathematically formulated or simulated. Even if one of these wear mechanisms appears alone less often in a real machine contact, normally one of them is dominating the wear process. This offers the possibility of finding out which parameters mainly influence wear and how they influence it, and thus of optimizing the contact process in a desired way.

The most common way to reduce wear is by lubrication, that is by introducing a fluid between the surfaces. This changes the contact

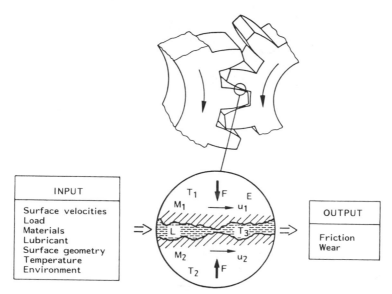

Fig. 1. The input parameters control the friction and wear produced in a tribological contact.

conditions and introduces even more parameters to be taken into account. Again, depending on the input tribological system parameters, the influence of the fluid on the contact can be divided into the four different lubrication mechanisms shown in Fig. 3. In hydrodynamic (HD) and elastohydrodynamic (EHD) lubrication, the two surfaces are separated by a fluid film and the behaviour of the contact can to a large extent be mathematically formulated. Surface asperity collisions take place frequently in boundary and mixed lubrication and the chemical reactions have a dominating influence on the tribological contact process.

If there is a good lubrication film separating the surfaces from each other and no disturbing particles appear in the contact, then the wear will be insignificant for a long time (curve 3 in Fig. 4). But this does not last indefinitely. Even if the surfaces do not touch each other, they will elastically respond to the load transmitted through the lubricating film. After a long time, maybe even five or ten years, the continuously repeating load cycle will cause a fatigue crack at the surface. In an instant, larger fatigue wear particles are released from the surface and a catastrophic failure results.

If the lubricating film is thin, as in boundary or mixed lubrication, then

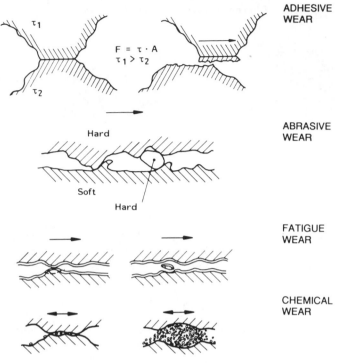

ADHESIVE
WEAR

$F = \tau \cdot A$
$\tau_1 > \tau_2$

ABRASIVE
WEAR

FATIGUE
WEAR

CHEMICAL
WEAR

Fig. 2. Basic mechanisms of wear.

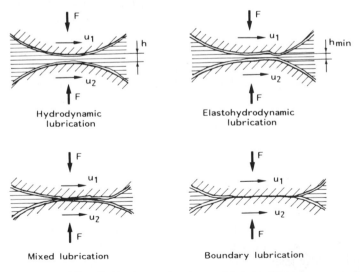

Hydrodynamic
lubrication

Elastohydrodynamic
lubrication

Mixed lubrication

Boundary lubrication

Fig. 3. Basic mechanisms of lubrication.

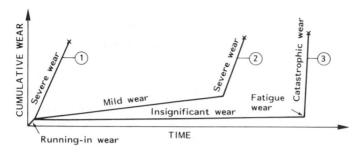

Fig. 4. Historiographs for three typical wear behaviours from first start to failure (x).

there is always some—often even detectable—wear present. This is called mild wear and does not normally disturb the performance of the machine (curve 2 in Fig. 4). It is possible in cases of mild wear to monitor the wear, follow its progress and detect if it reaches a critical level. After a longer period this often-linear accumulation of wear will result in a failure, but it does not appear suddenly and can be predicted by wear or vibration monitoring.

In well-designed machines where the material combination is tribologically correctly chosen, a stage of mild wear can be reached also in dry unlubricated contacts. This normally requires low load and low speed.

Excessively hard contact conditions result in severe wear. This may start as a fatigue wear crack or when the accumulated mild wear has reached a critical level. Alternatively it may be the result of a wrongly designed and thus overloaded contact (curve 1 in Fig. 4). The severe wear is often linear but rapid, and results in a short time in a catastrophic failure.

ACCELERATED TESTING

A high reliability of machine components can be achieved only by knowing their tribological behaviour and lifetime. In certain cases this can to some extent be estimated by theoretical analysis of the contact and by mathematical models. However, reliable information can often be achieved only by performing suitable tests on the components. In Chapter 1.1 it was shown how testing is an integrated part of the product development process. But the problem with wear and lifetime tests is that they are both time-consuming and expensive if performed in normal running conditions. The objective of accelerated testing is to provide the same information in a shorter time and to a lower cost.

Tribological accelerated testing of components can be performed by increasing load, speed, contact pressure, temperature or rate of contaminants, or by decreasing the lubricant viscosity or additive content. Many of these parameter changes are not easily done in real machines. It is often more appropriate to perform the accelerated testing in a laboratory environment on rigs where the real contact condition can be simulated and overloaded in a simplified mechanical device with more controlled parameter variation possibilities.

The simplification of a tribological test can be divided into six levels of simulation according to Uetz *et al.* (1979). The complexity of the test decreases when moving from field test level down to rig test, component test, miniature test, contact simulating test and simple sample test, as shown in Fig. 5. When moving to more simple tests, the interpretation of

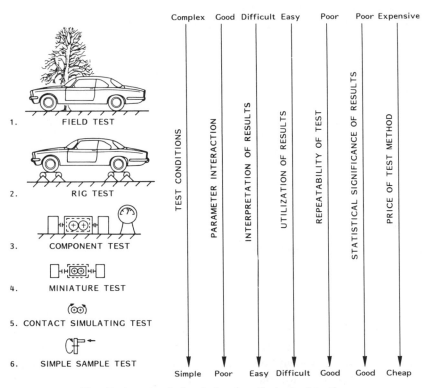

Fig. 5. Levels of simulation in tribological testing.

the results gets easier, the repeatability and the statistical significance of the results are improved and the cost of each test declines. On the other hand, the tests will show in a poorer way the interaction effects between different parameters and the utilization of the results gets more difficult.

Onsøyen (1990) has classified the different strategies that can be used in accelerated testing and he suggests that simplified tests are especially suitable for use when the cost of one component, including the surrounding equipment, is high. The use of simplified accelerated tests enables the performance of a larger number of tests, which makes it possible to treat the results statistically. Box et al. (1978) and Bergman and Klefsjö (1989) have shown that considerably more information can be gained from the tests when they are planned by factorial design techniques.

There are many advantages in using simplified accelerated tests, but there is also one considerable risk. If the simplification or the overloading of the contact considerably changes the wear or lubrication mechanism to be simulated, then the results of the tests are of no significance for the considered application.

Results from simplified and overloaded accelerated tests are reliable only if measures have been taken to assure that the simulated contact conditions are similar or in a controlled relation to the contact in the real component.

There are three ways to assure that the tests are performed in conditions relevant to the application:

(1) by using the wear and lubrication maps that recently have been devised on the basis of large collections of published test data;
(2) by monitoring test parameters such as friction, wear, film thickness or temperatures during the laboratory tests;
(3) by analysing and comparing the wear track and the wear debris from laboratory tests and from worn-out component surfaces in real machines.

WEAR AND LUBRICATION MAPS

A wear-mechanism map or a wear map is a figure which shows the regimes of different wear mechanisms depending on the two parameters varying along the coordinate axes. This is of course a simplified and only approximate way to present wear mechanism regimes, because only two parameters are varying and all the others are kept constant. If, however, the two parameters are those which have a dominating influence on wear, the wear map gives a good indication of how the wear mechanisms

Kenneth Holmberg

change and where the more uncontrolled transition regimes between two mechanisms are expected to appear.

Lim and Ashby (1987) have shown how wear maps can be developed for steel using a pin-on-disc configuration. The map, which is shown in Fig. 6, is produced on the basis of a detailed analysis of a large number

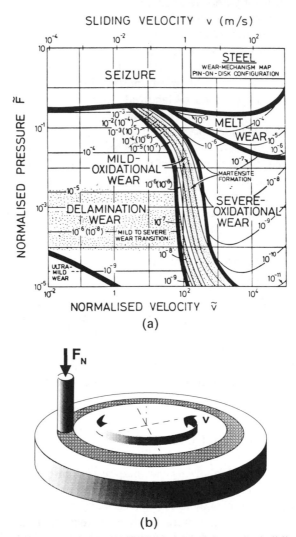

(a)

(b)

Fig. 6. (a) The Lim and Ashby (1987) wear map for a steel sliding pair using (b) the pin-on-disc test device.

of published wear test results and on a theoretical analysis of the wear mechanisms. It shows how the dominating wear mechanism changes with the speed and load given as normalized velocity and normalized pressure, respectively. Even levels for the normalized wear rates are given in the map as curves of constant wear rates.

The wear mechanisms used by Lim and Ashby in their map presentation are ultra-mild wear, delamination wear, mild and severe oxidational wear, melt wear and seizure. They give a simplified wear-rate equation for each mechanism as shown in Table 1. These wear mechanisms are

Table 1. The Lim and Ashby (1987) Simplified Wear-rate Equations. Symbols, Definitions and Units are Listed in the Appendix.

Seizure

$$\tilde{F}=\frac{1}{(1+a_1\mu^2)^{1/2}}\left[1-\frac{(T_b-T_o)}{20T_m}\ln\left(\frac{10^6}{\beta\tilde{v}}\right)\right]$$

Melt wear

$$\tilde{W}=\left(\frac{T_m-T_0}{T^*}\right)\frac{H_0}{L}\frac{1}{\beta\tilde{v}}\left[a\mu\tilde{F}\tilde{v}\frac{T^*\beta}{(T_m-T_0)}-1\right]$$

Mild-oxidational wear

$$\tilde{W}=\left(\frac{C^2A_0r_0}{Z_ca}\right)\exp\left[-\frac{Q_0}{RT_f}\right]\frac{\tilde{F}}{\tilde{v}}$$

Severe-oxidational wear

$$\tilde{W}=f_m\frac{K_{ox}(T_m^{ox}-T_b)}{L_{ox}a}\frac{(\tilde{F}N)^{1/2}}{\beta\tilde{v}}\left[a\mu\frac{aH_0\beta}{K_{ox}(T_m^{ox}-T_b)}\left(\frac{\tilde{F}}{N}\right)^{1/2}\tilde{v}-1\right]$$

Plasticity-dominated wear

$$\tilde{W}=k_A\tilde{F}\text{ with }k_A=\frac{2\gamma_0f_v}{f_A^*}$$

with the following definitions:

$$\tilde{W}=\frac{W}{A_n}\qquad a=\frac{1}{2+\beta(\pi\tilde{v}/8)^{1/2}}\qquad\qquad\mu=0.78-0.13\log_{10}(\tilde{v})$$

$$\tilde{F}=\frac{F}{A_nH_0}\qquad \Gamma^*=\frac{aH_0}{K_m}\approx222K\text{ for steel}\qquad N=\left(\frac{r_0}{r_a}\right)^2\tilde{F}(1-\tilde{F})+1$$

$$\tilde{v}=\frac{vr_0}{a}\qquad \beta=\frac{l_b}{r_0}=\frac{l_f}{r_a}\qquad\qquad T_0=300\text{ K}$$

mainly combinations of some of the basic wear mechanisms described above and can be related to these as shown in Table 2.

Table 2. The Wear Mechanisms Used in the Lim and Ashby (1987) Wear Maps are Combinations of the Basic Wear Mechanisms.

Wear mechanisms	Adhesion	Abrasion	Fatigue	Chemical wear
Seizure	×	×		
Melt wear	×			
Severe oxidational wear	×			×
Mild oxidational wear	×			×
Delamination wear	×		×	
Ultra-mild wear	×			

It is important to note that Lim and Ashby have limited their wear map to the rotational sliding pin-on-disc configuration and to steel pairs. For this reason this map is only applicable in applications with steel and with similar contact conditions. A method for developing similar wear maps for ceramics has been developed by Hsu *et al.* (1989). Wear maps for alumina ceramics have been published by Wang *et al.* (1989). Vingsbo *et al.* (1990) have developed fretting maps to show the wear behaviour in reciprocating moving contacts. They use displacement amplitude and frequency or tangential force amplitude and normal load as coordinate axes in their map presentations.

Similarly, Begelinger and de Gee (1981) earlier developed a kind of lubrication-mechanism map or lubrication map to show the changes from one lubrication regime to another. They represented the lubrication regime as elastohydrodynamic, boundary and scuffing in a map with velocity and load as coordinate axes, as shown in Fig. 7. Scuffing is not really a lubrication mechanism but can be considered as a contact mechanism for failed lubrication. These lubrication maps are also known as IRG transition diagrams.

These kinds of wear and lubrication maps are very useful when one performs an accelerated test. By comparing the actual test parameters to these maps, one gets a feeling of what kind of contact mechanisms can be expected and how close to the transition regions one is, even if the map presentation can by no means be considered as an exact diagram. The accelerated test results are best applicable to a real contact if they are both within the same wear or lubrication regime.

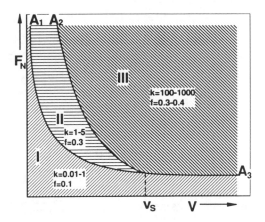

Fig. 7. Lubrication map for sliding concentrated steel contacts operating fully submerged in a liquid lubricant; f is the coefficient of friction and k the specific wear rate (10^{-6} mm^3/Nm) (Begelinger & de Gee, 1981).

TEST PARAMETER MONITORING

It is possible to get an indication of the dominating lubrication or wear mechanism by monitoring suitable test parameters like friction, lubricant film thickness, temperature, wear and surface roughness. The advantage of this method is that one gets an indication of the contact mechanisms during the whole process of wear and can notice possible changes in the mechanisms and the time when they take place.

Friction is generally measured in tribological accelerated tests. The coefficient of friction in lubricated contacts gives an indication of the lubrication regime, as shown in Fig. 8, but this information is not very accurate. Lim *et al.* (1989) have shown that typical values for the coefficient of friction can be plotted on the wear map for the dry steel contacts in Fig. 6, but this estimation is not very accurate either.

A better and recommendable way to define the lubrication regime in a contact is to measure the film thickness. This can most easily be done by sending an electrical current through the contact and measuring the electrical resistance or the capacitance. The oscilloscope traces in resistance measurements give very good and reliable information about the amount of metallic collisions in the contact, as shown in Fig. 9, because the current is much more easily conducted from one part to the other over the metallic asperity contacts than through the lubricating film

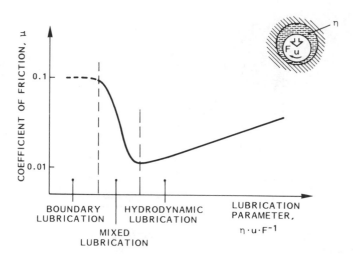

Fig. 8. The Striebeck curve indicates the relation between the lubrication regimes and the coefficient of friction.

(Dowson & Whomes, 1967–68; Georges *et al.*, 1983; Suzuki & Ludema, 1987). This gives a good indication of the transition region between boundary and full film (HD and EHD) lubrication, but not an absolute value for the film thickness. By measuring the capacitance between the two contacting parts, an absolute value for the film thickness can be found, but this technique and especially the calibration is somewhat more complicated (Schmidt, 1985; Alliston-Greiner *et al.*, 1987).

Accurate on-line wear measurements are difficult to perform. One possibility is to make the two samples radioactive and then register the amount of wear particles by radiation measurements (Ivkovic & Lazic, 1975). This method is certainly accurate but the handling of the radiated samples might create practical problems in the laboratory.

Wear particle analysis of samples of oil from the contact by the ferrography method is a well-established technique which gives a good indication of changes in the wear mechanism or the wear rate (Jones *et al.*, 1978; Lansdown, 1985; Corso & Adamo, 1989; this book, Chapter 3.2). The shortcoming of this method has so far been the amount of laboratory work that the analysis of each sample requires (about 1–2 h), but some promising attempts to automate this method for on-line measurements have recently been reported (Sato *et al.*, 1987; Chambers *et al.*, 1988; Kuoppala, 1988, this book, Chapter 3.2 and 3.3).

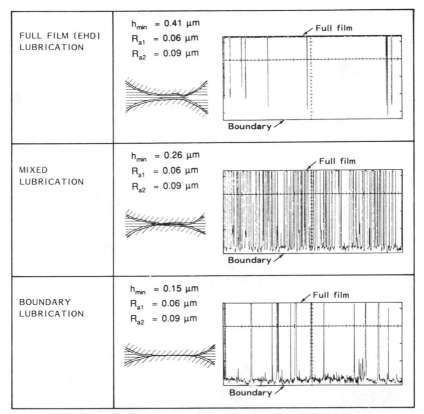

Fig. 9 The electrical resistance through the contact is related to the amount of metallic asperity contacts and is indicative of the lubrication regime. Measurements from the author's laboratory.

Monitoring the temperatures in the contact gives useful information but is not enough to draw conclusions about the wear or lubrication mechanisms. Optical on-line surface roughness measurements may be a practical future method of monitoring wear mechanisms and their changes.

WEAR TRACK ANALYSIS

During the action in a contact between two components, marks are caused on the sliding surfaces as they leave the contact. These marks

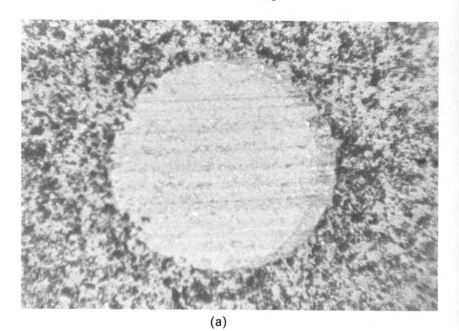

(a)

(b)

(c)

Fig. 10. Wear scars on spherical pins after pin-on-disc tests with ceramics: (a) mild wear in an alumina/alumina contact; (b) seizure in an alumina/alumina contact; and (c) severe oxidational wear in a silicon nitride/ silicon nitride (SSN/SSN) contact. Magnification: ×150.

carry useful information about the contacting process. Each wear mechanism leaves its own fingerprints or typical wear scar features on the surfaces and the mechanism can quite accurately be identified by these. This is illustrated by Fig. 10, which shows wear scars on spherical pins after pin-on-disc tests with a ceramic specimen. Figure 10(a) shows a surface after typical mild wear, Fig. 10(b) shows a surface after wear close to seizure with combined adhesion and abrasion, while Fig. 10(c) shows severe oxidational wear with chemical wear and abrasion, caused by the produced wear debris, as dominating wear mechanisms (Andersson, 1989).

De Gee *et al.* (1985) use in a similar way wear tracks on the specimen to define the lubrication regimes in Fig. 7 in their wear tests. Descriptions of how wear mechanisms can be identified from wear scars have been published by Vingsbo (1979) and Engel and Klingele (1981) and of how they appear on machine components by Jones and Scott (1981).

A good method for ensuring the reliability of tribological accelerated tests is to study the wear scars on the tested specimen and the wear scars from real components that have been working in industrial conditions similar to those which are to be simulated by the test. The applicability of the results is good if the wear scars indicate the same contact mechanisms.

CONCLUSION

Tribological accelerated testing can, in a short time and to a low cost, give useful information about component wear behaviour and lifetime. The results from accelerated testing are relevant to the performance of real components in machines only if the contact conditions are the same or similar, that is they are simplified and overloaded in a controlled way.

The reliability of accelerated tests can be increased by using wear or lubrication maps to predict the probable contact mechanisms. Another way is to use test parameter monitoring to control the contact mechanism during the test. In particular, measurements of the film thickness and wear particle analysis give reliable results. Thirdly, the contact conditions can be identified from the wear scars on the surfaces after the contacting action.

ACKNOWLEDGEMENTS

The author would like to thank Mr J. Vihersalo for skilfully performing the lubrication film measurements and Mr P. Andersson for the wear scar analysis and valuable comments. The financial support from the Nordic Industrial Fund and from the Technical Research Centre of Finland is gratefully acknowledged.

REFERENCES

Alliston-Greiner, A.F., Greenwood, J.A. & Cameron, A. (1987). Thickness measurements and mechanical properties of reaction films formed by zinc dialkyldithiophosphate during running. *Proc. Inst. Mech. Engrs*, **C178/87**, 565–72.
Andersson, P. (1989). Tribological aspects in design with ceramics. *Proc. 5th Scand. Symp. on Materials Science, New Materials and Processes*, Copenhagen, 22–25 May, pp. 109–15.

Begelinger, A. & de Gee, A.W.J. (1981) Failure of thin film lubrication—the effect of running-in on the load carrying capacity of thin-film lubricated concentrated contacts. *ASME J. Lubrication Techn.*, **103**, 203–10.

Bergman, B. & Klefsjö, B. (1989). *Kvalitet—från behov till användning* (Quality—from necessity to application) (in Swedish). Institute of Technology, Department of Mechanical Engineering, Linköping, Sweden.

Box, G.E.P., Hunter, W.G. & Hunter, J.S., (1978). *Statistics for Experimenters.* John Wiley, New York.

Chambers, K.W., Arneson, M.C. & Waggoner, C.A. (1988). An on-line ferromagnetic wear debris sensor for machinery condition monitoring and failure detection. *Wear*, **128**, 325–37.

Corso, S. & Adamo, R. (1989). The application of ferrography in monitoring motor oils during engine development. *STLE Lubrication Engineering*, **45**(9), 557–64.

de Gee, A.W.J., Begelinger, A. & Salomon, G. (1985). Failure mechanisms in sliding lubricated concentrated contacts. *Proc. 11th Leeds–Lyon Symp. on Tribology, Mixed Lubrication and Lubricated Wear.* Butterworths, London, pp. 105–16.

Dowson, D. & Whomes, T.L. (1967–68). Effect of surface quality upon the traction characteristics of lubricated cylindrical contacts. *Proc. Inst. Mech. Engrs*, **182**(14), 292–321.

Engel, L. & Klingele, H. (1981). *An Atlas of Metal Damage.* Wolfe Science Books & Carl Hanser Verlag, Munich, Germany, 1981.

Georges, J.M., Tonck, A., Meille, G. & Belin, M. (1983). Chemical films and mixed lubrication. *ASLE Trans.*, **26**(3), 293–305.

Hsu, S.M., Lim, D.S., Wang, Y.S. & Munro, R.G. (1989). Ceramic wear maps: concept and method development. *STLE/ASME Tribology Conf.*, Fort Lauderdale, FL, 16–19 October.

Ivkovic, B. & Lazic, M. (1975). Using radioactive techniques for tribological research. *Tribology International* (October), 209–13.

Jones, M.H. & Scott, D. (1981) *Industrial tribology.* Elsevier Tribology Series No. 8, Amsterdam, The Netherlands.

Jones, W.R., Nagaraj, H.S. & Winer, W.O. (1978). Ferrographic analysis of wear debris generated in a sliding elastohydrodynamic contact. *ASLE Trans.* 21(3), 181–90.

Kuoppala, R. (1988). Scanning technique for wear particle analysis. *9th European Maintenance Congress*, Espoo, Finland, 24–27 May.

Lansdown, A.R. (1985). Use of the rotary particle depositor in wear debris analysis. *Int. Conf. Friction, Wear and Lubricants*, Tashkent, USSR, 22–26 May.

Lim, S.C. & Ashby, M.F. (1987). Wear-mechanism maps. *Acta Metall.*, **35**(1), 1–24.

Lim, S.C. & Ashby, M.F. & Brunton, J.H. (1989). The effects of sliding conditions on the dry friction of metals. *Acta Metall.*, **37**(3), 767–72.

Onsøyen, E. (1990). *Accelerated testing and mechanical evauation of components exposed to wear.* Norwegian Institute of Technology, Division of Machine Design, Trondheim. 60 pp.

Sato, T., Ikeda, O., Hatsuzawa, T. & Linzer, M. (1987). Real-time evaluation of wear particles using electromagnetic forced rotation and laser scattering. *Wear*, **115**, 273–84.

Schmidt, U. (1985). Der Einfluss der Oberflächenrauheit auf die Schmierfilmaus-
bildung in realen EHD-Wälzkontakten. *VDI-Berichte*, **549**, 129–54.
Suzuki, M. & Ludema, K.C. (1987). The wear process during the 'running-in'
of steel in lubricated sliding. *ASME J. Tribology*, **109**, 587–93.
Uetz, H., Sommer, K. & Khosrawi, M.A. (1979). Übertragbarkeit von Versuchs-
und Prüfergebnissen bei abrasiver Verschleissbeanspruchung auf Bauteile.
VDI-Berichte, **354**, 107–24.
Vingsbo, O. (1979). Wear and wear mechanisms. In *Wear of Materials—1979*, ed.
K.C. Ludema, W.A. Glaeser & S.K. Rhee. American Society of Mechanical
Engineers, New York, pp. 620–35.
Vingsbo, O., Odfalk, M. & Shen, N. (1990). Fretting maps and fretting behavior
of some F.C.C. metal alloys. *Wear*, **138**, 153–67.
Wang, Y.S., Hsu, S.M. & Munro, R.G. (1989). Ceramic wear maps: alumina.
STLE/ASME Tribology Conf., Fort Lauderdale, FL, 16–19 October.

APPENDIX. SYMBOLS, DEFINITIONS AND UNITS

W	Wear rate (m^3/m)
$\tilde{W}$	Normalized wear
F	Normal force on sliding interface (N)
$\tilde{F}$	Normalized pressure on sliding interface
v	Sliding velocity (m/s)
$\tilde{v}$	Normalized velocity
A_n	Nominal area of contact (m^2)
A_r	Real area of contact (m^2)
r_0	Radius of pin (m)
r_a	Radius of an asperity (m)
l_b	Equivalent linear diffusion distance for bulk heating (m)
l_f	Equivalent linear diffusion distance for flash heating (m)
β	Dimensionless parameter for bulk heating ($= l_b/r_0$)
H	Hardness of sliding surface (N/m^2)
H_0	Room-temperature hardness of metal (N/m^2)
H_{ox}	Room-temperature hardness of oxide (N/m^2)
J	Heat flux ($J/m^2 s$)
q	Rate of heat input per unit area ($J/m^2 s$)
q'	Enhanced rate of heat input per unit area at an asperity ($J/m^2 s$)
q_c	Rate of heat conduction into the asperities per unit area ($J/m^2 s$)
Φ	Jaeger's dimensionless constant
α	Heat distribution coefficient
μ	Coefficient of friction
T	Temperature (K)
T_b	Bulk temperature (K)
T_f	Flash temperature (K)
T_0	Sink temperature for bulk heating (K)
T_0^f	Sink temperature for flash heating (K)
T_i	Temperature at the metal/oxide interface (K)

T^*	An equivalent temperature for metal (K)
T_c^*	An effective equivalent temperature for metal (K)
T_{ox}^*	An equivalent temperature for oxide (K)
T_c	Temperature for martensite formation (K)
T_m	Melting temperature of metal (K)
T_m^{ox}	Melting temperature of oxide (K)
T_{ox}	Oxidation temperature (K)
c	Specific heat (J/kgK)
ρ	Density of metal (kg/m^3)
ρ_{ox}	Density of oxide (kg/m^3)
ρc	Specific heat per unit volume (J/m^{3}K)
a	Thermal diffusivity of metal (m^2/s) ($=K/\rho c$)
a_{ox}	Thermal diffusivity of oxide (m^2/s)
K_m	Thermal conductivity of metal (J/msK)
K_{ox}	Thermal conductivity of oxide (J/msK)
K_c	Effective thermal conductivity (J/msK)
N	Total number of contacting asperities
N_T	True number of contacting asperities
P	Probability of forming a new asperity contact
η	Constant used in the calculation of N
s	Shear stress (N/m^2)
α_T	Constant used in Tabor's junction growth equation
$\dot{\varepsilon}$	Shear strain rate
$\dot{\varepsilon}_0$	Pre-exponential constant in low-temperature dislocation glide
ΔF	Activation energy for low-temperature dislocation glide (J/mol)
L	Latent heat of fusion per unit volume for metal (J/m^3)
L_{ox}	Latent heat of fusion per unit volume for oxide (J/m^3)
V_m	Volumetric rate of production of molten material (m^3/s)
f_m	Volume fraction of molten material removed during sliding
C	Constant used in the model for mild-oxidational wear
R	Molar gas constant (8·314 J/mol K)
Q_0	Activation energy for oxidation (J/mol)
A_0	Arrhenius constant for oxidation (kg^2/m^{2}s)
Δm	Mass of oxygen intake by the oxide film per unit area (kg/m^2)
k_p	Parabolic oxidation rate constant (kg^2/m^{4}s)
f	Mass fraction of oxygen in the oxide film
Z	Thickness of oxide film at an asperity (m)
Z_c	Critical thickness of oxide film (m)
Z_b	Thickness of oxide film due to bulk heating (m)
Z_f	Thickness of oxide film due to flash heating (m)
i_d	Pin-disc interaction time (s)
t_h	Heat diffusion time (s)
t_{ox}	Oxidation time (s)
t_c	Time taken to reach the critical oxide thickness (s)
X_o	Critical depth for void nucleation (m)
N_v	Number of inclusions per unit volume
r_1	Radius of an inclusion (m)
f_v	Volume fraction of inclusions

f_A Area fraction of voids
f_A^* Critical area fraction of voids
γ Cumulative plastic shear strain
γ^* Cumulative plastic shear strain needed to produce failure
γ_0 Plastic shear strain accumulated per pass
n^* Total number of passes to failure
λ Distance between asperity contacts
k_A Archard's dimensionless wear coefficient

1.3

Accelerated Testing of Components Exposed to Wear

ELDAR ONSØYEN

SINTEF, The Foundation for Scientific and Industrial Research at the Norwegian Institute of Technology, N-7034 Trondheim, Norway

ABSTRACT

This chapter describes the problem area of accelerated wear testing of mechanical components. Special challenges are component complexity and the possible transition from mild to severe wear, if a test is accelerated too severely. A scheme for 'mechanical evaluation' as a part of the test planning is suggested, and testing strategy based on available time and resources is discussed.

Oil hydraulic gear pumps have been tested in a case study. When reducing the oil viscosity step-wise to accelerate the tests, a temporary efficiency reduction often occurred, followed by a new running-in. No pumps failed within 2000–3000 hours of tests. In short-term experiments the instantaneous wear particle generation was studied using an on-line particle counter.

INTRODUCTION

The topic of this chapter is accelerated testing of mechanical components, in which wear is the main failure mechanism. A special challenge is the complexity of some components. The aim of the testing is to achieve information regarding the component's reliability, i.e. 'the ability to perform a required function under stated conditions for a stated period of time' (British Standard 4778, 1979).

As the lifetime of mechanical components is often much longer than the time available for testing, the tests must be accelerated. British

Standard 4778 (1979) gives the following definition of an accelerated test: 'A test in which the applied stress level is chosen to exceed that stated in the reference conditions in order to shorten the time required to observe the stress response of the item, or magnify the responses in a given time. To be valid, an accelerated test shall not alter the basic modes and mechanisms of failure, or their relative prevalence.'

Most of the earlier work on accelerated testing was carried out from the statistical point of view, and was aimed at components which fail suddenly, e.g. electronic components. Among literature covering parts of the selected area, the following is mentioned: reliability testing of simple components exposed to wear (Fleischer *et al.*, 1980), statistical methods for accelerated life testing (Viertl, 1988), analysis of lifetime data (Lawless, 1982), and reliability testing based on deterioration measurements (Lydersen, 1988).

This chapter gives some main points from a thesis (Onsøyen, 1990). The aim is to describe and demonstrate the problem area of accelerated wear testing, and to provide some methodology. The contents include:

— Purpose of reliability testing
— Description of wear processes in components
— Mechanical evaluation
— Accelerated wear testing
— Case study: Accelerated testing of hydraulic gear pumps

PURPOSE OF RELIABILITY TESTING

The needs for reliability evaluation and reliability testing may be illustrated by subsea components, used in petroleum exploration and production systems. Examples of such components are hydraulic control valves and hydraulically operated safety valves. The consequences may be serious if such equipment fails. In the worst case, an uncontrolled gas or oil release may occur, causing serious hazard to people and environment. Less drastic failure events may cause considerable economic consequences due to production losses and repair costs. The minimum lifetime required for subsea components, which operate under demanding conditions, is typically 5–20 years.

Against this background we see the need for effective methods for reliability evaluation and testing. Such methods are useful in different phases of the development of mechanical equipment:

— during the selection of components to be incorporated in a system (comparing alternative components);
— during the development of new components, or during the improvement and modification of existing component designs;
— during the evaluation of possible system concepts: some concepts may give special reliability requirements to the components involved.

The purpose of the evaluation and testing activities is to provide qualitative or quantitative knowledge regarding the component's reliability, such as the following.

(1) A basis for reliability improvement, by either modifying the design or changing the operational conditions.
(2) Weak points in the design, and the most critical sub-components.
(3) Dominating failure causes and mechanisms.
(4) Type of failure and performance (efficiency, power output, etc.) progression throughout the component lifetime, in particular, whether the loss of performance is sudden or gradual.
(5) The influence of the operational conditions (load, speed, etc.) on the component lifetime. This information may be more or less quantitative.
(6) Data connected with the expected time to failure, e.g. the time for 90% probability of survival, at specified operational conditions.
(7) Other quantitative information related to reliability, such as performance as a function of time, wear rate in critical sub-components, etc.

DESCRIPTION OF WEAR PROCESSES IN COMPONENTS

As a background for the planning of accelerated wear tests, some basic knowledge about wear processes in both simple and complex mechanical components is needed.

Wear

Wear is defined as 'damage to a solid surface, generally involving progressive loss of material, due to relative motion between that surface and a contacting substance or substances' (ASTM G40–88). When studied under a microscope, every surface is like a landscape with 'hills' and 'valleys', see Fig. 1.
There are two main conditions for a wear process to take place: first

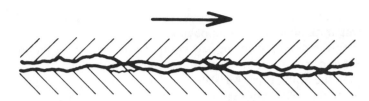

Fig. 1. Typical interacting surfaces, microscopic.

there must be an interaction between two surfaces, or between a fluid flow and a surface, and secondly, loose 'wear particles' must be generated from at least one of the surfaces. In sliding interaction, wear takes place when asperities or hard particles scratch or plough against a surface, causing wear particles to loosen from the surface. In rolling situations, fatigue cracks are intiated, causing flakes of the material to be released (surface fatigue).

Based on the mechanisms of material removal, different wear mechanisms have been defined: adhesive wear, abrasive wear, surface fatigue, delamination, fretting, erosion (including cavitation), corrosion wear, oxidation wear and impact wear. More information about wear and lubrication is given in Chapter 1.2 of this book and in textbooks such as Czichos (1978) and Jones and Scott (1983).

Factors Influencing the Wear Rate

The wear rate of a surface is the depth or volume of removed material per unit of sliding or rolling distance, or per unit of time. Wear is a rather complex failure mechanism, and a large number of factors influence the wear rate of a given pair of interacting surfaces:

— Macro-geometry: are the interacting surfaces conformal, or do they interact through a point or line contact?
— Type of interaction: sliding, rolling, impact; adhesion, abrasion or force transfer through a fluid film
— Normal (perpendicular) force
— Relative velocity
— Materials (hardness, ductility, etc.) and material combination
— Surface roughness (micro-geometry) and surface layers
— Friction coefficient, friction force
— Temperatures

— Type of lubrication: hydrodynamic, boundary or elastohydrodynamic lubrication, or no lubrication at all
— Lubricant properties and means of lubricant supply
— Type of surface deformation due to the interaction force: elastic or plastic
— Contamination in the lubricant: particles, water, chemical contamination, etc.
— The possibilities for wear debris to escape from the interaction zone
— Environment and atmosphere

Wear Rate as a Function of Load, and the Possibilities for Severe Wear

A natural way to speed up a wear test is to increase the load between interacting surfaces beyond the normal level. If then the relation between load and wear rate is known, the time to reach a certain wear depth under normal conditions may be estimated from the results of testing at higher load. Thus, knowledge about the wear rate as a function of load is needed.

This relationship is illustrated schematically in Fig. 2. When two dry, unlubricated metal surfaces rub against each other, the wear rate is often a linear function of the contact pressure. However, when increasing the contact pressure above a certain limit, a transition from mild wear to a severe wear process occurs, causing a more rapid increase in wear rate. The figure also shows the case of a lubricated sliding bearing. Up to a certain load, the surfaces are completely separated by an oil film (hydrodynamic lubrication). In this situation the wear rate depends only

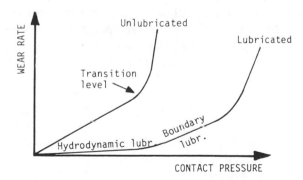

Fig. 2. Wear rate as a function of contact pressure, schematic.

on the content of hard particles in the oil. When the load is increased further, the surfaces start to rub against each other (boundary lubrication), and the wear rate rises. Also in the boundary lubrication situation there may be a transition from mild to severe wear.

The conclusion so far is that to avoid the transition from mild to severe wear, a component test must not be accelerated too severely. More information about the transition to severe wear is given in Chapters 1.1 and 1.2 of this book and by Salas-Russo (1990).

However, in some components, severe wear may occur even under normal operational conditions, causing too short a service life. Generally, the causes of severe wear are related to the following sources.

(1) Design errors: unsuitable material selection, too high local loads or temperature, too rough surface finish, etc.
(2) Fabrication errors: wrong materials, tolerances or surface finish, insufficient cleaning, etc.
(3) The component is operated under conditions other than those intended by the designer. In particular, some components need a gentle running-in, in order to attain sufficient conformity and smoothness of the interacting surfaces.

The first point is most likely to occur if the component is a new design, if it is produced in a small number, or if it is a modification of another component version.

Wear Depth as a Function of Time

According to Needleman (1978) there are in principle two types of performance deterioration of a component as a function of time: progressive and cumulative. The author suggests that the same terms should be used also when characterizing the wear progression. See examples in Fig. 3. An example of the progressive type of wear process is the wear volume of a plain journal bearing, operating with some metal-to-metal contact. After running-in, there might be a stable period with a constant wear rate, until the bearing clearance is high enough to change the dynamic behaviour of the shaft, causing an accelerating wear process.

A ball-bearing gives an example of the cumulative type of wear process. After some minor running-in wear, the wear rate is almost zero for a long period of time. During this period, a surface fatigue damage accumulates. Fatigue cracks are initiated, and after some time the first metal flakes start to loosen from the surface of a bearing ring.

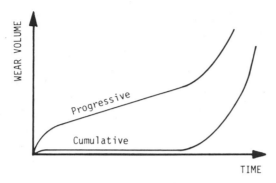

Fig. 3. Progressive and cumulative wear progression, schematic.

Complex Components

One of the challenges in accelerated wear testing is the complexity of some components. A complex component has some of the following characteristics.

(1) It has several critical sub-components. If there is no interaction between them, the component can be dealt with as a number of independent simple sub-components. But in some cases the wear process in one sub-component may cause an increased strain on another, e.g. due to the wear particles generated.

(2) Only some measure of performance (efficiency, leakage, etc.) may be monitored during testing, and not the actual material loss, which is the primary effect of the wear process.

(3) The shape of the component performance as a function of the wear depth or material loss is unpredictable.

Regarding point (3), some components are designed to compensate for wear, for example the hydraulic gear pump described in the case study later in this Chapter. The pump performance might then follow a curve as illustrated in Fig. 4, where the efficiency is expressed tentatively as a function of material loss in the pump.

A SCHEME FOR ACCELERATED WEAR TESTING

Having in mind a test where the aim is, for example, the time t_{90} for 90% probability of survival, the following general scheme for accelerated wear

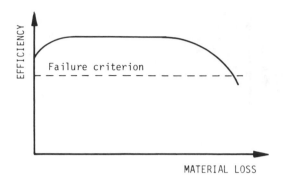

Fig. 4. Efficiency of a hydraulic pump as a function of material loss due to wear, schematic.

testing is suggested:

(1) Mechanical evaluation
(2) Definition of objectives of the test
(3) Choice of test strategy
(4) Stochastic modelling of the time to failure
(5) Design and fabrication of test system
(6) Experiment design
(7) Experiments
(8) Investigation of tested components
(9) Analysis and evaluation of test results; conclusions

These stages are described in the following two sections.

MECHANICAL EVALUATION

The term 'mechanical evaluation' is used by Lydersen and Rausand (1987) as a necessary part of the preparations for accelerated life tests. In the present section the task is detailed further, for the purpose of components exposed to wear. The main objectives of a mechanical evaluation are typically to find out why and how the component may fail, and to give a basis for the planning of reliability tests.

The mechanical evaluation may be based on:

(1) dismantling and study of new or used components;
(2) information from the manufacturer: drawings, design criteria, material

specifications, test results, operational experience, etc. It may be useful to visit the manufacturer, and task (1) might be carried out here;
(3) information from earlier reliability studies and testing;
(4) operational experience from users;
(5) information from reliability data sources.

In some cases component testing is too expensive, too time-consuming or unfeasible for other reasons. Then the mechanical evaluation may be the main phase of a reliability study, in addition to the analysis of possible field experience data. In other cases, the decision about possible testing is made after the mechanical evaluation. A limited test programme may, however, be compensated through a thorough mechanical evaluation.

A procedure for the mechanical evaluation of a component with respect to wear is suggested below.

(1) Description of the component as an element in the system where it is intended to operate:

  — A brief system description
  — The functions of the component in the system
  — The component's operational conditions and specifications, as a part of the system, e.g.:

  • Component load: forces, torques, speed, etc.
  • Demands for capacity, efficiency, precision, leakage, noise level, etc.
  • Minimum lifetime required
  • Environment: temperature, atmosphere, dust, humidity, etc.
  • Working medium and type of lubricant
  • Maintenance strategy and plan

  — Strains on the component as a result of possible failure processes in the surrounding system

(2) Description of the component:

  — Working principle
  — Detail design and function
  — Operational conditions, as specified by the manufacturer

(3) Possible failure modes of the component from the system point of view, and consequences on the system. For the last task, the FMECA method (Failure Mode, Effects and Criticality Analysis, MIL-STD-1629A, 1980) is a convenient tool.

(4) Summary of operational experience.

(5) Identification and discussion of possible causes of the different failure modes, i.e. failure processes in the various sub-components. For some complex components, Fault-Tree Analysis† and FMECA (see above) are useful methods.

(6) Identification and study of the most important sub-components in which wear may cause a failure:
 — Description of the main factors influencing the wear rate, referring to the list given earlier in this chapter.
 — Expected wear mechanisms.
 — The importance of the operational conditions (stress parameters) on the wear rate

(7) Evaluation of the possibilities of a severe wear situation in any of the sliding or rolling contacts (see the section above on wear rate as a function of load).

(8) Expected type of failure progression throughout the component lifetime, and consequences on the component performance (see the sections above on wear depth as a function of time, and on complex components), in particular whether the loss of performance will be sudden or gradual.

(9) Survey of possible ways to measure or monitor the component deterioration.

(10) Evaluation of the complexity of the component, referring to the section on complex components.

(11) Selection of failure criteria.

(12) Conclusions from the mechanical evaluation, including needs and possibilities for component testing and ways to accelerate the tests.

ACCELERATED WEAR TESTING

Alternative Test Strategies

Some alternative test objectives were given in seven points in the first main section of this chapter. The specific test objectives and strategy must

† The concept of fault-tree analysis was originated in 1961 by H.A. Watson of Bell Telephone Laboratories, and the method is described in, e.g., Ireson and Coombs (1988).

be decided, based on the resources available and on the mechanical evaluation results. Alternative strategies for accelerated testing are discussed below.

Two main constraints in the planning of accelerated tests are the budget and the time available. Possible test strategies are visualized in a simplified way in Fig. 5. The two axes in the diagram are the component

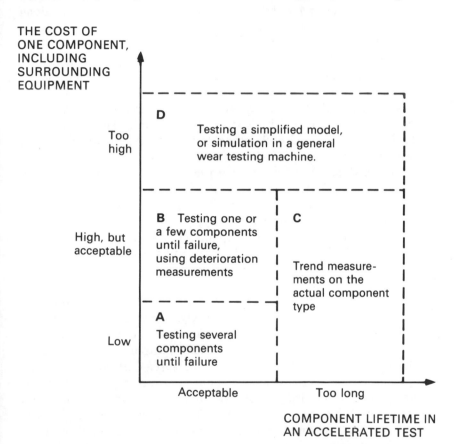

Fig. 5. Testing strategy, depending on costs and on expected lifetime.

lifetime in an accelerated test, and the cost of one component, including surrounding equipment needed for testing. Because the transition from one wear mechanism to another must be avoided, a wear test must not be accelerated too much. In some cases the component lifetime will be too long, or the operational costs (e.g. energy expenses) too high to allow testing until failure. Depending on the parameters above, Fig. 5 is divided into four regions, A to D:

A. *Accelerated life testing of several components.* This is the traditional type of accelerated life testing, with an acceptable time to failure and low costs. The mean time to failure under normal conditions (or another measure of reliability) is estimated, based on the observed times to failure and/or based on deterioration measurements along the test. This type of testing assumes that a sufficient number of equal components are run, and that it is possible to develop a stochastic model for the lifetime as a function of the stress parameters (pressure, temperature, etc.) selected to accelerate the tests. Such modelling is commented on in the next section.

Andersson (1983) describes how the time needed to test rolling bearings can be limited by 'sudden death' testing. The bearings are tested in groups, and each group test is terminated when the first failure occurs.

B. *Accelerated life testing of one or a few components.* Here the time to failure is acceptable, as above, but the costs are such that only one or a few components can be tested. Then measurements of the component deterioration (wear depth, leakage, efficiency, etc.) along the test are more important than above, in order to assure sufficient statistical confidence in the results. Qualitative results from the test, such as weak points and main failure mechanisms, may be as important as the quantitative information.

C. *Trend measurements.* The expected lifetime is in this case too long, even in an accelerated test. Alternatively, one might want to run as many tests as possible within a limited time, using the same test system or even the same component. Then the trend of the component deterioration (e.g. wear depth) can be measured during a short period of time. Trend measurements require accurate measuring methods and sufficient knowledge about the type of deterioration progression throughout the component lifetime. The section on trend measurements in the case study below describes trend measurements using an on-line particle counter to study the generation of wear debris.

D. *Simplification and simulation.* Sometimes it would be too expensive to test a complete component, or one might have sufficient knowledge of the main problems of the component. The critical parts and the main failure processes may then be isolated and investigated, using a simple model of the component or a general wear testing machine (e.g. a pin-on-disc machine). In some cases there is a further alternative of testing a less expensive component type, which has relevance to the actual component. Simplification and simulation are described further in Chapters 1.1 and 1.2 of this book.

Modelling the Time to Failure

Stochastic modelling of the time to failure, when using deterioration measurements, includes the following steps:

(1) Selection of 'normal' levels of all operational conditions affecting the component reliability
(2) Selection of 'stressors' to be increased or decreased beyond their normal levels to accelerate the tests, e.g. pressure, oil viscosity, etc.
(3) Modelling of the wear rate as a function of the selected stressors
(4) Modelling the wear progression, which is the wear depth or wear volume as a function of time
(5) Stochastic modelling of the time to failure, i.e. the time until a pre-defined deterioration limit is reached

Examples of qualitative 'models' were presented earlier: wear rate as a function of contact pressure (Fig. 2), wear depth as a function of time (Fig. 3) and performance as a function of wear depth (Fig. 4). It is beyond the scope of this chapter to give details on how to model the time to failure. An indication is given below, however, and an example for a simple sliding bearing is given in Onsøyen (1990). A method for wear prediction by stochastic filtering is given in Chapter 3.4 of this book.

For the situation in Fig. 6, a simple model for the wear depth as a

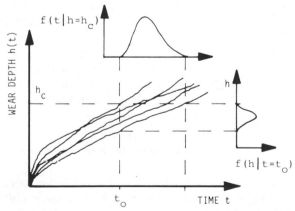

Fig. 6. Probability densities for the wear depth and the time to failure, based on Fleischer *et al.* (1980).

function of time would be

$$h(t) = h_0 + h't$$

where $h(t)$ is wear depth, t is time, h_0 is the contribution from running-in and h' is the wear rate (the increase of wear depth per unit of time). h' is a function of the selected stressors. The time to failure is the time until $h(t)$ reaches a critical wear depth h_c.

This type of failure progression is treated by Fleischer et al. (1980), Ahmad and Sheikh (1984) and Lydersen (1988). Both h_0 and h' are stochastic variables, following the normal distribution. Assuming that the statistical variation is determined only by the initial conditions (fabrication and running-in), and that h_0 and h' are independent, the time to failure follows a Bernstein distribution. If h_0 is fixed and the variations are determined mainly by changes in the wear process and operational conditions throughout the component life, the time to failure may be modelled using a Birnbaum–Saunders or an inverse Gaussian distribution.

The lifetime of a component is normally reported in terms of operation time or the number of cycles. But sometimes the calendar time is also important, because of corrosion effects, chemical degradation, etc. When planning accelerated tests, we must consider how much of the 'dormant' time can be cut out without changing the failure processes too much.

Test System and Experiment Design

The test system must be designed and fabricated such that all external factors influencing the possible failure processes of the tested components can be monitored and controlled.

If the cost is acceptable, a component may be sacrified to assure that the test system provides repeatable results, and to find stressor levels which are sufficiently high to give acceptable test times. If the component cost is low, it is advisable to start at a relatively high stress level. If the cost is higher, one may start at a level which is assumed not to be destructive, and then increase the stress step by step. Such an experiment might also give an indication of the level for transition to severe wear.

Statistical experiment design and data analysis is not covered in this chapter. It is treated in general by, e.g., Montgomery (1984), and in connection with accelerated testing in Chapter 1.4 of this book.

CASE STUDY: ACCELERATED TESTING OF HYDRAULIC GEAR PUMPS

Possibilities and problems of accelerated wear testing have been investigated and demonstrated by testing oil hydraulic pumps. A full report from the case study is given in Onsøyen (1990). In this section some results which illustrate the methodology and problem area of testing are presented.

Mechanical Evaluation

A small and inexpensive hydraulic gear pump type has been selected. The principle of such a pump is seen in Fig. 7. The pump is a positive displacement pump, designed to supply a fixed quantity of fluid per revolution, almost independent of the delivery pressure. It gives about 1 litre fluid per minute at 3000 rpm, and is designed for maximum 17 MPa continuous pressure, 20 MPa peak pressure and minimum 25 mm²/s oil viscosity.

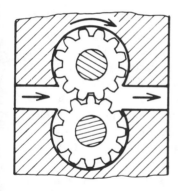

Fig. 7. The principle of an external gear pump.

A mechanical evaluation has been carried out according to the scheme outlined earlier in this chapter, and some of the main results are given below.

— The main failure mode is insufficient fluid flow, at the specified pressure, and is a result of increased internal leakage.
— Based on operational experience, the main factors influencing the lifetime seem to be oil cleanliness, delivery pressure and oil viscosity.

— Three critical parts of the pump were identified: the journal bearings, the gear faces against the end plates, and the gears.
— The journal bearings are plain sliding bearings, with steel shafts running in bores in aluminium bearing housings. Calculations indicate that both the combination of load and speed, and the combination of oil film thickness and surface roughness may cause severe wear, even with clean oil.
— The easiest way to monitor the pump condition during testing is by frequent measurements of the volumetric efficiency, and from the user's viewpoint this is the main measure of performance. Wear depths or material loss cannot be measured easily without dismantling the pump.
— It is not possible to predict the relationship between the wear depth in critical parts and the pump performance, because the pump is designed to compensate for wear. In addition, there is a possible interaction between the wear processes in different critical sub-components: debris from surface fatigue of the gears may cause abrasive wear on other interacting surfaces. Therefore, the simple and inexpensive pump is regarded as a complex component.

General experience from the mechanical evaluation includes the following.

— The complete mechanical evaluation, which is reported in Onsøyen (1990), is rather extensive. In general, it is necessary to limit the extent of mechanical evaluation according to the needs in the actual case, and to concentrate on the main potential problem sources.
— In order to carry out a mechanical evaluation, a thorough understanding of the component's way of operation and the possible failure processes is essential. Teamwork may therefore be necessary.
— The mechanical evaluation results in a survey of potential problems, critical sub-components, failure processes, etc. It is, however, difficult to foresee which failure processes are most probable, and the next sections will show that testing of pumps has given some surprising results. Therefore, only testing (or relevant operational experience) can confirm which are really the main problems of a component.

Objectives and Strategy

The objectives of the pump test programme were:

(1) identifying weak points in the design, and the most critical sub-components;

(2) studying the volumetric efficiency as a function of time, throughout the whole pump lifetime, and thereby giving a basis for modelling the time to failure;

(3) studying the importance of the operational conditions on wear rate or pump lifetime;

(4) if possible, estimating the expected lifetime at normal operational conditions.

Before the tests, it was uncertain to which degree these aims could be fulfilled. It was therefore decided to carry out the test programme step by step. A natural test strategy to achieve points (1), (2) and (4) above is type B in Fig. 5: testing a few pumps until failure, using deterioration measurements. In addition, more or less quantitative data on the importance of the operational conditions (point (3)) can be obtained by trend measurements (strategy type C). When planning long-term tests, the hope was to be able to run the pumps until failure within about 2000 running hours (3 months).

Long-term Accelerated Tests

It was decided to test the pumps using relatively clean oil. Traditionally, tribological testing of hydraulic pumps has been carried out with an artificial abrasive contaminant, such as 'Air Cleaner Fine Test Dust' (ACFTD), in the hydraulic fluid. Comprehensive studies of pump deterioration due to abrasive wear are reported by Milwaukee School of Engineering (1980), BHRA (1984), Hong and Fitch (1986) and Winner (1987). However, good methods are available to assure satisfactory cleanliness in hydraulic systems, and less work is done aiming at other wear mechanisms than abrasive wear. In practice, the oil cleanliness was ISO Standard 4406 (1987) class 15/12 or better during the tests.

A test system was designed, capable of running three pumps at a time. Figure 8 shows the results from an introductory experiment at moderate operational conditions: 20 MPa pressure (18% above maximum continuous pressure), 2900 rpm, a typical hydraulic oil (32 mm²/s viscosity at 40°C) and a typical oil temperature (35°C). The volumetric efficiency has been measured at approximately fixed intervals during 2000 hours of operation. The figure shows that the volumetric efficiency improved significantly during the first 200 hours for all three pumps, then it remained stable until the experiment was stopped.

Similar experiments with 65% overload by increasing the delivery pressure, and with pressure cycling, gave the same kind of results. The

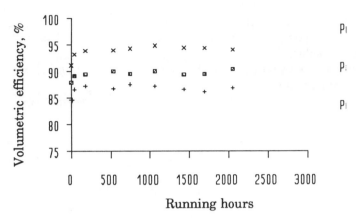

Fig. 8. Volumetric efficiency as a function of running hours, measured at 20 MPa.

experiments showed a large difference in efficiency between the nine pumps tested so far, but none of the pumps showed any indications of efficiency reduction within 1500–2000 running hours. It was then decided to try trend measurements to go deeper into what are the conditions for pump wear.

Trend Measurments Using On-line Particle Counting

Trend measurements were commented on earlier in the section on Alternative Test Strategies. The approach in this study was to measure the wear particle generation by using an on-line optical particle counter immediately after the pump, counting particles from 2 µm and up. Background knowledge on the characteristics of wear particles generated in different wear regimes is given by Reda *et al.* (1975) and Beerbower (1981).

A pump which had operated for 1500 hours during a long-term test was selected for the tests. The test system was made such that particles should not be able to get trapped anywhere, and 2 µm filtration was provided (Beta$_2$ ⩾ 75, according to ISO Standard 4572, 1981), so that the instantaneous generation of wear particles could be measured.

Tests were run at three pressure levels, 15, 20 and 25 MPa. The speed was 3000 rpm and the oil was the same type as in the previous expriments. In each test the oil temperature was increased slowly (less than 0.3°C/min), starting at a temperature giving a low particle generation.

The particle concentrations in the 2–3, 3–4, 4–5 and 5–10 µm size ranges were measured during 50 seconds (50 ml) every 2 or 3 minutes.

Figure 9 shows particle counts as a function of temperature and pressure, and Fig. 10 presents the 20 MPa data on a logarithmic scale. In

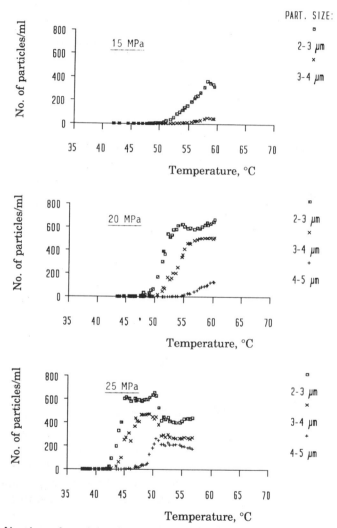

Fig. 9. Number of particles per millilitre in the hydraulic oil after the pump, as a function of inlet oil temperature. The pump has been run at three different pressure levels.

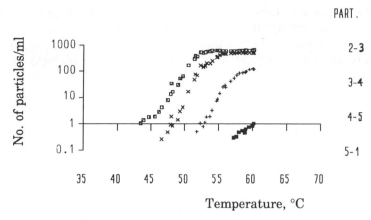

Fig. 10. The 20 MPa data from Fig. 9, presented on a logarithmic scale.

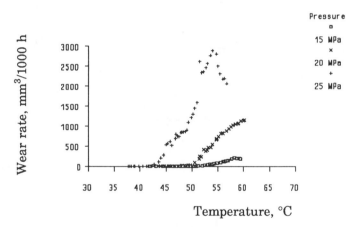

Fig. 11. Calculated wear rate as a function of pressure and oil temperature.

Fig. 11 the wear rate is calculated roughly in mm³/1000 h, based on the particle counts. As the oil viscosity decreases with increasing temperature, it is rather the viscosity which is critical, and not the temperature. Figure 12 gives a closer view of the data from Fig. 11 in the 0–5 mm³/1000 h wear rate range, as a function of oil viscosity. A calculation has shown that this range is the order of magnitude of 'mild' wear in the selected pump.

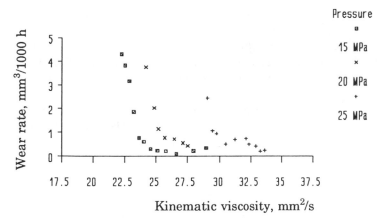

Fig. 12. Calculated wear rate as a function of oil viscosity, in the 0–5 mm³/1000 h wear rate range.

The conclusions regarding the gear pump are as follows.

— A transition from mild to severe wear occurs almost suddenly at a critical oil viscosity. This probably means that a transition from hydrodynamic lubrication to mixed or boundary lubrication occurs at a critical place inside the pump. We do not know where this critical part is located, but the author would suggest the journal bearings. The critical viscosity increases with increasing pressure.
— After passing the transition to severe wear, both the wear rate and the average wear particle size increase with decreasing oil viscosity and with increasing pressure.
— Wear rates have been observed which would ruin the pump within a few hours. However, the final long-term test described in the next section confirms that the very severe wear was of a temporary nature, resulting in a new running-in. After the most severe test at 25 MPa, the pump could tolerate more demanding conditions than before.

The conclusions regarding the trend measurement method are as follows.

— The method makes it possible to study the conditions for transition from mild to severe wear.
— It was possible to measure the instantaneous generation of wear particles in the pump, from the mild wear rate of about 0·5 mm³/1000 h up to 3000 mm³/1000 h, which in this case is very severe wear.

— The method is more suitable for more simple components than the complex gear pump.

— The repeatability was not satisfactory, and the main reason seems to be the temporary running-in effects of the pump. The measuring results depend on what the test item has been through prior to the test.

— A major limitation of the test system was that it was not possible to keep a constant temperature, and therefore only transient effects were measured.

— In the optical particle counter, anything which blocks or disturbs the light beam is counted as particles. Therefore, soft compounds such as 'friction polymers', which have been observed in the oil, will disturb the counts.

— A tendency for many small particles to agglomerate and thereby be counted as one large particle was also observed.

Trend measurement by particle counting is an interesting topic for further research. The test object must then be simpler and easier to control and monitor than the gear pump. In addition, the test system must be made such that all factors influencing the wear process can be monitored, controlled and kept constant. Challenges regarding the test method include:

— controlling the 'noise level' and error sources in the instrumentation, to be able to measure mild wear accurately;

— finding the conditions for repeatable measurements, from the wear and lubrication points of view.

— measuring smaller particles, i.e. down to 1 μm or less.

After the test method has been sufficiently developed, basic studies could be carried out on the transition between different wear regimes, and on the wear rate as a function of material combination, surface roughness, load, relative velocity, oil viscosity, oil additives, etc.

Final Long-term Test

Based on the results from the trend measurements, a final experiment lasting 3100 h was run with three new pumps. After running-in, the test conditions were accelerated step by step by lowering the oil viscosity (high oil temperature and using a lower viscosity oil) and by using an oil without anti-wear additives. The pressure was 20 MPa, which is a mild overload (18%).

The test started at $17 \, \text{mm}^2/\text{s}$ viscosity (60°C), and according to the results from trend measurements, this should give severe wear. Two pumps showed a new running-in, but no volumetric efficiency reduction was observed during 840 h. The viscosity was then reduced further to $13 \, \text{mm}^2/\text{s}$. One of the pumps had a new running-in and a slight efficiency improvement during the 1440 h at this viscosity, while the performance of the two other pumps was practically stable.

The oil was then replaced by a type without anti-wear additives. The viscosity was reduced step-wise until the final phase, which is seen in Fig. 13. Here the viscosity was $3 \cdot 5 \, \text{mm}^2/\text{s}$, which is one-seventh of the manufacturer's specification. At first in this phase, the drive motors almost stopped due to high internal friction in the pumps. But after less than 1 h, the motor speed became normal again. A running-in process occurred once again, and the volumetric efficiency improved significantly for all three pumps during the 410 h at this viscosity. Pump 10 had an odd performance progression, and might possibly have been degrading towards the end of the test.

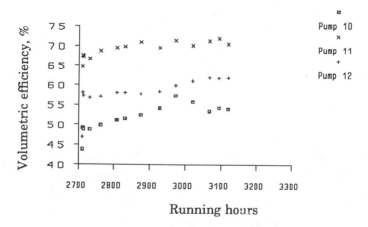

Fig. 13. Volumetric efficiency at 20 MPa pressure and $3 \cdot 5 \, \text{mm}^2/\text{s}$ oil viscosity, during the last phase of the final long-term test.

A final efficiency measurement at the initial operational conditions confirmed that the efficiency improvement observed during several phases of the experiment had been the result of temporary efficiency reduction when worsening the operational conditions. High internal friction has caused increased local temperatures in the pump, causing higher internal leakage. But a new running-in has occurred every time, which means that critical surfaces have become smoother and/or more conformal.

Study of the pumps after the tests revealed that the most critical part of the selected pump is the gear teeth. In most of the 12 pumps tested, severe surface fatigue (pitting) was observed. The pumps from the final experiment had most damage. This, however, did not seem to influence the volumetric efficiency. The other sub-components pinpointed in the mechanical evaluation, i.e. the bearings and the gear faces against the end plates, did not show any significant sign of wear.

Conclusions from the long-term experiments include the following.

— Except for two pumps out of 12 the volumetric efficiency improved significantly during the first 100–200 running hours. This is a long running-in period. The improvement is largest for the pumps having the lowest efficiency after running-in.
— After running-in, the volumetric efficiency was principally constant for all the pumps until the tests were terminated. Exceptions are the temporary effects in the final experiment.
— Even with 65% overload, heavy pressure cycling or oil viscosity down to $3.5 \, \text{mm}^2/\text{s}$ (one seventh of the manufacturer's specification), it was not possible to run any of the pumps until failure, within a 2000–3000 h test. It was therefore not possible to model or estimate the time to failure.
— Several times when the operational conditions were worsened during the final experiment, a temporary efficiency reduction and a new running-in were observed.
— The experiments illustrate the difference between various stressors when accelerating a test. Because the predominant effect of increasing the pressure is that the internal leakage increases, the pressure was increased only by a factor of 1·65. The viscosity, however, was reduced by a factor of 7 relative to the manufacturer's specification.
— The main factor influencing the pump performance seems to be the production tolerances. The tested pumps originate from two different production series, A and B. There is a significant difference in volumetric efficiency between the two series, and also between the pumps within series B. It should be added that the pumps are simple and inexpensive, and that the displacement is small compared to most gear pumps.

CONCLUSIONS

Accelerated wear testing is a useful tool in the development, improvement and selection of mechanical components. A thorough mechanical evaluation should be carried out as a part of the test preparations. It identifies important failure modes, critical sub-components and potential failure causes and processes. However, only testing (or relevant operational experience) can confirm which are really the main problems of a component.

Wear tests must not be accelerated too severely, to avoid the possible transition from mild to severe wear. Another challenge is the complexity of many mechanical components. Qualitative information, such as weak points, suggested modifications and conditions for achieving a long service life, may be the main results from the testing. The extent of testing is often limited by cost and time constraints, and therefore quantitative reliability data such as the mean time to failure may be hard to attain. Ways to limit costs and time during testing include trend measurements and simplification and simulation of the wear process. To maximize the amount of test data, some measures of the component deterioration should be monitored along the tests.

Possibilities and problems of accelerated wear testing have been demonstrated by testing oil hydraulic gear pumps. The tests were accelerated by a step-wise reduction of the inlet oil viscosity. In the worst case the viscosity was one-seventh of the maufacturer's specification. Often when the test conditions were worsened, a temporary efficiency reduction occurred, followed by a new running-in. It was not possible to run any of the pumps until failure within the time available. The only trace of wear observed was surface fatigue in the gear teeth, and the main factor influencing the pump efficiency was the production tolerances.

Trend measurements were carried out by using an on-line particle counter to measure the instantaneous generation of wear particles in the pump. The conditions for transition from mild to severe wear, and the wear rate as a function of pressure and oil viscosity, were studied. The method is more suitable for less complex components than the gear pump, and is an interesting topic for further research.

REFERENCES

Ahmad, M. & Sheikh, A.K. (1984). Bernstein reliability model: derivation and estimation of parameters. *Reliability Engineering*, **8**, 131–48.

Andersson, T. (1983). Endurance testing in theory. *Ball Bearing Journal*, **217**, SKF Engineering & Research Centre, Postbus 50, 3430 AB Nieuwegein, The Netherlands.

ASTM G40–88 (1988). *Standard terminology relating to wear and erosion.* American Society for Testing and Materials.

Beerbower, A. (1981). Wear rate prognosis through particle size distribution. *ASLE Trans.*, **24**, 285–92.

BHRA (1984). *Contaminant sensitivity—Standard test methods. Contamination control in fluid power systems 1980–1983. Volume VII.* Research Contractor: British Hydromechanics Research Association. Dept. of Trade and Industry, NEL, East Kilbride, Glasgow.

BS4778 (1979). *Glossary of terms used in quality assurance (including reliability and maintainability terms).* British Standards Institution, London.

Czichos, H. (1978). *Tribology—A Systems Approach to the Science and Technology of Friction, Lubrication and Wear.* Elsevier, Amsterdam, The Netherlands.

Fleischer, G., Gröger, H. & Thum, H. (1980). *Verschleiss und Zuverlässigkeit.* VEB Verlag, Berlin.

Hong, I.T. & Fitch, E.C. (1986). Wear of gear pump under abrasive fluid conditions. *Proc. 41st Nat. Conf. on Fluid Power*, Detroit, MI.

Ireson, W.G. & Coombs, C.F. (eds) (1988). *Handbook of Reliability Engineering and Management.* McGraw-Hill, New York.

ISO Standard 4406 (1987). *Hydraulic fluid power—Fluids—Method for coding level of contamination by solid particles.*

ISO Standard 4572 (1981). *Hydraulic fluid power—Filters—Multi-pass method for evaluating filtration performance.*

Jones, M.H. & Scott, D. (eds) (1983). *Industrial Tribology—The Practical Aspects of Friction, Lubrication and Wear.* Elsevier, Amsterdam, The Netherlands.

Lawless, J.F. (1982). *Statistical Models and Methods for Lifetime Data.* John Wiley, New York.

Lydersen, S. (1988). *Reliability testing based on deterioration measurements.* Dr. Ing. dissertation 1988:32, Norwegian Institute of Technology, Trondheim.

Lydersen, S. & Rausand, M. (1987). A systematic approach to accelerated life testing. *Reliability Engineering*, **18**, 285–93.

MIL-STD-1629A (1980). *Procedures for performing a failure mode, effects and criticality analysis.* Department of Defense, Washington, DC.

Milwaukee School of Engineering (1980). *Final report on the investigation into hydraulic gear pump efficiencies in the first few hours of the pump's lives and a comparative study of accelerated life test methods on hydraulic fluid power gear pumps–Part III.* Fluid Power Institute, Milwaukee School of Engineering, AD-A089 848.

Montgomery, D.C. (1984). *Design and Analysis of Experiments*, 2nd edition. John Wiley, New York.

Needleman, W.M. (1978). Fluid particulate contamination, component wear and performance. *Proc. Int. Conf. on the Fundamentals of Tribology*, Massachusetts Institute of Technology, June 1978.

Onsøyen, E. (1990). *Accelerated testing and mechanical evaluation of components exposed to wear.* Dr. Ing. dissertation, 1991:17, Norwegian Institute of Technology, Division of Machine Design, Trondheim, December 1990.

Reda, A.A., Bowen, R. & Weatcott, V.C. (1975). Characteristics of particles generated at the interface between sliding steel surfaces. *Wear*, **34**, 261–73.

Salas-Russo, E. (1990). *Failure in lubricated sliding steel contacts*. Licentiate Thesis TRITA-MAE-1990:8, Royal Institute of Technology, Stockholm.

Viertl, R. (1988). *Statistical Methods in Accelerated Life Testing*. Vandenhoeck & Ruprecht, Göttingen, Germany.

Winner, D.P. (1987). *Untersuchung der Verschmutzungsempfindlichkeit von hydraulischen Verdrängereinheiten*. Dr. Ing. dissertation, Technischen Hochschule Aachen, Germany.

1.4

Accelerated Life Testing
for Reliability Improvement

Bo Bergman and Mohsen Hakim

*Linköping University, Department of Design and Production,
Division of Quality Technology, S-581 83 Linköping, Sweden*

ABSTRACT

Today, there is an increasing demand for improved quality and reliability because of increasingly complex systems putting severe reliability requirements on system components and parts. Reliability improvement is needed. Accelerated life testing as treated in the reliability literature has mostly been used to measure reliability, not to improve it. A change has to be made.

In this chapter we discuss accelerated testing from a reliability improvement point of view. Statistically designed experiments are important in order to find factors affecting reliability. Simple factorial designs, often fractional, as well as more advanced plans, can be used. Robust design methodology is a concept which has to be incorporated into the reliability field. Some simple illustration will be given.

INTRODUCTION

The general purpose of reliability technology is product reliability improvement. The demand for reliability improvement is increasing due to increasing system complexity and increasing demands from customers on quality. Reliability is one of the important dimensions of quality. A means of finding weak points and other important areas for reliability improvement is the use of accelerated life testing; see also Chapter 1.1 in this book.

Traditionally, accelerated life testing has been used to estimate or measure reliability. The new emphasis on improvements puts new requirements on the planning of accelerated life testing experiments. Not only the acceleration effect is of interest. We have to find the effects of different disturbing factors as well as the effects of different design parameters on reliability. Thus, the traditional one-factor-at-a-time strategy for life testing cannot be recommended. Statistically designed life testing experiments have to be utilized. Only recently has design of experiments been discussed in the life testing literature, though an exception is the work of Zelen (1959).

Today, it has been realized that design of experiments is important in life testing situations; see for example O'Connor (1985) and Taguchi (1986). In a later section of this chapter some basic ideas are presented. We shall also discuss the role of accelerated life tests in robust design methodology. Another area of application is for the selection of condition monitoring techniques. Finally, we shall give some ideas concerning diagnostic checking of life testing experiments—here different types of TTT-plotting techniques are important.

ACCELERATION MODELS

We can see an acceleration model as an equation modifying a distribution scale parameter, or percentile, as a function of the operating stress. Some of the most common models are the Arrhenius, Eyring and Power Rule models.

In order to describe the relationship between life distributions $F(t|S_1)$ and $F(t|S_2)$ at two different stress levels S_1 and S_2, the acceleration function $a(t; S_1, S_2)$ is defined such that

$$F(t|S_2) = F(a(t; S_1, S_2)|S_1); \quad t \geq 0$$

Here we assume that S_2 is more severe than S_1. This implies that $a(t; S_1, S_2) > t$. See also Fig. 1.

The analysis of a accelerated life test is very dependent on the model assumptions made. Acceleration models are discussed by, for example, Viertl (1987) and Mazzuchi and Singpurwalla (1987); see also Xie et al. (1990) in which some concepts of acceleration are discussed. Acceleration may be considered as a speeding-up of time or as an increase in failure rate. In the simplest types of models these increased rates (time and

probability
density

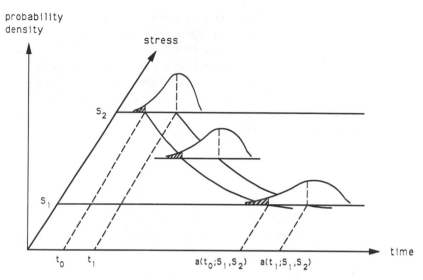

Fig. 1. Illustration of the acceleration function $a(t; S_1, S_2)$.

failure rate) are modelled by using a proportionality constant pertinent to the degree of acceleration.

Simple graphical analysis methods are considered in the recent book by Nelson (1990). A thorough survey of classical statistical methods applied to acccelerated life tests is given in Bhattacharya (1987) while Mazzuchi and Singpurwalla (1987) take a Bayesian point of view, utilizing ideas from Kalman filtering.

FACTORIAL DESIGNS

The one-factor-at-a-time strategy for life testing, which is unfortunately still used in most industrial situations, should be substituted by factorial design because the latter takes less time, costs less money and gives more information. Moreover, the effect of interaction between factors cannot be found using the one-factor-at-a-time strategy.

Factorial designs, complete or fractional, are excellent for the planning of experiments for finding important quality-affecting factors. To illustrate the idea we shall use the illustration by Box and Bisgaard (1987). We refer to that paper for a more complete discussion on the role of design of experiments for quality improvement.

Assume we want to find factors of importance for fatigue life of a component, in this case a spring. Three factors are assumed to be important: S = steel temperature, O = oil temperature, and C = carbon content. For each factor two levels are selected, one low and one high. The low level is symbolized by '−' and the high level is symbolized by '+'. Eight combinations of factor levels may be formulated. These eight combinations may be illustrated in a three-dimensional cube, where each dimension corresponds to a factor, see Fig. 2.

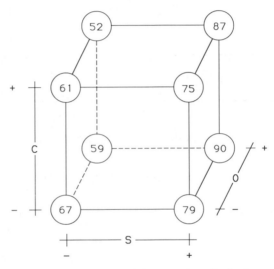

Fig. 2. Reliability figures illustrated in a cube displaying all experiment conditions studied.

For each combination, a number of springs are manufactured and exposed to accelerated life testing. The percentages of springs surviving without cracks for the prescribed testing time are noted, and can be shown in the corners of the cube in Fig. 2.

The numerical evaluation of the effect of each of the three factors and their interactions is easy to do but here, just by looking at the cube, we can comprehend which factors are active. Steel temperature seems to be important and its level should be kept high. Steel and oil temperatures seem to interact—we estimate a positive effect of increasing the oil temperature while the steel temperature is high, but the opposite is true while the steel temperature is low. Perhaps also the carbon percentage has some importance. This can also be illustrated as in Fig. 3.

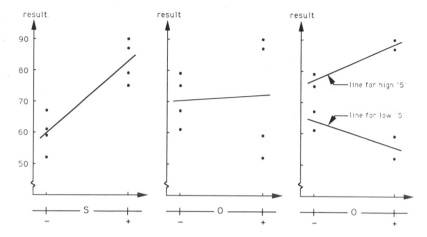

Fig. 3. Some results from Fig. 2 displayed in a different way.

Of course the above statements might be wrong if random fluctuations are large. Here we assume that a sufficient number of springs have been tested at each combination of factor levels to make the above statements reasonable. A formal discussion can be made utilizing properties of the binomial distribution.

FRACTIONAL FACTORIAL DESIGN

The number of different combination of factor levels increases very much when we try to apply the above type of plan in situations with many factors of interest. Having for example 4 factors, we should have to investigate $2^4 = 16$ different combinations of factor levels and it doubles for every additional factor. But we can reduce the number of combinations with little loss of information by observing only a fraction of all possible combinations.

In the case illustrated by Fig. 4, which is a 2^{4-1} design, the information we lose is that the effect of main factors will not be distinguishable from the three-factor-interactions. The two-factor-interaction effects will also be inseparable. If needed, we can complete this design afterwards by doing the remaining eight combinations of factor levels. This can be seen in Fig. 4(a) and (b) or alternatively in Fig. 4(c). We also observe that if one of the factors can be ignored, the 2^{4-1} design can be considered as a complete design for the other three factors.

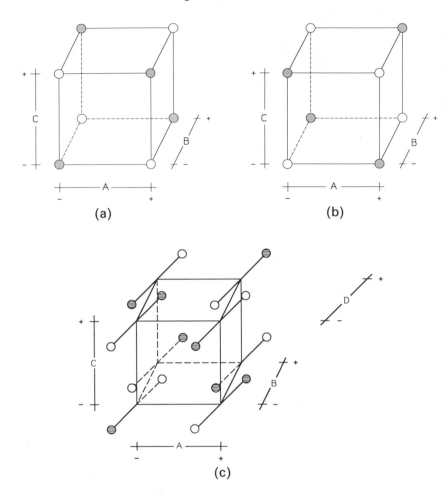

Fig. 4 A complete factorial design for four factors A, B, C and D requires 2^4 combinations of factor levels but these can be halved by choosing only the dashed corners. This can be illustrated by either (a) in which D is ' − ' and (b) in which D is ' + ', or by (c) in which all four factors are illustrated.

The fractional factorial design is very useful particularly for selecting among numerous factors at the beginning of a reliability improvement process. In cases where the interaction effects can be considered negligible, then up to seven factors can be evaluated using only eight factor combinations. This means a 2^{7-4} design. After this first design, the number of factors can be reduced and more complete designs will be applicable. Those factors which seem not to have any effect on the quality might be economically very interesting. By a suitable change of their levels, we may reduce the cost without affecting the function.

Without special reference to life testing experiments, many questions regarding factorial designs, complete and fractional, are discussed in Box et al. (1978). A book in Swedish on the design of experiments is in progress (Bergman, 1991b). In general a sequence of life tests should be used to find good combinations of design parameters. In a general setting this is discussed in Box and Draper (1987), an excellent book on response surface methodology. These ideas should be more exploited in the area of life testing.

SOME SPECIAL PROBLEMS

When accelerated life tests are utilized for the evaluation of the effects of the studied factors special problems occur. Some of these are discussed below.

In the life testing experiment above we used estimated reliability as a response. But usually we are interested in the complete life distribution. Is the improvement due to an increased mean life or is it due to a decreased left tail of the life distribution? A good decision can in many situations be different depending on the answer to the above question.

Another problem area is the possibility of an interaction between the factors under study and the stress factor. A stress factor not always affects only the time scale, which perhaps is the ideal case, but it may also affect the shape of the distribution. This effect is illustrated later in Fig. 7. Currently this question is being addressed in ongoing work at the Division of Quality Technology, Linköping University. The concept of total time on test (TTT) which will be described in a later section, as well as measures of IFR-ness, developed by Professor R.E. Barlow, will be utilized in these studies.

Another problem area involved in the analysis of (fractional) factorial designs utilizing (accelerated) life tests is the uncertainties in the results of the analysis. Thyr Andersson, of SKF-ERC in The Netherlands, has tried to find out about these uncertainties by using a boot-strapping type of technique. He shows, for example, the uncertainty which is related to the selection of the proper test strategy for a reliable L_{10} life (10% failed bearings) in Fig. 5. These diagrams are obtained by computer-simulated

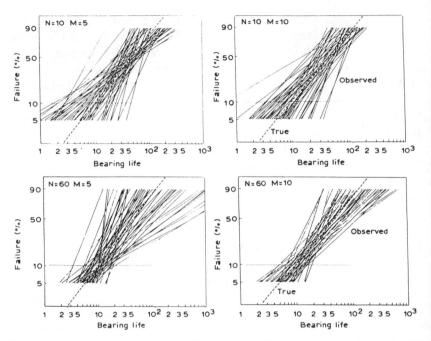

Fig. 5. Computer-simulated sampling can visualize the uncertainty of the life distribution under different conditions. From Andersson (1984).

sampling and testing from a given quantity of bearings with known Weibull life parameters:

$$\beta = 1 \cdot 2; \ L_{10} = 10 \cdot 0; \ L_{50} = 48 \cdot 1.$$

In Fig. 5, the number N is the size of the test series and M is the number of failed bearings. Each full line represents an individual test result of N bearings run up to M failures which the dashed line represents the true life distribution of the given quantity of bearings in a Weibull probability plot: see Andersson (1984).

ROBUST DESIGN METHODOLOGY

Robustness against disturbing factors is a very important way to find highly reliable solutions.

Many failures occur due to premature deterioration because of manufacturing defects or because of product measures, which are manufactured far from their target values. These defects and deviations from target values usually are due to manufacturing variations. Other failures occur due to a varying environment in use or due to different handling by the users.

The purpose of robust design methodology is to make the product insensitive to these and similar sources of variation out of control of the designer. The idea is to find and to utilize interactions between design parameters and disturbing factors: see Bergman (1989). A general description of robust design methodology is given in, for example, Phadke (1989); see also the forthcoming book by Bergman (1991).

CONDITION MONITORING

Inferences from accelerated life testing should include not only inference about life distribution properties and affecting factors but also state changes before a failure. If efficient condition monitoring techniques can be found, failure consequences may be reduced drastically. Replacements can be made before the occurrence of catastrophic failures. The selection of condition monitoring techniques is discussed in Chapters 1.2 and 3.1 of this book, while some questions regarding maintenance planning are discussed in Chapters 4.2 and 4.3.

DIAGNOSTICS

All inference from data is dependent on more or less severe model assumptions. After the data analysis we shall always perform a diagnostic check. Are the data consistent with the model we have assumed? A number of types of residual plotting techniques should be performed. Here we shall only draw attention to TTT (total time on test) plotting techniques. For a general survey see Bergman and Klefsjö (1984).

In many cases it has been assumed that acceleration affects only the scale of the life distribution. By drawing TTT-diagrams based on life data from several stress levels this assumption is easily checked.

In Fig. 6, the result of an accelerated life test on small light bulbs is illustrated in a TTT-diagram. The normal stress level is supposed to be 6 V but the voltage has been increased from 8 up to 14 V. We see that, based on these data, the common assumption that the form parameter

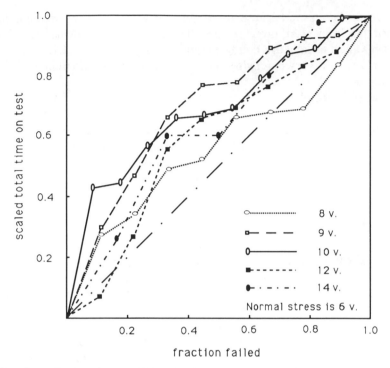

Fig. 6. TTT-plots for small light bulbs tested under different stress levels.

will be the same for all stress levels seems to be reasonable in this case.

The constancy of the form parameter, however, may sometimes be questionable. In Fig. 7, the life time distribution seems to become more and more DFR (Decreasing Failure Rate) as the stress level increases. The reason for this may be the existence of some special failure modes under higher stress levels. For more discussion, we refer to Xie *et al.* (1990).

SOME FURTHER COMMENTS

The use of factorial design in combination with accelerated life testing has not been much studied. More research in this area needs to be done. Another interesting area which deserves further study is how to use the information regarding variables which indicate the state changes before

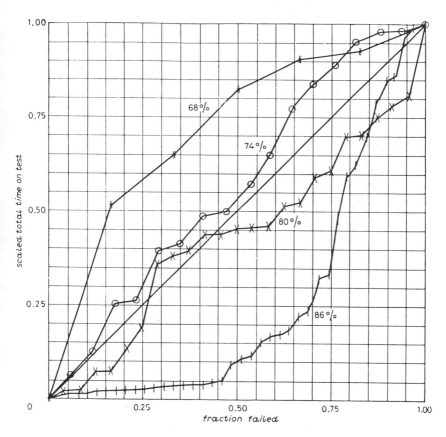

Fig. 7. Total Time on Test (TTT) plots for Kevlar spherical pressure vessel life test data. From Barlow *et al.* (1988).

a failure. The use of this information can be very effective: see Lydersen (1988).

REFERENCES

Andersson, T. (1984). Endurance testing in theory. *Ball Bearing Journal*, 217.

Barlow, R.E., Toland, R.H. & Freeman, T. (1988). A Bayesian analysis of the stress-rupture life of Kevlar/Epoxy spherical pressure vessels. In *Accelerated Life Testing and Experts' Opinions in Reliability*, ed. C.A. Clarotti & P.V. Lindley, North-Holland, Amsterdam.

Battacharyya, G.K. (1987). Parametric models and inference procedures for accelerated life tests. *Proc. 46th Session ISI*, Tokyo, Japan, invited paper 24.1.

Bergman, B. (1989). On robust design methodology for reliability improvement. In *Reliability Achievement, the Commercial Incentive*, ed. T. Aven. Elsevier Applied Science, London.

Bergman, B. (1991). *Industrial Design of Experiments and Robust Design Methodology*, in Swedish, book to appear.

Bergman, B. & Klefsjö, B. (1984). The total time on test concept and its use in reliability theory. *Operations Research*, **32**, 596–605.

Box, G.E.P. & Bisgaard, S. (1987). The scientific context of quality improvement. *Quality Progress*, June.

Box, G.E.P. & Draper, N.R. (1987). *Empirical Model-building and Response Surfaces*. John Wiley, New York.

Box, G.E.P., Hunter, W. & Hunter, S.J. (1978). *Statistics for Experimenters*. John Wiley, New York.

Lydersen, S. (1988). *Reliability testing based on deterioration measurements*. PhD dissertation, Norwegian Institute of Technology, Trondheim.

Mazzuchi, T.A. & Singpurwalla, N.D. (1988). Inferences from accelerated life tests—some recent results. In *Acceleration life testing and experts' opinion in reliability*, eds C.A. Clarottti & D.V. Lindley, North Holland, Amsterdam.

Nelson, W. (1990). *Accelerated Testing, Statistical Models, Test Plans and Data Analyses*. John Wiley, New York.

O'Connor, P. (1985). *Practical Reliability Engineering*, 2nd ed., John Wiley, Chichester.

Phadke, M.S. (1989). *Quality Engineering Using Robust Design*. Prentice-Hall, London.

Taguchi, G. (1986). *Introduction to Quality Engineering*. Asian Productivity Organization, Tokyo, Japan.

Viertl, R. (1987). Bayesian inference in accelerated life testing. *Proc. 46th Session ISI*, Tokyo, Japan, invited paper 24.2.

Xie, M., Zhao, M. & Hakim, M. (1990). When is the life really accelerated? *Proc. SRE Conf.*, Studsvik, Sweden.

Zelen, M. (1959). Factorial experiments in life testing. *Technometrics*, **1**, 269–88.

PART 2

Failure data information

2.1

Reliability Information from Failure Data

PER-ANDERS AKERSTEN

Akersten Tillförlitlighetsteknik AB, PO Box 9055, S-650 09 Karlstad,
Sweden

BO BERGMAN

Linköping University, Department of Design and Production,
Division of Quality Technology, S-581 83 Linköping, Sweden

KURT PÖRN

Studsvik Nuclear AB, S-611 82 Nyköping, Sweden

ABSTRACT

To build new systems fulfilling increasing requirements on reliability and
performance, reliability information is needed. Sources of information are
specially designed, usually accelerated, reliability tests or field data from
similar systems and components in use. In this chapter we address the latter
situation.

From operational use we obtain failure data. However, these data have
to be transformed to reliability information to be useful to the designer. Any
interpretation of data must take into account some model of reality and
some assumption concerning the relevance of the observed situation to a
future similar situation of a new system. These two questions are to some
extent addressed in this chapter.

Most systems in operation are repairable. However, most reliability
analysis methods are addressed to nonrepairable systems. Simple graphical
techniques to find the relevance of different modelling approaches are
discussed in a forthcoming dissertation by the first author. Some results are
given in this chapter.

Usually we have many sources of potential reliability information concerning a component under study. All these sources should be utilized as far

as possible. In a recent dissertation the third author of this chapter studied problems of taking failure data from several sources into account. Some of the ideas are presented.

INTRODUCTION

In any reliability analysis and for many reliability improvement efforts, information on the reliabilities of components under study is required. Reliability information is obtained from failure data. In this chapter we shall study some different aspects on the transformation from failure data to reliability information.

The most common assumption upon which failure data banks are based is that component failures occur according to a Poisson process, the intensity of which is given in the data bank. The two questions addressed in this chapter are the following:

— Shall we study just one Poisson process connected to each component, or can we find more information utilizing also failure data from similar components?
— Is the Poisson assumption, i.e. constant failure intensity, really a relevant one?

Both questions have been studied within the PhD programme at the Division of Quality Technology, Linköping University.

POISSON PROCESSES

Empirical Bayesian Inference

The first of the two questions mentioned in the introduction is addressed in a PhD thesis by Pörn (1990), the theme of which has its origin in the work on a Reliability Data Handbook (Bento *et al.*, 1985) for nuclear power plants of Swedish design. The Handbook, providing uncertainty distributions for constant (independent of time) failure rates or failure probabilities per demand of important safety related groups of components, has been developed in order to facilitate the performance of probabilistic safety studies for nuclear power plants. In these studies the failure rates of the Handbook are normally converted to average unavailabilities according to the operating mode and testing scheme of the component in question. The distributions of the Handbook are estimated on the basis of operational (field) data, systematically and continuously gathered into a central data bank (Ekberg *et al.*, 1985).

Although the components are grouped on the basis of their type, operating mode, size and capacity, there are certainly factors such as various environmental, operating and maintenance conditions that make it unrealistic to assume complete homogeneity within the groups with regard to reliability. The similarities, however, are considered so significant that the groupwise treatment is deemed beneficial from the statistical or informational point of view.

To use a more or less deeply established terminology, the statistical approach in the earlier versions of the Handbook can be characterized as 'parametric empirical Bayes' (PEB) according to Deely and Lindley (1981) and Singpurwalla (1986). This terminology derives from the fact that the prior distribution of the primary parameter is specified to its form, the (secondary) parameters of which are estimated on the basis of empirical evidence and sampling theory models.

Thus the PEB approach is not logically consistent because we use sampling theory methods to estimate the prior distribution but otherwise interpret the densities as measures of knowledge rather than in a frequency sense. Among the more apparent consequences of this inconsistency one may mention the difficulty in finding reasonable estimates of the secondary parameters. Therefore, it was quite natural to extend the Bayesian view to include also the treatment of the secondary parameters. The resulting approach, called 'Bayes empirical Bayes' (BEB) by Deely and Lindley (1981), will be used in the third version of the Reliability Data Book (1991).

Bayes Empirical Bayes

Let us assume that the Poisson probability model is valid. According to this model the number x of events follows a Poisson distribution with a given intensity λ. The density of this distribution reads

$$p(x|\lambda) = \exp(-\lambda T) \cdot (\lambda T)^x / x!$$

where T denotes the exposure time. On the basis of the observable x we have to estimate the unknown λ, where by estimation we mean specification of the uncertainty distribution. The Bayesian solution of this problem is very simple if we have a well-grounded prior distribution $p(\lambda)$.

Then the posterior distribution is proportional to

$$p(\lambda|x) \propto \lambda^x \exp(-\lambda T) \cdot p(\lambda)$$

In the empirical Bayesian situation we presuppose the existence of n additional, related observations, x_n, and on the basis of these data we try to uniquely determine the prior distribution $p(\lambda)$. On the contrary, according to the Bayes empirical Bayes method used here the distribution $p(\lambda)$ is considered uncertain, and this uncertainty is expressed in the same way as the uncertainty of $p(x)$, namely by introducing a hyperparameter θ as a conditioning parameter. Thus we have

$$p(\lambda) = \int p(\lambda|\theta)p(\theta)\,d\theta$$

which means that the uncertainty concerning λ has been transferred to the uncertainty of the hyperparameter θ. The Bayes empirical Bayes method is based on the following assumptions or judgements:

(1) The hyperparameter θ has density $p(\theta)$.
(2) Given θ, the parameters $\{\lambda_i\}$ are identically and independently distributed (iid) with density $p(\lambda|\theta)$.
(3) Given θ and $\{\lambda_i\}$, the data $\{x_i\}$ are independent, x_i having density $p(x_i|\lambda_i)$, independent of θ and of all λ's other than λ_i.

These assumptions lead to an inferential distribution, here written in the form

$$p(\lambda_{n+1}|x_{n+1}) \propto p(x_{n+1}|\lambda_{n+1}) \cdot p(\lambda_{n+1}|x_n)$$

where

$$p(\lambda_{n+1}|x_n) = \int p(\lambda_{n+1}|\theta)p(\theta|x_n)\,d\theta$$

Thus the inferential problem of specifying the uncertainty concerning λ_{n+1} on the basis of the direct, 'unit specific' observation x_{n+1} and the related, 'generic' data x_n is, in principle, transferred to the problem of defining a hyperparameter θ, specifying its prior distribution $p(\theta)$ and calculating the posterior distribution $p(\theta|x_n)$.

Hyperparameters

In this section we propose the choice of a specific class of distributions $\{p(\lambda|\theta),\ \theta \in D\}$, which are more flexible and, in particular, lead to more robust posterior estimates than the family of pure *conjugate* distributions. Still this class D of distributions is mathematically tractable.

When the Bayes method is used in practice a *natural conjugate* prior distribution is very often chosen, mostly for reasons of mathematical convenience. A family of prior distributions is conjugate with respect to a given statistical model if the posterior distribution in each case belongs to the same family. This preservation property was conveniently utilized in the parametric empirical Bayes application (Bento *et al.*, 1985) previously referred to, which means that gamma distributions were used as $p(\lambda|\theta)$ for Poisson probability models. However, according to Berger (1984, p. 98), for example, many authors have found that conjugate prior distributions are often not robust, in the sense that they are leading to posterior estimates which are too much influenced by the prior distribution also in cases when this prior distribution seems to be less realistic. This lack of robustness has also been demonstrated in applications: see, e.g., Pörn (1986).

The purpose of the density $p(\lambda|\theta)$ is to describe the uncertainty concerning λ of a specific unit. Prior to having any observation of this unit, the uncertainty may be specified quantitatively through the study of related units acting in a similar environment. These latter units, however, are not necessarily so closely related that their intensities could be assumed equal to each other. On the contrary, according to the basic assumption (2), the intensities $\{\lambda_i\}$ are assumed to follow a common distribution with the density $p(\lambda|\theta)$. Thus this density (for given θ) may be interpreted as a measure of the natural variability between the units of the population. Therefore, with observations of the related units, $\{x_i\}$, it seems reasonable to use these observations to 'estimate' $p(\lambda|\theta)$. In any parametric approach, the attention is restricted to a certain class or family of distributions, characterized by the parameter θ.

In the choice of the distribution class D it is important that at least the following requirements are fulfilled.

(1) Distributions in D are flexible enough to describe various population variabilities, and in general the uncertainty of the intensities $\{\lambda_i\}$. Further it is an advantage if the distributions are easy to interpret.
(2) D leads to robust inferential solutions, which means in particular that the influence of the prior distributions in D will be small for units which are outside the main area of population support.
(3) D represents distributions which are mathematically tractable.

If the last requirement is considered first, it seems quite reasonable to start with the previously mentioned class of conjugate distributions, i.e. gamma distributions,

$$G = \{g(\lambda|\alpha, \beta); \ \alpha > 0, \beta > 0\}$$

In order to increase the flexibility and improve the robustness proper-ties, the class G is expanded or *contaminated* to encompass the mixed distributions:

$$D' = \{(1 - c)g(\lambda|\alpha, \beta) + c \cdot f(\lambda); \ \alpha > 0, \ \beta > 0, \ 0 < c < 1\}$$

where the parameter c denotes the mixing coefficient between the informative distribution $g(\lambda|\alpha, \beta)$ and the *noninformative distribution* $f(\lambda)$. The role of $f(\lambda)$ is twofold. By choosing a noninformative $f(\lambda)$ we introduce the desired property of robustness. Secondly, by adding the contamination term we can correct the 'error' of a pure gamma distribu-tion in describing the natural population variability. To cite deGroot (1982): 'All good Bayesian statisticians reserve a little pinch of probability that their model is wrong'. In other words, specifying the uncertainty concerning λ we want to emphasize the complete uncertainty in the 'tail'-areas of $g(\lambda|\alpha, \beta)$ in particular. Even if a substantial amount of observations $\{x_i\}$ were available, these observations would seldom give any clue to the specification to the 'tail'-area of their distribution.

Concerning the concept of noninformative distribution several defini-tions or principles can be found in the literature. In this study we found it workable to use the definition proposed by Box and Tiao (1973) and based on the concept of *data translated likelihood*. This means that one seeks a transformation of the probability model such that the trans-formed density is approximately a location density. The transformed parameter is then assigned the uniform density, which via the inverse transformation determines the noninformative prior distribution of the original problem. Applying Box and Tiao's approach to the Poisson probability model, the noninformative distribution of λ will be

$$f(\lambda) \propto \lambda^{-\frac{1}{2}}$$

As with many noninformative distributions this one is also improper. With this distribution we are not even able to calculate the marginal distribution or the likelihood function for $\theta = (\alpha, \beta, c)$. To avoid these difficulties the contamination distribution is substituted by the closely related and proper distribution,

$$g(\lambda|\tfrac{1}{2}, \beta_0)$$

Here the scale parameter β_0 is given a small (fixed) positive value just in order to make the distribution proper. Thus our arguments concerning the choice of suitable uncertainty distributions of λ result in the following class of distributions:

$$D = \{(1-c)g(\lambda|\alpha, \beta) + c \cdot g(\lambda|\tfrac{1}{2}, \beta_0); \ \alpha > 0, \ \beta > 0, \ 0 < c < 1\}$$

Hyperpriors

As we have seen above, the solution of the inferential problem requires the specification of a prior distribution on D, a distribution describing the uncertainty concerning the parameter $\theta = (\alpha, \beta, c)$ before we have obtained any observations at all. Such a distribution we have designated by $p(\theta)$. In a Handbook application like the one we are interested in here, it is reasonable to look for a prior distribution, which we could call a reference or standard prior distribution. Box and Tiao (1973) mean by such a prior distribution one which is noninformative and thereby allows the data to 'speak for themselves'. And then, by *noninformative distribution* they mean a distribution 'that does not represent *total ignorance* but an amount of prior information which is small relative to what the particular projected experiment can be expected to provide'.

In a multiparameter problem like this the choice of prior distribution is substantially simplified if certain parameters can be judged *a priori* to be distributed independently. In the case of interest here it is appropriate to assume the mixing parameter c to be distributed independently of the parameters α and β. Instead of the latter parameters, we consider the parameters 'mean' (μ) and 'coefficient of variation' (v) (standard deviation divided by mean), which are assumed *a priori* to be independent of each other. Applying Jeffreys' rule (which is a rule for finding data translated likelihoods) to these two parameters separately and going back to the original parameters α, β, c, an approximate noninformative distribution for these is

$$p(\alpha, \beta, c) \propto [\alpha(\alpha + \beta/T)]^{-\frac{1}{2}} \beta^{-1} \cdot c^{-\frac{1}{2}}$$

Starting with this noninformative hyperprior, all steps of the *two-stage contaminated hierarchical model* can be calculated. For the purpose of these numerical calculations a computer code, TSEBA, has been developed.

The calculation of $p(\theta|\mathbf{x}_n)$ and the robustness of $p(\lambda_{n+1}|\mathbf{x}_{n+1})$ have been demonstrated by examples. In addition the robustness properties of $p(\lambda_{n+1}|\mathbf{x}_{n+1})$ have been discussed in a decision oriented framework. By using the concepts of 'expected utility' and 'expected value of information', we have found significant differences in the sensitivity, with respect to additional information, between the three-dimensional (contaminated) BEB approach proposed here on the one hand and the corresponding two-dimensional (noncontaminated) BEB and the pure PEB approach on the other hand. The latter group of models, based on natural conjugate prior distributions for the Poisson intensity λ, lead to a posterior distribution that is too 'stubborn' in the sense that there is not much value in getting more observations. Without giving any formal definition of robustness, it is quite clear that there is a close relationship between robustness and the expected value of more information as applied in this study.

The inferential approach outlined above has been restricted to Poisson probability models. It is to be noted, however, that the main features of this approach are generally applicable. The next section addresses exploratory methods for the investigation of the relevance of the Poisson assumption.

THE RELEVANCE OF THE POISSON ASSUMPTION

Event Epochs

The question whether or not a Poisson assumption is relevant may be addressed by exploratory graphical methods. One simple approach is to plot the number of failures against the calendar time. This 'total time on test' plot in itself does not provide all the information needed for performing stringent model inference. However, it is used to identify interesting properties to be studied in more depth. The usefulness for pointing out interesting properties is greatly affected by the way data are gathered and by the model assumptions made. In the case of monitoring a single system there are virtually no problems. When pooling data from several systems problems usually appear. Without due consideration of censoring and differences in operating and calendar time, a simple pooling of failure events may distort existing patterns.

The continuous monitoring of a system, or a group of systems, results in a plot with an open time axis. The retrospective analysis may be performed, using the fact that the number of events, falling in the time interval chosen, is known. Here we suppose that the time interval of study is $[0, T]$, during which n events occur at the successive epochs t_1,

$t_2, \ldots, t_n$. Then we may base our plot on the normalized failure epochs

$$w_i = t_i/T, \ i = 1, \ldots, n$$

for the abscissa, and the number of failures for the ordinate. It is quite possible to normalize the ordinate, too, giving the plotting positions $(t_i/T, i/n)$, $i = 1, 2, \ldots, n$.

Figure 1 gives a plot of the data in Lambe (1974), concerning the sequence of repairs of a Ford Sedan.

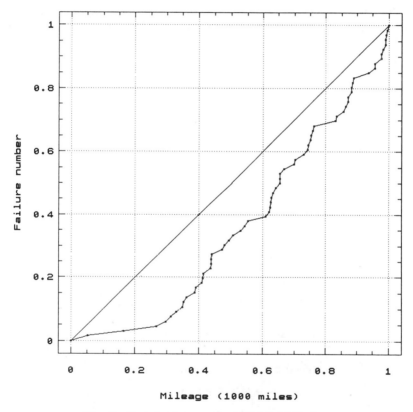

Fig. 1. Repair history of a 1956 Ford Sedan.

Deviation from a straight line in the plot of the number of failures vs the total time on test are to be expected, especially for small numbers of failures. Large deviations indicate the presence of a trend, or other systematic variation in the rate of occurrence of failures. Very small deviations should also cause suspicion. This might be an indication of a strong dependence between successive inter-event times.

Various formal tests for trend exist, among which the Laplace test (see e.g. Cox & Lewis, 1966) is the most widely known. A suitable test statistic is then

$$V = \left(\frac{n}{12}\right)^{-1/2} \left(\sum_{i=1}^{n} w_i - n/2\right)$$

Under the hypothesis of a homogeneous Poisson process, this test statistic follows approximately a normal distribution with mean 0 and variance 1. In many cases, however, the deviations from the diagonal are so apparent that no formal tests are needed.

Inter-event Times

The sequence of event epochs $t_1, t_2, \ldots$, gives rise to a sequence of inter-event times, or times between failures,

$$x_1 = t_2 - t_1, \; x_2 = t_3 - t_2, \ldots$$

A common error in the analysis of repairable systems is to consider the set of inter-event times as a set of independent and identically distributed random variables.

Let us consider $x_1, x_2, \ldots, x_n$, a sample from a distribution F with $F(0-) = 0$. The ordered sample is denoted by

$$x_{(1)} \leqslant x_{(2)} \leqslant \cdots \leqslant x_{(n)}$$

with $x_{(0)} = 0$ for convenience. We then define the successive TTT-statistics,

$$z_i = \sum_{j=1}^{i} (n-j+1)[x_{(j)} - x_{(j-1)}]$$

for $i = 1, 2, \ldots, n$, and the scaled TTT-statistics as

$$u_i = z_i/z_n \quad \text{for } i = 1, 2, \ldots, n$$

$$u_0 = 0$$

Plotting the points $(i/n, u_i)$, corresponding to an observed sample of size n, in a diagram and connecting the points by line segments, we get the familiar TTT-plot.

In the exponential case, corresponding to data from a homogeneous Poisson process, it is well known that the joint distribution of the random variables $u_1, \ldots, u_{n-1}$ is the same as that of an ordered sample of size $n-1$ from a uniform distribution on $[0, 1]$. Large deviations from the diagonal in the TTT-plot indicate non-exponentiality of the inter-event times. However, if the assumptions of independent and identically distributed inter-event times cannot be justified, this type of TTT-plot is of very limited value.

Formal tests are made possible, e.g. by the statistic

$$W = \left(\frac{n}{12}\right)^{-1/2} \left(\sum_{i=1}^{n} u_i - n/2\right)$$

Under the hypothesis of a homogeneous Poisson process, this test statistic also follows approximately a normal distribution with mean 0 and variance 1.

Combination

If the homogeneous Poisson process assumption is relevant, both the aforementioned types of TTT-plots should be used. A large deviation from the diagonal in any one of them is enough for rejection. The test data given in Littlewood (1980) result in the patterns of Fig. 2. It is quite obvious that a homogeneous Poisson process model gives very bad fit.

The scatter-plot in the upper right is another example of TTT-plot combinations. Its details and interpretation are presented in Akersten (1991). There it is further shown that the two test variables V and W are asymptotically independent in the case of a homogeneous Poisson process. This independence assumption is valid also for small numbers of observations, a result strongly supported by simulation experiments. In this case the sum of squares

$$T = V^2 + W^2$$

follows approximately a χ^2-distribution with two degrees of freedom. This statistic T may then be used for testing the hypothesis of a homogeneous Poisson process against alternatives, not necessarily of monotone trend type.

CONCLUSIONS

The questions raised in the introduction have been answered, to some extent at least, by the studies described in this chapter. The second main

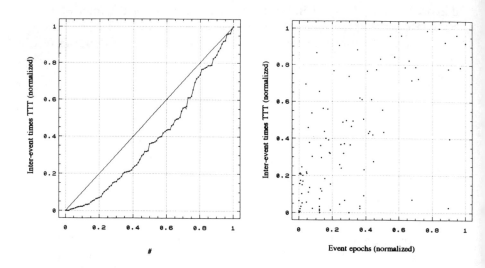

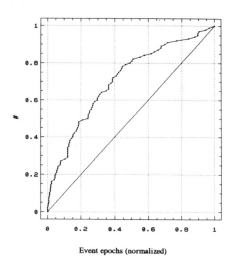

Event epochs (normalized)

Fig. 2. Combinations of TTT-plots, applied to Littlewood's data.

section presents some useful graphical techniques, especially a combination of two types of TTT-plots, for testing the validity of homogeneous Poisson processes. The first main section describes a two-stage contaminated model to be used for Bayesian estimation of component-specific Poisson intensities. This model is applicable in cases where the assumption of homogeneous Poisson processes is valid and when field data from similar components are available. By applying this method the similarities within the group of components can be fully utilized from the statistical point of view.

REFERENCES

Akersten, P.A. (1991). Repairable systems reliability, studied by TTT-plotting techniques, Linköping Studies in Science and Technology (forthcoming).

Bento, J.-P., Björe, S., Ericsson, G., Hasler, A., Lydén, C.-D., Wallin, L., Pörn, K. & Åkerlund, O. (1985). *Reliability Data Book for Components in Swedish Nuclear Power Plants.* Swedish Nuclear Power Inspectorate and Nuclear Training & Safety Center of the Swedish Utilities, Stockholm, RKS 85-25.

Berger, J. (1984). The robust Bayesian viewpoint. In *Robustness of Bayesian Analysis*, ed. J.B. Kadane. North-Holland, Amsterdam.

Box, G.E.P. & Tiao, G.C. (1973). *Bayesian Inference in Statistical Analysis.* Addison-Wesley, Reading, MA.

Cox, D.R. & Lewis, P.A.W. (1966). *The Statistical Analysis of Series of Events.* Methuen, London.

Deely, J.J. & Lindley, D.V. (1981). Bayes Empirical Bayes. *J. Amer. Statist. Assoc.,* **76**, No. 376.

deGroot, M.H. (1982). Comment on Glenn Shafer's article: Lindley's Paradox. *J. Amer. Statist. Assoc.,* **77**, No. 378, 336–9.

Ekberg, K., Andersson, M. & Bento, J.-P. (1985). The ATV-System and its use. *ANS/ENS International Topical Meeting on Probabilistic Safety Methods and Applications*, San Francisco, 24 February–1 March 1985. Vol. 1, paper 43.

Lambe, T.A. (1974). The decision to repair or scrap a machine. *Oper. Res. Quart.,* **25**, 99–110.

Littlewood, B. (1980). Theories of software reliability: how good are they, and how can they be improved. *IEEE Trans. Software Engineering*, **6**, 489–500.

Pörn, K. (1986). On robustness of empirical prior distributions. In *On uncertainty and robustness estimating reliability parameters for safety studies*, Thesis No. 68, Linköping Studies in Science and Technology, Lin-Tek-Lic-1986:8, Linköping University, Sweden.

Pörn, K. (1990). *On empirical Bayesian inference applied to Poisson probability models.* Linköping Studies in Science and Technology, Dissertation No. 234, ISBN 91-7870-696-3, Linköping University, Sweden.

'*Reliability Data Book for Components in Nordic Nuclear Power Plants*', Version 3, prepared for Swedish Nuclear Power Inspectorate and Nuclear Training & Safety Center of the Swedish Utilities (to be published in 1991, Stockholm).

Singpurwalla, N.D. (1986). *A unified perspective on Bayes, Empirical–Bayes, Bayes–Empirical–Bayes and sample theory models*. George Washington University School of Engineering and Applied Science, GWU/IRRA/Serial TR-86/4, Washington DC, USA.

2.2

Bayesian Methods and Expert Opinions Applied to System Reliability Estimation and Management

A.B. Huseby and B. Natvig

University of Oslo, Institute of Mathematics, PO Box 1053, Blindern, N-0316 Oslo 3, Norway

ABSTRACT

Managing the reliability of a complex system is a problem involving many different decisions. Typically, these decisions are made on different points of time, and thus are based on unequal sets of information. In the first part of this chapter we discuss the effects these decisions have on reliability evaluations. We also suggest a general methodology for optimizing decisions under such circumstances. To illustrate the ideas we consider a simple example where a multicomponent system is inspected regularly during its lifetime. At each inspection time a decision is made whether to repair failed components or just to leave the system in its present state.

In the second part of this chapter, combining the opinions of k experts about the reliabilities of n components of a binary system is considered, the case $n = 2$ being treated in detail. Our work in this area generalizes results in papers by Huseby (1986, 1988) on the single component case. Since the experts often share data, he argues that their assessments will typically be dependent and that this difficulty cannot be handled without making judgments concerning the underlying sources of information and to what extent these are available to each of the experts. In the former paper the information available to the experts is modelled as a set of observations $Y_1, \ldots, Y_m$. These observations are then reconstructed as far as possible from the information provided by the experts and used as a basis for the combined judgment. This is called the retrospective approach. In the latter paper, the uncertain quantity is modelled as a future observation, Y, from the same distribution as the Y_i's. This is called the predictive approach. For *the case n > 1, where each expert is giving opinions about more than one component, additional dependencies between the reliabilities of the components come into play. This is for instance true if two or more components are of similar type, are sharing a common environment or are exposed to common cause failures. In this chapter the generalized predictive approach is considered. Our complete work in this area is presented in Natvig (1990).*

INTRODUCTION

When making decisions under uncertainty it is not sensible to base these on the classical theory for testing hypotheses. This theory is constructed for testing scientific hypotheses and hence is not very suitable in decision making. When making decisions in real applications it would in most cases be unwise not to take informed subjective assessments into account, in addition to more basic data from experiments, for instance. A member of a jury in a murder case is forced to make a subjective assessment of the credibility of key witnesses in addition to evaluating the concrete evidence at hand. A medical doctor who is thinking of heart surgery for a patient cannot just base the decision on general estimates for the probability of a successful operation. The doctor must in addition, partly subjectively, take the patient's physical and psychological condition into account. An insurance company that is offered to insure a nuclear power plant must do this on the basis of a risk analysis of the plant. Such an analysis can in no way be reasonably acceptable if the assessments and experience of the engineers on the technological components and of the psychologists and sociologists on the human factor are not taken into account. The Bayesian approach is constructed to deal with such assessments and experience in a way that is consistent with the laws of probability, and is hence especially suitable as a basis for decision making under uncertainty. A good application of this approach is given in a PhD thesis by Pörn (1990), the theme of which has its origin in the work on a Reliability Data Handbook for nuclear power plants of Swedish design. For further details see Chapter 2.1 of this book. An introduction to Bayesian methods is given in Natvig (1989a) whereas a comprehensive treatment of reliability and Bayesian methods in this area is given in Natvig (1989b).

When a decision problem is to be analyzed, one has to establish a mathematical model describing the quantities involved, and their corresponding uncertainties. From a Bayesian point of view uncertainty about some unknown quantity, θ, has to be formulated in terms of a probability distribution for θ. Thus, modelling the uncertainties of a decision problem involves a description of probability distributions for all the unknown quantities. If there is dependence among these quantities, this has to be taken into account in the probability model. Concerning assessment of probability there have been quite a large number of papers lately on combination of experts' opinions. For a fairly recent approach we refer to Huseby (1986, 1988). A review of the literature on this topic is provided in Genest and Zidec (1986). In the second part of this chapter results in Huseby (1988) are generalized.

Secondly, one must consider all the different decisions involved in the problem. Especially, one must describe when these decisions have to made, or at least the logical order of the decisions. In the simplest decision problems, only one decision is involved, and typically, this decision has to be made based on the present state of information. However, in more complicated situations, the problem may consist of a sequence of decisions, all taken at different points of time and thus also on different states of information. A typical example of this is project management. A Bayesian approach to such decision problems can be found in Huseby (1989). In the first part of this chapter, however, we shall focus on sequential decision problems in reliability management. In our setting reliability management of some technological system includes both evaluation of reliability before the system is operative as well as making decisions concerning maintenance during the system lifetime. Hence this part of the chapter is very much linked to the two subsequent chapters of the present book on condition monitoring and operational reliability.

SEQUENTIAL DECISION PROBLEMS IN RELIABILITY MANAGEMENT

When it comes to the structuring of a decision problem, this has often been done using decision trees. However, recently an alternative method has been developed, based on so-called influence diagrams. Besides offering a more compact graphical representation of the problem, such diagrams appear to make it possible to implement more effective software tools for performing decision analysis. An introduction to influence diagrams can be found in Howard and Matheson (1984). See also the discussion of this topic in Howard (1988). Concerning computational issues of influence diagrams, we refer to Olmsted (1983) and Shachter (1986). For a review of Bayesian statistics and analysis of influence diagrams, see Barlow and Pereira (1987).

Influence diagrams are also closely related to so-called Markov fields. Thus, such diagrams appear to be useful in a purely probabilistic setting, where no actual decisions are involved. Some recent papers on this are Lauritzen and Spiegelhalter (1988) and Spiegelhalter and Lauritzen (1989).

Although the influence diagram methodology appears to be promising as a tool for structuring decision problems, the number of calculations needed to find the exact solution to the problem grows very rapidly. Thus, in order to apply the methods to large scale problems, it is typically necessary to make considerable simplifications. Especially, this is true in cases involving many decisions. In this chapter we shall explore these problems in the light of some simple examples. We shall also briefly outline a way to obtain certain simplifications which can be used to obtain estimates of the solutions in situations where the exact solution is unobtainable.

Risk Evaluation with One Delayed Decision

In order to present the principle of sequential decision making in the context of reliability, we now consider a very simple example. The system to be analysed is an undirected 2-terminal network system shown in Fig. 1.

The components of this system are the edges of the graph, and are denoted by $1, ..., 9$. The system is functioning if and only if the source node S and the terminal node T can communicate through the network.

We assume that the system is monitored continuously, so whenever a

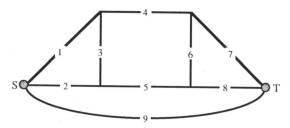

Fig. 1. An undirected 2-terminal network system.

component fails, its exact lifetime is known to the reliability manager. However, due to some practical reasons, the components of the system can only be repaired at certain points of time. That is, the system is inspected at regular time intervals and, if judged necessary, repaired. Specifically, let τ denote the time between two inspections. If one decides to repair the system, all failed components are replaced. For simplicity we assume, however, that the repair cost is the same irrespective of the number of replaced components. We denote this cost by C_r. Moreover, if the system fails during the time between two inspections, one has to pay a penalty cost of C_p. This cost is assumed to be independent of the point of time in this interval, when the system fails. Typically, of course C_p is much larger than C_r.

An example of such a system could be a subsea oil drilling installation. Such systems are usually operated from a remote control unit, so irregularities in the system are detected more or less immediately. Repairing components in such systems, however, requires expensive special equipment. For obvious economic reasons it is not possible to have such equipment available at the installation permanently. Moreover, bad weather conditions during the winter typically make it impossible to repair failed components. Thus, one has to concentrate the maintenance operations to certain periods of the year. When such a system is repaired, the rental cost of necessary equipment, and not each particular component replacement, represents most of the expenses. Thus, assuming a fixed repair cost independent of the number of replaced components is indeed quite realistic. If the main effect of a system failure is loss of production, the assumption of a penalty cost independent of the failure time cannot be fully justified. It may, however, serve as a reasonable approximation.

Let:

$$T_{i,1} = \text{Time to first failure of edge } i, i = 1,\ldots, 9 \qquad (1)$$

$$T_{i,j} = \text{Time to failue of edge } i \text{ after the } (j-1)\text{th repair}, i = 1,\ldots, 9,\ j = 2, 3,\ldots \qquad (2)$$

Given failure rates $\lambda_1, \ldots, \lambda_9$, we assume that the $T_{i,j}$'s are independent and exponentially distributed. Especially, λ_i is the failure rate of $T_{i,j}$, $i = 1, \ldots, 9, j = 1, 2, \ldots$

The failure rates are unknown, and the prior uncertainties about these parameters are assessed as:

$$\lambda_i \sim \text{Gamma}(\alpha_i, \beta_i), i = 1, \ldots, 9 \qquad (3)$$

It is also assessed that the λ_i's are independent *a priori*.

First we consider the system in a period of time corresponding to two inspection periods. At time zero, all the components are fresh and functioning. After time τ the system is inspected, and a judgment is made whether or not to repair all (if any) failed components. Yet τ units of time later, the system is inspected again, and the total bill is made up. Our main concern now is to evaluate the risk of this system. That is, we want to compute the expected cost of running the system during these two periods. However, before we can do so, we need to derive a decision rule for the judgment made at the first inspection. That is, we must find a criterion for when the system should be repaired. Let d_1 denote the decision corresponding to repairing the system, while d_2 denotes the opposite alternative. We now stress the point that this decision is made at time τ, and not at time zero. Thus to choose between the two, we must compute the expected cost for each alternative, given the information available at time τ. At this point we will know which of the components survived the first period, and which did not. Moreover, for the failed components we will also know the exact lifetimes. In the light of this information the priors for the failure rates may be updated. Using these updated distributions, we may calculate the probability of surviving the next period for each of the components.

Let p_i denote the probability of surviving the next period for component i, $i = 1, \ldots, 9$, and let $\mathbf{p} = (p_1, \ldots, p_9)$. Standard calculations now yield:

$$
p_i = \begin{cases}
\left(\dfrac{\beta_i + \tau}{\beta_i + 2\tau}\right)^{\alpha_i} & \text{if edge } i \text{ did not fail} \\[2ex]
\left(\dfrac{\beta_i + T_{i,1}}{\beta_i + T_{i,1} + \tau}\right)^{\alpha_i + 1} & \begin{array}{l}\text{if edge } i \text{ failed and was} \\ \text{repaired}\end{array} \\[2ex]
0 & \text{otherwise}
\end{cases} \quad i = 1, \ldots, 9 \qquad (4)
$$

Furthermore, let $h = h(\mathbf{p})$ denote the probability of surviving the next period for the system as a function of the corresponding probabilities for the components. By edge factoring and series-parallel-reductions it is easily established that:

$$
\begin{aligned}
h(\mathbf{p}) = p_9 \amalg [& p_3 p_6 (p_1 \amalg p_2)(p_4 \amalg p_5)(p_7 \amalg p_8) \\
& + p_3 (1 - p_6)(p_1 \amalg p_2)(p_4 p_7 \amalg p_5 p_8) \\
& + (1 - p_3) p_6 (p_1 p_4 \amalg p_2 p_5)(p_7 \amalg p_8) \\
& + (1 - p_3)(1 - p_6)(p_1 p_4 p_7 \amalg p_2 p_5 p_8)]
\end{aligned} \qquad (5)
$$

In particular, let h_1 and h_2 denote these probabilities given respectively that the system is repaired and not repaired. In order to make a decision we can now compute the expected cost for each of the two alternatives as:

$$E(\text{Cost}|d_1) = C_p(1-h_1) + C_r \qquad (6)$$

$$E(\text{Cost}|d_2) = C_p(1-h_2) \qquad (7)$$

and choose the alternative with the minimal expected cost.

We observe that since h_1 and h_2 both depend on all the failure data from the first period, so will the decision rule. Hence, the cost one has to pay for the last period also depends on these data. As a result, it becomes very difficult to derive exact expressions for the distribution of the total cost. Thus, evaluating the risk, even in this simple case, is a complicated task. Since, however, we have found an explicit decision rule, it is possible to investigate the risk by using Monte Carlo simulation. This is a well-known numerical technique; for details see Ripley (1987).

In Table 1 we list the main results of simulations on five different parameter sets, each being simulated 5000 times. The only difference between the parameter sets is the value of τ, the time between inspections, which runs through the values $2, \ldots, 6$. The other parameter values are as follows:

$$\alpha_i = 1 \cdot 1, \ \beta_i = 7 \cdot 0, \ i = 1, \ldots, 9; \quad C_r = 1 \cdot 0, C_p = 5 \cdot 0 \qquad (8)$$

Table 1. Output from the Monte Carlo Simulation.

		Mean cost		Obs. freq. of decision	
τ	Optimal dec.	d_1 always	d_2 always	d_1	d_2
2	0·96	1·48	1·16	21·9	78·1
3	1·79	2·11	2·19	51·6	48·4
4	2·66	2·85	3·13	70·0	30·0
5	3·36	3·58	3·94	45·7	54·3
6	3·99	4·27	4·62	50·1	49·9

In the table we have listed the mean simulated total cost under the optimal decision rule described above. It is important to understand the difference between this rule where the decision is made after time τ, and rules where the decision is made at time zero. To focus on this, we have also calculated the expected cost when the decision is fixed initially as d_1 and d_2 respectively. These numbers can be found using the following exact expressions:

$$E(\text{Cost}|d_1 \text{ fixed}) = C_p(1 - h(\tau)) + C_r \qquad (9)$$

$$E(\text{Cost}|d_2 \text{ fixed}) = C_p(1 - h(2\tau)) \qquad (10)$$

where $h(t)$ denotes the probability that the system does not fail before time t $(t > 0)$. Equation (9) can easily be verified by first conditioning on the failure rates. Under this condition the component lifetimes are exponentially distributed. Thus, we may use the well-known 'lack of memory' property of the exponential distribution and then obtain the result by integrating with respect to the prior distributions of failure rates. Equation (10) is derived by straightforward calculations. Finally, we have tabled the frequencies of the two different decisions made according to the optimal rule.

Table 1 clearly indicates the difference in expected total cost for the optimal decision rule and the fixed rules. We stress this point particularly because many risk assessments are based on fixed decisions. As a consequence, the risk may be rather badly estimated. Note especially that it does not help to investigate all possible fixed decisions. A decision rule which is a function of the information available at the time the decision is to be made, represents something qualitatively different compared to any fixed decision. As is seen from the table, the mean cost using the optimal rule is typically less than the mean cost using any of the fixed decisions. This is of course intuitively fairly obvious.

We also note that the observed frequency of decision d_1 appears to have a peak somewhere around $\tau = 4$. One might perhaps think that as τ grows, it should be more and more important to replace failed components. However, a large τ-value also implies that the probability of no system failure in the last period is small. Thus, there will be less to gain by repairing the system.

Multiple Decisions

In the example discussed in the previous section, only one decision was involved. However, since this decision had to be made during the system lifetime (in order to obtain optimal risk performance) rather than at the beginning, the problem of evaluating the risk became computationally complex. If several decisions are to be made, even finding the optimal decision rules may be very complicated. This is due to the fact that the decision made at one point of time, t, must be based on an evaluation of the risk of the remaining parts of the project. Thus, since these parts may involve other later decisions, the problem of making the right decision at time t becomes at least as difficult as the risk evaluation discussed in the example above.

One might think that a way to solve the problem of making the right decision at a time t would be to simulate the remaining parts of the system lifetime for each possible decision, and then choose the one which is optimal with respect to some given criterion. However, the decision to be made at time t should be a function of the information available at that time. Thus, as before, we are not looking for *one* fixed decision, but rather a complete function. In order to determine this function or decision rule, it may in the worst case be necessary to simulate the remaining parts of the system lifetime, for all possible sets of information available at time t. In most practical situations this is a hopeless task.

In order to explore these problems, we consider the same system as above. This time, however, the system is operative in k inspection periods instead of just two. At each inspection, except the last one, a judgment is made whether or not to repair failed components. The prices and distributions are the same as before.

Rather than attempting to solve the problem directly, we shall proceed in a stepwise fashion. As a first suggestion of a solution, one may use the same decision rule as we did before. That is, when the system is inspected, only the probability of no system failure in the next inspection period is considered, and the decision is made so that the expected cost in this period is minimized. The effects this decision may have on later periods are simply neglected. Using the same parameters as in the previous computations, and keeping $\tau = 3$, we simulated the system once again. In this case we let the number of inspection periods run through the numbers 2, 4, 6, 8 and 10, and simulated the system 5000 times for each of these numbers. By doing so we obtained estimates of expected total cost. As a comparison we also computed the corresponding numbers for the two fixed strategies, d_1 and d_2.

In Fig. 2 we have plotted estimated expected total costs as functions of the number of inspections. As one can see, the difference in performance of the three strategies becomes more important as the number of inspections increases. In particular, the expected cost using d_2 always increases considerably compared to the other two. Again this is not surprising at all.

The next question we ask is whether the decision rule described above can be improved. Intuitively, it seems reasonable that when the system is

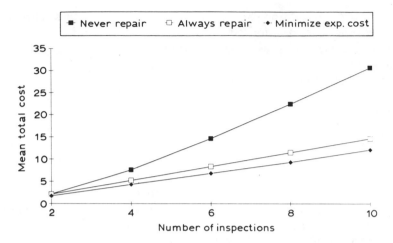

Fig. 2. Estimated expected total cost as functions of the number of inspections.

operative in more than two periods, one should have a slightly more restrictive replacement policy. Although repairing the system may be sensible on a short time perspective, replacing components too early may result in more repairs as well as system failures later on. In order to investigate this closer we consider decision rules of the following form:

$$\text{Replace all failed components if } E(\text{Cost}|d_1) - E(\text{Cost}|d_2) > c \quad (11)$$

where c is a number to be determined. We observe that if $c = 0$, we get the old decision rule back. Thus eqn (11) is a generalization of this rule.

By simulating the system for different c-values, it is possible to get an estimate of the optimal c. As an example we varied c 1000 times at random between -5 and $+5$ and simulated the system cost over 10 inspection periods using these c-values. The results are presented as a scatter plot in Fig. 3. As one can see, the dots in the diagram are spread around in such a way that it is difficult to carry out any optimization. To see things a little more clearly, we have fitted a polynomial of degree 4 to the data. This curve is also shown in the same diagram. We observe that the fitted curve has a minimum at 0·87. This number is of course not very reliable. Indeed the procedure we used for finding it is very *ad hoc*. However, these calculations at least indicate that the decision should be made according to eqn (11) with $c > 0$. In fact we simulated the system 5000 times using the decision rule described in eqn (11) with $c = 0·87$, and

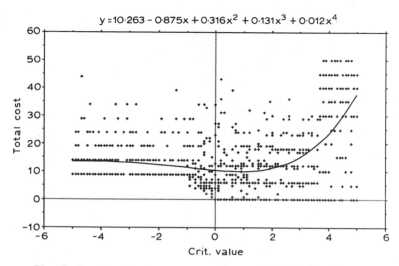

$$y = 10.263 - 0.875x + 0.316x^2 + 0.131x^3 + 0.012x^4$$

Fig. 3. Scatterplot of c versus total cost in 1000 simulations.

observed a slightly better performance than with $c=0$. $c=0.87$ implied a mean total cost of 11.783, while the corresponding result for $c=0$ was 12.042.

The last step now is to allow c to vary from inspection to inspection. Since we know that $c=0$ is optimal in the inspection before the last period, while c should be positive in earlier inspections, it is clear that a constant c cannot be optimal. However, by allowing c to vary, the complexity of the optimization increases. Instead of optimizing one single parameter, one will have to carry out a multidimensional optimization. To reduce the problem one may model c as a parametric function of the inspection number. We carried out a simulation study where we let c be a linear decreasing function. The gain in terms of reduced expected total cost was, however, very little; we skip the details here. Thus, at least in this particular case, the rule based on a constant c-value appeared to be acceptable.

Conclusions

In the first part of this chapter we have studied the problem of finding optimal decision rules in the case of sequential decisions. It has not been our intention to provide an extensive discussion of this topic in this chapter. We just wanted to briefly outline the problem to explain why even in seemingly simple cases this very soon becomes a complex task. We did this by considering some simple examples. A main point, however, is that by considering decision rules of a special form, it is possible to reduce the dimension of the problem considerably. In fact, the problem is reduced to optimizing the response with respect to a few controllable variables. This reduction may of course have the unfortunate side effect that relevant information is ignored.

We believe, however, that if the form of the decision rule is chosen in a sensible way, the described method will yield a good approximation to the optimal solution. Furthermore, by allowing sequential decisions, one obtains a far more realistic model, and thus the risk analysis is improved.

In our study we have made extensive use of Monte Carlo simulation. Considered just as a numerical method, this is a convenient way to obtain answers relatively quickly without sacrificing model flexibility. However, while we started out with a problem of pure decision analysis, we end up with a problem of analysing statistical data from the simulations. From a Bayesian point of view, this should of course be done by applying Bayesian statistical methods. Thus, all uncertainty about unknown variables should be described probabilistically. In this paper, however, we have chosen a more simplified approach, just calculating mean total costs and not providing any distributions for these parameters. This is done in order to focus on the main issue here: the dynamics of a sequential decision problem.

USING EXPERT OPINIONS IN A TWO COMPONENT SYSTEM—THE PREDICTIVE APPROACH

Consider, for a fixed point of time, t, a binary system like a nuclear power plant of n binary components. Let $(i = 1, \ldots, n)$:

$$X_i = \begin{cases} 1 & \text{if the } i\text{th component functions} \\ 0 & \text{otherwise} \end{cases}$$

$$\mathbf{X} = (X_1, \ldots, X_n)$$

$$\phi(\mathbf{X}) = \begin{cases} 1 & \text{if the system functions} \\ 0 & \text{otherwise} \end{cases}$$

Let furthermore:

$$E(X_i \mid p_i) = p_i = \text{the reliability of the } i\text{th component}$$

$$E(\phi(\mathbf{X}) \mid h) = h = \text{the reliability of the system}$$

If we assume that $X_1, \ldots, X_n$ are independent given $\mathbf{p} = (p_1, \ldots, p_n)$, we write:

$$h = E(\phi(\mathbf{X})|\mathbf{p}) = h(\mathbf{p})$$

Natvig and Eide (1987) assumed that the joint prior distribution of the reliabilities, before running any experiments on the component level, $\pi(\mathbf{p})$, can be written as:

$$\pi(\mathbf{p}) = \prod_{i=1}^{n} \pi_i(p_i)$$

where $\pi_i(p_i)$ is the prior marginal distribution of p_i, i.e. we assumed that the components have independent prior reliabilities. $\pi_i(p_i)$ describes our initial uncertainty in p_i, by for instance allocating most of the probability mass close to 1, indicating a very reliable component.

In this chapter we assume that k experts will provide the information about the reliabilities of the components. Our work in this area generalizes papers by Huseby (1986, 1988) on the single component case. Since the experts often share data, he argues that their assessments will typically be dependent and that this difficulty cannot be handled without making judgments concerning the underlying sources of information and to what extent these are available to each of the experts. In the former paper the information available to the experts is modelled as a set of observations $Y_1, \ldots, Y_m$. These observations are then reconstructed as far as possible from the information provided by the experts and used as a basis for the combined judgment of a decision maker (DM). This is called the *retrospective* approach. In the latter paper, the uncertain quantity is modelled as a future observation, Y, from the same distribution as the Y_i's. This is called the *predictive* approach.

For the case, $n > 1$, where each expert is giving opinions about more than one component, additional dependencies between the reliabilities of the components come into play. This is for instance true if two or more components are of similar type, are sharing a common environment or are exposed to common cause failures. In the case of $X_1, \ldots, X_n$ independent given $\mathbf{p}$, and the lifetimes being exponentially distributed with unknown failure rates $\lambda_1, \ldots, \lambda_n$, this problem is considered by Lindley and Singpurwalla (1986). Then obviously:

$$p_i = \exp(-\lambda_i t), \quad i = 1, \ldots, n$$

In the latter paper the jth expert, $j = 1, \ldots, k$, expresses his opinion about λ_i and hence of p_i in terms of a normal distribution for

$\theta_i = \ln\lambda_i$, $i = 1, \ldots, n$. He provides its mean m_{ji} and standard deviation s_{ji} but also ρ_{jir} being the personal correlation between θ_i and θ_r, $j = 1, \ldots, k$; $i, r = 1, \ldots, n$, $i \neq r$. In addition the DM has to provide his personal correlations between the m_{ji}'s for fixed expert j and different components, for fixed component i and different experts and finally for both different experts and components. The great drawback of this approach is the difficulty of assessing these correlations directly without having an underlying model as in the papers by Huseby.

Lindley and Singpurwalla (1986) use an approximation technique suggested by Laplace, which has been pointed out to be quite good by Tierney and Kadane (1986) to arrive at the corresponding uncertainty in $h(\mathbf{p})$ for a parallel system of independent components. They claim that the results may easily be generalized to cover any coherent system of independent components. This is not true since representing a coherent system of independent components by a series-parallel structure introduces replicated components which of course are dependent. For details see the excellent textbook by Barlow and Proschan (1975) or Natvig (1989b).

The generalized predictive approach is treated in the next section for the case $n = 2$. Here the uncertain quantities (Z_1, Z_2) are the lifetimes of the two components. These are assumed to have a bivariate exponential distribution. As an example of such a two component system consider a module of the lubricating system for the main bearings of a power station turbine presented in Chapter 4.3 of the present book. In this system an oil pump driven by an electromotor is delivering oil from a reservoir, the oil being cleaned by a filter on its way. Our module of interest is a series system of the oil pump and the electromotor. In the paper above the lifetimes of these components are assumed to be independent and exponentially distributed, neglecting that they are sharing a common environment or may be exposed to common cause failures, which are basic assumptions in our research in this area presented as a whole in Natvig (1990). If in addition the oil pump and the electromotor are of a new design, there are no data to rely on in the beginning. Hence the best one can do as a start is to let experts help in specifying the joint distribution of the lifetimes of these components.

The Predictive Approach

The deductions in this section follow the main lines of the example given in section 3 of Huseby (1988). The jump from the univariate to the bivariate case, however, gives sufficient obstacles to overcome. Let (Z_1, Z_2) be the lifetimes of the two components. The DM specifies a set of vectors of nonnegative numbers:

$$\mathbf{z}_s = (z_{11s}, z_{21s}, z_{12s}, z_{22s}, z_{13s}, z_{23s}), s = 1, \ldots, r$$

He then asks the jth expert to describe his uncertainty about (Z_1, Z_2) by specifying a set of vectors of probabilities:

$$\boldsymbol{\pi}_{js} = (\pi_{j1s}, \pi_{j2s}, \pi_{j3s}), s = 1, \ldots, r$$

such that:

$$P(Z_1 > z_{1vs}, Z_2 > z_{2vs}) = \pi_{jvs}, v = 1, 2, 3; s = 1, \ldots, r \qquad (12)$$

For $s = r = 1$ the jth expert can for instance be asked to specify the probabilities that both the oil pump and the electromotor survive 5000 h, that the oil pump survives 5000 h and the electromotor 10 000 h and that the oil pump alone survives 10 000 h. The DM then faces the problem of computing his posterior distribution for (Z_1, Z_2) given $\boldsymbol{\pi}_{js}$, $j = 1, \ldots, k$; $s = 1, \ldots, r$.

We assume that the DM assesses that given the hyperparameters $\theta_1, \theta_2, \theta_3$, (Z_1, Z_2) and the imaginary observations (Z_{1i}, Z_{2i}), $i = 1, \ldots, m$ are mutually independent with a bivariate exponential distribution of the Marshall–Olkin type, i.e.

$$P(Z_1 > z_1, Z_2 > z_2 | \theta_1, \theta_2, \theta_3) = \exp(-\theta_1 z_1 - \theta_2 z_2 - \theta_3 z_3)$$

where $z_3 = \max(z_1, z_2)$. Remember for this distribution that:

$$Z_1 = \min(V_1, V_3)$$
$$Z_2 = \min(V_2, V_3)$$

where the V_l's are mutually independent and exponentially distributed with failure rates $\theta_l, l = 1, 2, 3$. Hence $\theta_l, l = 1, 2$ is the failure rate knocking out the lth component alone, whereas θ_3 is the failure rate knocking out both at the same time. For further details on the properties of this distribution we refer to Barlow and Proschan (1975). Furthermore, we assume that the prior distributions of $\theta_l, l = 1, 2, 3$, for both the DM and the jth expert are independent gamma distributions with shape parameter and scale parameter respectively equal to (a_l, b_l) for the DM and (a_{jl}, b_{jl}) for the jth expert, $j = 1, \ldots, k; l = 1, 2, 3$. In Huseby (1988) just a vague gamma distribution with parameters close to zero is used as a prior for the single parameter θ.

As in the latter paper let $B_0, B_1, \ldots, B_k$ be disjoint subsets of the index set $\{1, \ldots, m\}$ such that:

$$B_0 \bigcup B_1 \bigcup \cdots \bigcup B_k = \{1, \ldots, m\}$$

It is then assessed that the jth expert has access to information on the (Z_{1i}, Z_{2i})'s with indices in the set $A_j = (B_0 \cup B_j)$, $j = 1, \ldots, k$. Thus B_0 is the set of common information, while the B_j's are the sets of individual informations. As opposed to Huseby (1988) we express the information as *survivals* of the two components beyond specific time points; i.e.

$$\{Z_{1i} > z_{1i}, Z_{2i} > z_{2i}\}, \quad i = 1, \ldots, m$$

instead of just observed lifetimes. This turns out to be at least mathematically advantageous.

Introduce:

$$z_{3i} = \max(z_{1i}, z_{2i})$$

$$t_{jl} = \sum_{i \in A_j} z_{li}, j = 1, \ldots, k; \ l = 1, 2, 3$$

$$t_l = \sum_{i=1}^{m} z_{li}, l = 1, 2, 3$$

Here t_{jl}, $l = 1, 2$, is the total survival of the lth component and t_{j3} the total survival of both components from a common failure, corresponding to the information from the jth expert. t_l, $l = 1, 2, 3$, are similarly the total survivals corresponding to the whole set of information. We now have by standard calculations involving Bayes' theorem:

$$P\left[(Z_1 > z_1, Z_2 > z_2) \middle| \bigcap_{i=1}^{m} (Z_{1i} > z_{1i}, Z_{2i} > z_{2i}) \right]$$

$$= k \int_{\theta_1 = 0}^{\infty} \int_{\theta_2 = 0}^{\infty} \int_{\theta_3 = 0}^{\infty} P(Z_1 > z_1, Z_2 > z_2 | \theta_1, \theta_2, \theta_3)$$

$$\times P\left[\bigcap_{i=1}^{m} (Z_{1i} > z_{1i}, Z_{2i} > z_{2i}) \middle| \theta_1, \theta_2, \theta_3 \right] \tag{13}$$

$$\times \prod_{l=1}^{3} \frac{b_l^{a_l} \theta_l^{a_l - 1}}{\Gamma(a_l)} \exp(-b_l \theta_l) \, d\theta_1 \, d\theta_2 \, d\theta_3$$

$$= \prod_{l=1}^{3} \left(\frac{b_l + t_l}{b_l + t_l + z_l} \right)^{a_l}$$

The constant k is determined by noting that $z_1 = z_2 = 0$ gives a joint survival probability of 1. Similarly we get:

$$P\left[(Z_1 > z_1, Z_2 > z_2)\middle| \bigcap_{i \in A_j} (Z_{1i} > z_{1i}, Z_{2i} > z_{2i})\right]$$

$$= \prod_{l=1}^{3} \left(\frac{b_{jl} + t_{jl}}{b_{jl} + t_{jl} + z_l}\right)^{a_{jl}} \tag{14}$$

Introducing $z_{3vs} = \max(z_{1vs}, z_{2vs})$, $v = 1, 2, 3$; $s = 1, \ldots, r$, we get by combining eqns (12) and (14) the following r sets of three equations to determine, for fixed $j = 1, \ldots, k$, the information t_{jl}, $l = 1, 2, 3$:

$$\prod_{l=1}^{3} \left(\frac{b_{jl} + t_{jl}}{b_{jl} + t_{jl} + z_{lvs}}\right)^{a_{jl}} = \pi_{jvs}, \quad v = 1, 2, 3; \ s = 1, \ldots, r \tag{15}$$

Note that for fixed s there is no guarantee that we end up by a unique solution to these three equations satisfying the obvious claim:

$$t_{j3} \geqslant \max(t_{j1}, t_{j2}) \geqslant \min(t_{j1}, t_{j2}) \geqslant 0 \tag{16}$$

Furthermore, even if all of the r sets of equations give a unique, acceptable solution these will in general be different. Ideally we should calculate a posterior distribution for t_{jl}, $l = 1, 2, 3$, based on the assessments π_{jvs}, $v = 1, 2, 3$; $s = 1, \ldots, r$. However, as an approximation we will at the present stage of research suggest as Huseby (1988) did that one should base the subsequent calculations for fixed $j = 1, \ldots, k$ and fixed $l = 1, 2, 3$ on the *averages* of t_{jl}, for the sets of equations having a unique, acceptable solution. If an expert provides a small fraction of acceptable solutions, he should perhaps better be dismissed.

A general investigation into the set of equations (15), for instance by a computer program performing algebraic manipulations, is outside the scope of this chapter. However, the DM can design his experiment in a clever way leading to both easier assessments for the experts and simpler calculations. For instance he can specify:

$$\mathbf{z}_s = (z_s, z_s, z_s, 0, 0, z_s), s = 1, \ldots, r \tag{17}$$

leading to rather easy assessments in eqn (12). For $s = r = 1$ the jth expert can now be asked to specify the probabilities that both the oil pump and the electromotor survive 5000 h and that the oil pump and the electromotor alone respectively survives 5000 h. Let us furthermore for simplicity assume that the jth expert assesses:

$$a_{jl} = a_{j1}, \quad j=1,\dots,k; l=2,3 \tag{18}$$

Introducing

$$x_{jl} = b_{jl} + t_{jl}$$
$$y_{jvs} = (\pi_{jvs})^{a_{j1}^{-1}}, \quad j=1,\dots,k; v=1,2,3; s=1,\dots,r$$

and then suppressing the indices j and s eqn (15) reduces to:

$$\begin{aligned}
x_1 x_2 x_3 &= y_1(x_1+z)(x_2+z)(x_3+z) \\
x_1 x_2 x_3 &= y_2(x_1+z)x_2(x_3+z) \\
x_1 x_2 x_3 &= y_3 x_1(x_2+z)(x_3+z)
\end{aligned} \tag{19}$$

Disregarding unacceptable solutions involving either $x_1=0$, $x_2=0$ or both, the system above is easily solved for the variables $x_l/(x_l+z)$, $l=1,2,3$. This leads to the following solution:

$$\begin{aligned}
x_1 &= y_1 z/(y_3-y_1) \\
x_2 &= y_1 z/(y_2-y_1) \\
x_3 &= y_2 y_3 z/(y_1-y_2 y_3)
\end{aligned} \tag{20}$$

Hence we get ($j=1,\dots,k; s=1,\dots,r$):

$$t_{j1} = \pi_{j1s}^{a_{j1}^{-1}} z_s \Big/ \left(\pi_{j3s}^{a_{j1}^{-1}} - \pi_{j1s}^{a_{j1}^{-1}} \right) - b_{j1}$$

$$t_{j2} = \pi_{j1s}^{a_{j1}^{-1}} z_s \Big/ \left(\pi_{j2s}^{a_{j1}^{-1}} - \pi_{j1s}^{a_{j1}^{-1}} \right) - b_{j2} \tag{21}$$

$$t_{j3} = \pi_{j2s}^{a_{j1}^{-1}} \pi_{j3s}^{a_{j1}^{-1}} z_s \left(\pi_{j1s}^{a_{j1}^{-1}} - \pi_{j2s}^{a_{j1}^{-1}} \pi_{j3s}^{a_{j1}^{-1}} \right) - b_{j3}$$

Let us give some comments on when eqn (21) satisfies the claim (eqn (16)) of being a set of acceptable solutions.

A necessary condition for t_{j1} to be nonnegative is that:

$$\pi_{j3s} = P(Z_1>0, Z_2>z_s) \geqslant P(Z_1>z_s, Z_2>z_s) = \pi_{j1s}$$

which is always true. The same argument applies to t_{j2}. Hence a necessary and sufficient condition for $\min(t_{j1}, t_{j2})$ to be nonnegative is that

$$\pi_{j1s}^{a_{j1}^{-1}} z_s \Big/ \left(\pi_{j4-ls}^{a_{j1}^{-1}} - \pi_{j1s}^{a_{j1}^{-1}} \right) \geqslant b_{jl}, \quad l=1,2$$

This is always true for the vague gamma distribution with parameters close to zero. A necessary condition for t_{j3} to be nonnegative is that:

$$\pi_{j1s} = P(Z_1 > z_s, Z_2 > z_s) \geqslant P(Z_1 > z_s, Z_2 > 0)P(Z_1 > 0, Z_2 > z_s)$$

$$= \pi_{j2s}\pi_{j3s}$$

This is again always true if the expert's assessments are consistent with the bivariate exponential distribution. *Sufficient* conditions for having $t_{j3} \geqslant \max(t_{j1}, t_{j2})$ are

$$b_{j3} \leqslant \min(b_{j1}, b_{j2})$$

$$\pi_{j1s}^2 \leqslant \pi_{j2s}\pi_{j3s}\min(\pi_{j2s}, \pi_{j3s}) \tag{22}$$

Due to eqn (18) the first of the conditions in eqn (22) means that the jth expert assesses the prior mean of θ_3 not less than the prior means of θ_1 and θ_2. Anyway, this condition is always true for the vague gamma distribution. The latter condition is true if the expert's assessments of the π_{jvs}'s are consistent with the bivariate exponential distribution having $\theta_3 \leqslant \min(\theta_1, \theta_2)$, which in a way is the opposite condition. This makes sense since if the first condition is true the expert is allowed to be consistent by breaking the second one. If on the other hand the first one is not true, the expert is forced to be consistent by satisfying the second one.

Assume now that we have found $t_{jl}, j = 1, \ldots, k; l = 1, 2, 3$ for instance by taking averages of the acceptable solutions to eqn (21). The final aim of the DM is to compute his posterior distribution for (Z_1, Z_2) given the information $t_{jl}, j = 1, \ldots, k; l = 1, 2, 3$. When $B_0 = \emptyset$, i.e. when the experts share no *common* information, this information is sufficient. Let $T_{jl}, j = 1, \ldots, k; l = 1, 2, 3$ be mutually independent and exponentially distributed with failure rates θ_l. Then the DM calculates, similar to eqn (13),

$$P\left[Z_1 > z_1, Z_2 > z_2 \, \middle| \, \bigcap_{j=1}^{k} \bigcap_{l=1}^{3} (T_{jl} > t_{jl}) \right] = \prod_{l=1}^{3} \left(\frac{b_l + \sum_{j=1}^{k} t_{jl}}{b_l + \sum_{j=1}^{k} t_{jl} + z_l} \right)^{a_l} \tag{23}$$

This is nothing else than eqn (13) since $\sum_{j=1}^{k} t_{jl}$ are the calculations of t_l, $l = 1, 2, 3$, based on eqn (21).

When $B_0 \neq \emptyset$, the situation is more complicated. Let $T_{0l}, l = 1, 2, 3$, be mutually independent and exponentially distributed with failure rates $\theta_l, l = 1, 2, 3$, and also independent of the T_{jl}'s. Let us now assume that the k experts agree to specify their common information as:

$$\bigcap_{l=1}^{3} (T_{0l} > c_l), \quad \text{where } 0 \leqslant c_l \leqslant t_{jl}, j = 1, \ldots, k; l = 1, 2, 3$$

Here $c_l, l = 1, 2$, is the total survival of the lth component and c_3 the total survival of both components from a common failure, that all experts agree on as a minimum. A reasonable choice without any additional specification is:

$$c_l = \sum_{i \in B_0} z_{li} = \min_{1 \leqslant j \leqslant k} t_{jl}, l = 1, 2, 3$$

A choice for the DM is now to calculate:

$$P\left[Z_1 > z_1, Z_2 > z_2 \middle| \bigcap_{j=1}^{k} \bigcap_{l=1}^{3} (T_{jl} > t_{jl} - c_l) \cap \bigcap_{l=1}^{3} (T_{0l} > c_l) \right]$$

corresponding to a censoring of the common information at $c_l, l = 1, 2, 3$. By Bayes' theorem this probability equals:

$$k \int_{\theta_1 = 0}^{\infty} \int_{\theta_2 = 0}^{\infty} \int_{\theta_3 = 0}^{\infty} P(Z_1 > z_1, Z_2 > z_2 | \theta_1, \theta_2, \theta_3)$$

$$\times P\left[\bigcap_{j=1}^{k} \bigcap_{l=1}^{3} (T_{jl} > t_{jl} - c_l) \cap \bigcap_{l=1}^{3} (T_{0l} > c_l) \middle| \theta_1, \theta_2, \theta_3 \right]$$

$$\times \prod_{l=1}^{3} \frac{b_l^{a_l} \theta_l^{a_l - 1}}{\Gamma(a_l)} \exp(-b_l \theta_l) d\theta_1 d\theta_2 d\theta_3$$

$$= \prod_{l=1}^{3} \left[\frac{b_l + \sum_{j=1}^{k} t_{jl} - (k-1)c_l}{b_l + \sum_{j=1}^{k} t_{jl} - (k-1)c_l + z_l} \right]^{a_l} \tag{24}$$

For $k = 1$ or $c_l = 0$ eqn (24) reduces to eqn (23) as it should. Hence eqn (24) is a generalization of eqn (23). Also eqn (24) is a decreasing probability in c_l as is intuitively obvious.

Conclusion

It seems that generalizing this work to the case $n \geqslant 3$ is more a matter of stamina than of new ideas. Hence there remains some research and development to implement the present ideas and result in real applications of larger systems. Some important steps in this direction are reported in Gåsemyu and Natvig (1991). It should, however, be noted that the use of expert opinions is actually implemented in the regulatory work for nuclear power plants in the US. In addition there is no reason why this approach should not be used for instance in the offshore oil industry when new or redesigned systems are analysed. A general problem when using expert opinions is the selection of the experts. This problem is not addressed directly in this chapter except for suggesting when a selected expert should be dismissed. However, asking experts technical questions on the component level as in this chapter, where the consequences for the overall reliability assessment on the system level are less clear, seems very advantageous. Hence one can avoid the problem that to any risk assessment on system level there is an expert who will strongly support it.

Acknowledgements

This chapter is based on research carried out in the project 'Failure Data Information with Bayesian Statistics'. The papers by Natvig (1989a, b, 1990) were also written as a part of this project. This project was carried out within the Nordic cooperative programme for Terotechnology, supported by the Royal Norwegian Council for Scientific and Industrial Research and the Nordic Industrial Fund. The authors are grateful to these institutions for making this research possible.

REFERENCES

Barlow, R.E. & Pereira, C.A.B. (1987). *The Bayesian operation and probabilistic influence diagrams*. Tech. Rep., ESRC 87-7, University of California, Berkeley, CA.

Barlow, R.E. & Proschan, F. (1975). *Statistical Theory of Reliability and Life Testing. Probability Models*. Holt, Rinehart and Winston, New York.

Gåsemyu, Y. & Natvig, B. (1991). Using expert opinions in Bayesian estimation of component lifetimes in a shock model—a general predictive approach.

Paper presented at the 48th Session of the International Statistical Institute, Cairo, 9–17 September 1991.

Genest, C. & Zidek, J. (1986). Combining probability distributions: A critique and an annotated bibliography. *Statistical Sci.* 1, 114–48.

Howard, R.A. (1988). Decision analysis: Practice and promise. *Management Sci.*, 34, 679–95.

Howard, R.A. & Matheson, J.E. (1984). Influence diagrams. *Readings on the Principle and Applications of Decision Analysis*, Vol II, Strategic Decision Group, Menlo Park, CA.

Huseby, A.B. (1986). *Combining experts' opinions, a retrospective approach.* Tech. Rep. Center for Industrial Research, PO Box 350, Blindern, Oslo 3.

Huseby, A.B. (1988). Combining opinions in a predictive case. In *Bayesian Statistics* 3, ed. J.M. Bernardo, M.H. DeGroot, D.V. Lindley & A.F.M. Smith. Oxford University Press, pp. 641–51.

Huseby, A.B. (1989). Economic risk assessment in the case of sequential decisions. In *Reliability Achievement: The Commercial Incentive*, ed. T. Aven. Elsevier, pp. 203–14.

Lauritzen, S.L. & Spiegelhalter, D.J. (1988). Local computations with probabilities on graphical structures and their application to expert systems (with discussion). *J. Roy. Statist. Soc. Ser. B*, 50, 157–224.

Lindley, D.V. & Singpurwalla, N.D. (1986). Reliability (and fault tree) analysis using expert opinions. *J. Amer. Statist. Assoc.*, 81, 87–90.

Natvig, B. (1989a). På tide med Bayes-analyse i Norge nå? (Time for Bayes analysis in Norway now?) *Tilfeldig Gang* 6(3), 7–13, Norwegian Statistical Association.

Natvig, B. (1989b). *Pålitelighetsanalyse med Teknologiske Anvendelser* (Reliability Analysis of Technological Systems). Institute of Mathematics, University of Oslo.

Natvig, B. (1990). Using expert opinions in Bayesian estimation of system reliability. Revised version of a paper presented at the Course-Congress on Reliability and Decision Making, Siena, Italy, 15–26, October.

Natvig, B. & Eide, H. (1987). Bayesian estimation of system reliability. *Scand. J. Statist.*, 14, 319–27.

Olmsted, S.M. (1983). *On representing and solving decision problems.* PhD Thesis, Engineering-Economic Systems Dept, Stanford University, Stanford, CA.

Pörn, K. (1990). *On Empirical Bayesian inference applied to Poisson probability models.* PhD thesis, Linköping University, Sweden.

Ripley, B.D. (1987). *Stochastic Simulation.* John Wiley, New York.

Shachter, R.D. (1986). Evaluating influence diagrams. *Oper. Res.*, 34, 871–82.

Spiegelhalter, D.L. & Lauritzen, S.L. (1989). *Sequential updating of conditional probabilities on directed graphical structures.* Res. Rep., R-88-32, Inst. Elec. Syst., Aalborg University, Denmark.

Tierney, L. & Kadane, J.B. (1986). Accurate approximations for posterior moments and marginal densities. *J. Amer. Statist. Assoc.*, 81, 82–6.

2.3

Systematic Analysis of Operating Experiences— An Application to Motor Operated Valve Failure and Maintenance Data

KAISA SIMOLA, KARI LAAKSO, SEPPO HÄNNINEN

Technical Research Centre of Finland,
Laboratory of Electrical Engineering and Automation Technology,
SF-02150 Espoo, Finland

MIKKO KOSONEN and ESA UNGA

Teollisuuden Voima Oy, SF-27160 Olkiluoto, Finland

ABSTRACT
The analysis of operating experiences, e.g. using failure and maintenance data, gives valuable information on components' behaviour in their operational environment. This knowledge can be used to reveal weaknesses and ageing in components, and to plan more effective maintenance and test practices to improve the component reliability.

Reliability engineering offers both qualitative and quantitative methods for data analyses. Failure mode and effects analysis (FMEA) and maintenance effects and criticality analysis (MECA) are systematic analysis methods which are commonly used in the design stage. In this chapter their use in the analysis of operating experiences is demonstrated through a case study.

The efficient use of operating experiences requires systematic data collection practices, which are widely used in the nuclear industry. Our study is based on data obtained from TVO 1 and 2 nuclear power plants' failure data collection system. We describe an analysis of motor operated valve operating experiences in four safety related systems. The data consist of 181 failure and maintenance descriptions, which have been reported during the observation period 1 January 1981 to 31 December 1989. The analyses cover failures of both the closing valve itself and its electromechanical actuator.

In the qualitative analyses, classifications were made on valve parts, failure modes, causes, effects, detection, and criticality, and recurring failure causes and significant problem areas in valve operability were studied and identified. The failure and maintenance descriptions are documented on particular FMEA and MECA sheets, from which data are easily retrievable and updatable for further analyses. As examples of quantitative studies, statistical analyses concerning repair and unavailability times and failure trends are demonstrated.

INTRODUCTION

A study on motor operated closing valve failures in four safety systems of two boiling water reactor (BWR) plants in Finland is reported. This study has been initiated from previous results of motor operated valve (MOV) studies of Finnish and Swedish BWRs performed within the NKA/RAS-450 project (Laakso, 1990). Analyses showed notable variations in the number of valve failures between plants and their systems. The comparison of test and accident conditions revealed some significant deviations in operating conditions and thus the reliability of some MOVs can be questioned in real demand situations (Eriksen & Knochenhauer, 1988). The classification and description of failures in the failure reporting system is also in some cases incomplete or misleading and a careful qualitative study would be required before making quantitative analyses and drawing conclusions on significant problem areas.

The reports from the failure reporting systems of two Finnish nuclear power plants, TVO 1 and 2, have been analysed in detail. In total 181 reported failure events in altogether 104 valves have been re-analysed and sorted according to a new classification developed for the MOV. The failure mode and effects analysis (FMEA) method is used for qualitative analyses. Additionally the repair actions are studied by a maintenance effects and criticality analysis (MECA). These analyses have been performed by filling and storing FMEA and MECA sheets in a computerized spread-sheet data base from which the information is obtainable for further statistical analyses. Quantitative analyses concerning repair and unavailability times and failure trends were performed and ageing-related failures were surveyed.

The chapter is based on the work done within the Nordic Terotechnology programme funded by the Nordic Industrial Fund, and the project 'Reliability Assessment of Maintenance in Nuclear Power Plants' which is funded by the Ministry of Trade and Industry in Finland.

MOTOR OPERATED CLOSING VALVE DATA

The TVO 1 and 2 nuclear power units, located in Olkiluoto, Finland, are operated by Teollisuuden Voima Oy (TVO). TVO 1 and TVO 2 are two identical ASEA-ATOM (nowadays ABB Atom) BWR units, 710 MWe each. The units were connected to the national grid in September 1978 (TVO 1) and February 1980 (TVO 2). Both units have thus been in commercial operation for about 10 years. The valve operating experience from the TVO 1 and 2 nuclear power units have been the basis for this study.

The data have been obtained from the plant failure reporting systems and include the failure events reported between 1 January 1981 and 31 December 1989. In total 104 (52 at each plant) motor operated closing valves in four safety systems have been considered; 72 of these valves are external isolation valves, and among the remaining 32 valves there are 16 back-up valves for external isolation valves and 16 'normal' closing valves. The systems and valve types are described in detail in Eriksen and Knochenhauer (1988) and short descriptions are given here.

The studied valves are located in the following safety systems (the system identification code is given in brackets):

— Shut-down cooling system (321)
— Containment vessel spray system (322)
— Core spray system (323)
— Auxiliary feed water system (327)

The systems 322, 323 and 327 have a $4 \times 50\%$ subsystem structure and design capacity. These three systems are in stand-by during normal plant operation. These systems are presented in Fig. 1 (Laakso, 1990). The shut-down cooling system (321) is continuously operating because it has additionally the reactor water cleaning function. In this system 321 the operational position of the valves is open, and there is a continuous water flow through these four closing valves.

The isolation valves have a dual function: they should isolate the space inside/outside the containment tightly from each other in possible accident conditions, and in some plant transient or accident conditions they should start up or stop the water flow in the safety system by opening or closing the valve. The valves are thus mostly activated only in periodic tests but some valves are also activated between tests (in systems 322 one valve in each subsystem with an approximately 3-day period for operational reasons).

The valves are mostly wedge gate valves, but eight are ball valves

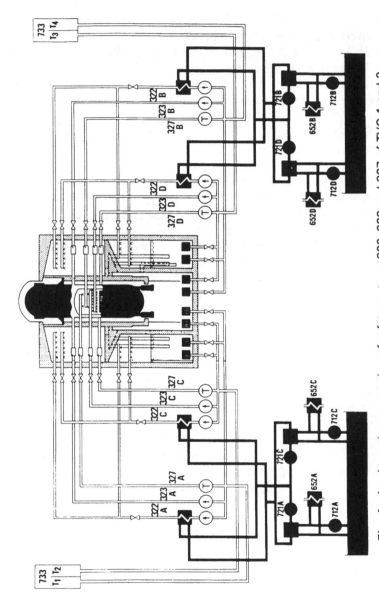

Fig. 1. A schematic presentation of safety systems 322, 323 and 327 of TVO 1 and 2.

manufactured by NELES. The gate valves are manufactured by NAF (24) and STENBERG (72). Nominal sizes of studied valves vary between 100 and 300 mm. The manufacturer of the actuators of all valves is AUMA and the actuator sizes vary with closing torques from 40 up to 1400 Nm.

Because the closing or opening of most of these valves is not needed during the normal plant operation, the functional availability of valves is tested periodically. The test intervals are defined in safety technical specifications. Additionally, valves in system 321 are tested every three months and most valves in other three systems are tested each month. A tightness test is performed on all these valves once a year during the revision outage.

Preventive maintenance of MOVs includes overhaul of actuators every 10 years. An overhaul/repair of a valve is done if the result of the annual tightness test is not approved. The safety significant MOVs have a preventive maintenance programme depending on valve type. According to the present programme the valves are maintained at intervals of 1–6 years.

The valve failure data are obtained from the failure reporting systems of the TVO power plants. The systems contain information on failure events in a coded form and time points related to the detection of failure and repair actions. In addition to classified and coded information, reports include also short descriptions of failure and repair in plain language. The failure reporting system data are further transmitted to the ATV-system (Ekberg *et al.*, 1985) which stores data from Swedish nuclear power plants and Finnish BWR units.

The data collected during the observation period of nine years include a total of 181 reported events in 67 valves. No failures were reported for 37 valves studied; 120 failures were reported from TVO 1 and the remaining 61 from TVO 2. These failure events include failures detected in the valve actuator and its electric power supply and control systems, too.

ANALYSIS METHODS

The failure reports are first studied qualitatively using failure mode and effects analysis (FMEA) and maintenance effects and criticality analysis (MECA) methods. These methods, especially FMEA, are widely used in reliability engineering, and usually applied in the design stage to identify the possible failure modes and their impact. The basic idea in FMEA is to systematically 'think through' the possible failure mechanisms and their effects on the system and list them in the form of a table on specific FMEA sheets. The procedure for FMEA is described in an IEC standard (IEC Standard 812, 1985). In connection with the FMEA, the maintenance actions and the effects of the isolation of the maintenance object can be analysed using MECA (Laakso & Burns, 1985).

In this study, the qualitative analysis methods are used primarily to classify the failures and repair actions reported in the plant failure reporting system. Before the reports were analysed, a specific classification for failures was formed in order to identify valve parts failed, failure modes, causes, effects and ways of failure detection. This classification was further completed and updated during the analysis of failure reports.

This follow-up analysis of failure and repair information is rewritten on FMEA and MECA sheets for each individual valve. Thus the failure and maintenance history is systematically presented for each valve individually in its own FMEA and MECA sheet stored in a microcomputer using a spread-sheet data base. In addition to separate sheets, all the information concerning 181 failure events is collected in one large file, enabling quick updating or selection of desired information and calculations. Calculated results are automatically updated if changes are made in FMEA or MECA sheets. The accomplishment of statistical analyses is helped by using coding in classification. The description of FMEA and MECA sheets is given in the next section.

After the analysis and classification of reported failures and repair actions, further statistical analyses can easily be applied. Statistical analyses of the collected data include quantification of failed subcomponents, failure modes and effectiveness of failure detection, estimation of repair and unavailability time distributions, and failure trend analyses based on the parameter estimation of the Weibull process. The computer codes used in these analyses are described in detail in Huovinen (1989). Methods to obtain reliability information from failure data are also discussed in Chapter 2.1 of this book.

CLASSIFICATION FOR FMEA AND MECA

Examples of FMEA and MECA sheets are presented in Fig. 2. The header of each sheet contains general information on the valve: identification, function, type, size, manufacturer, and activation interval. Addi-

Failure mode and effects analysis (FMEA)

Plant: TVO1
Comp. identif.: 322V204
Function: External isolation valve, basic operational position closed

Activation interval: 3 d
Valve type: Gate, Stenberg, DN 150

Name of analyst: KS/SH   Date: 4.1.90

ITEM	I	FAILURE MODE	FM	FAILURE CAUSE	FC	FAILURE EFFECT ON VALVE OPERABILITY	FE	FAILURE DETECTION	FD	COMMENTS	DATE OF FAILURE DETECTION
stem	M	stuck	M	normal wear	W	does not close	C	revision test	R	revision	3-Jun-81
circuit board	C	missing control	C	electrical damage	E	no effect	N	control-room monitoring	C		1-May-87
torque switch	T	wrong operation of torque switch	T	wrong adjustment	A	does not close	C	revision test	R	revision	30-May-89

Maintenance effects and criticality analysis (MECA)

Plant: TVO1
Comp. identif.: 322V204
Function: External isolation valve, basic operational position closed

Activation interval: 3 d
Valve type: Gate, Stenberg, DN 150

Name of analyst: KS/SH   Date: 20.7.89

ITEM	DATE OF FAILURE DETECTION	CORRECTIVE MAINTENANCE ACTIVITY	ISOLATION FROM SYSTEM	CRITICALITY LEVEL	UNDET. UNAV. TIME (h)	DELAY TIMES (h)	MAN HOURS/ MEN	ACTIVE REPAIR TIME (h)	UNAVAIL. TIME (h)	COMMENTS
stem	3-Jun-81	control circuits checked, stem lubricated, box tightness checked	isolation	latent critical	36	3	8 / 2	28	67	repair during revision
circuit board	1-May-87	circuit board replaced	no	monitored non critical	0	430	2 / 1	2	0	
torque switch	30-May-89	torque switch adjusted	-"-	latent critical	36	9	4 / 2	4	49	repair during revision

Fig. 2. Examples of FMEA and MECA sheets.

tionally, the name of the analyst(s) and date of analysis is included. The activation interval is given as the same as the test interval, except for some valves that are activated for operational purposes often between tests.

FMEA sheets contain information on the failed item and the cause, mode, effect and detection of the failure. Additionally, one column is reserved for comments. Under the titles of columns, a classification into specified groups was made in order to facilitate the statistical analysis. These classifications are defined in more detail in the subsections of this chapter. The classification used in this study has been developed specifically for the motor operated valves. This contrasts with the classification of the plant failure reporting system which is common for all kinds of components and thus less problem-specific.

In MECA sheets for maintenance analyses, the item and date of failure from the FMEA are repeated. Repair actions are described and information on required safe isolation of the repair object from the line operability, failure criticality and time durations related to repair and unavailability of the valve are given.

Division into Subcomponents

A gate valve and a motor actuator are presented in Fig. 3 (Eriksen & Knochenhauer, 1988). The valve (including the actuator) is divided into 12 subcomponents. These items were defined so that each reported failure can be assigned to one hardware item. The mechanical valve itself includes the following five parts: stem, bonnet packings, stem packings, slide and sealing surfaces, and leakage piping. The bonnet and stem packings are considered together if their separation in the identification of the failed item is not possible.

The division of valve into electrical and electromechanical subcomponents follows the T-book (T-boken, 1985), but with some deviations. In our study the electrical equipment for an individual valve is classified as follows: gear box, torque switch, limit switches, switchgear equipment, circuit board, electric motor, and indications and push buttons. Switchgear equipment includes fuses, relays, contactors and the power supply cables to the motor. Logic and automation for control of the valve are partly included in the class of circuit board.

The breakdown of the motor operated valve into subcomponents is presented in Fig. 4.

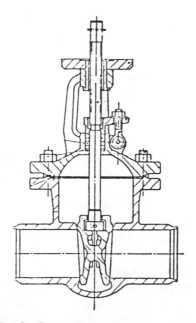

Fig. 3. Gate valve and motor actuator.

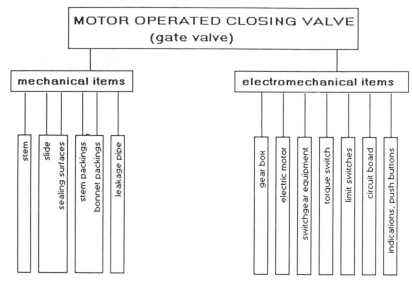

Fig. 4. Breakdown of a MOV into subcomponents failed.

Failure Modes

In the classification of failure modes only the most typical modes related to failed items are specified. The typical failure modes of bonnet and stem packings are leakages. Lack of stem lubrication may cause mechanical stiffness in the stem and cause a torque trip of the actuator because the torque needed to open the stuck valve exceeds the torque setting. Also the valve may be stuck due to dirt and sediment accumulated on the slide and may hinder the opening of the valve. The failure mode related to slide and sealing surfaces is a leak from sealing surfaces through the valve detected in the tightness test.

The failure mode associated with the torque switch is a torque switch trip which cuts the power supply to the electrical actuator and stops the operation of the valve. As already mentioned, mechanical stiffness of the stem can also cause trip of the torque switch and it is difficult to separate if the torque switch or stem was incorrect during the trip. During the start of the normal close/open cycle for a valve there is a hammerflow load that may be very high and thus could exceed the torque switch setting. In this analysis, failures to open/close due to a torque trip are classified as torque failures only if new adjustment of the torque setting was required.

Wrong positioning of the limit switch results in the valve stopping in an inadequate position. It may cut the power supply to the actuator too early. On the contrary, it can lead to a torque switch trip. Also loosening of contacts or mechanical stiffness of the limit switch can cause faulty operation of the limit switch.

Voltage cut-off means in most cases that the power supply to the motor actuator was terminated by some cause. Often the poor contacts of the contactor due to dirt and oxidation cut off the power supply to the actuator motor. Missing or wrong control means that indications (lamps or push buttons) operate incorrectly.

Other failures that cannot be classified in any more specific group are collected under the heading 'fault in electrical or mechanical items'.

Human factors include, e.g., temporary repairs which require later corrective actions, or positioning of a valve in a wrong position.

Failure Cause

In the classification of failure causes, the intention is to determine the root causes of failures. Often, however, the cause cannot be identified from the original failure reports or the cause description is clearly incorrect. In such cases it is often impossible to identify the cause afterwards, although discussions with maintenance foremen have given some help.

The most difficult aspect of the failure modes concerning the valve actuator is that they generally cannot be translated to a specific root cause. The failures have been related to several possible areas that include setting of limit switches and torque switches, inadequate operation of protective devices, possible deficiencies in maintenance procedures or methods, incorrect assembly, misuse of equipment, and unanticipated effect of the control circuit. A major problem identified concerned incorrect torque switch settings due to drifting, incorrect adjustment or deficient design specifications. Ageing of torque switch springs and their greasing may also contribute to torque switch trip in an inadequate valve position. These failures are indicative of a very complex interaction among the diverse mechanical and electrical failures of an integrated valve function, separately maintained by mechanical and electrical maintenance groups.

The principal failure cause is classified in one of 11 defined groups, as follows: (1) normal wear, (2) wrong adjustment, (3) mechanical damage, (4) electrical damage, (5) dirt, oxidation, sediment and corrosion, (6) loosening, (7) vibration, (8) poor maintenance and other human factors, (9) foreign objects, (10) design or material deficiency, and (11) unknown. Failure causes which are unidentifiable or cannot be clarified due to clearly erroneous reporting are classified in the group 'unknown'.

Effect on Valve Operability

The failure of a subcomponent may affect the valve operability in different ways. When the valve is actuated, the possible effects are maloperations of the valve, i.e. not closing or not opening. Additionally, while the valve is in stand-by, the degradation of, e.g., sealings and packings may lead to leakages. These leakages are divided into internal leakages (through the valve) and external leakages (e.g. to the system collecting controlled leakages or out to room). In many cases, the failure of an item has no effect to the valve operability but the effects of the repair actions on the valve operability must still be considered. In Table 1 we present the principal failure modes related to failure effects on valve operability.

Failure Detection

A failure can be detected either when the valve is actuated (in test or on demand) or during the stand-by time in local monitoring, preventive maintenance or control-room monitoring. Failures detected during opening or closing the valve are thus classified in one of the following groups: periodic test, revision test, leakage test or on demand. Revision tests are periodic tests performed during annual revision outage. The valve stem packings may then be subject to preventive replacement and parts of the actuators are dismantled for electrical workshop tests. Preventive testing of the actuator is done according to a plan with a 10-year intervals in the workshop. Control-room monitoring includes here only alarms detected outside test and demand instands, e.g. external leakages to system 352 (system for collection of controlled leakages). Local monitoring consists of visual inspections by plant personnel.

Criticality Definitions

In the analyses, the reported events are classified according to their impact on component availability. Failures directly preventing the function of the valve are called critical. Other failure events requiring repair actions are further divided into two groups: repair-critical failures which prevent valve function during corrective maintenance, and non-critical failures which are repaired without any effect on component operability. These definitions are illustrated in Fig. 5.

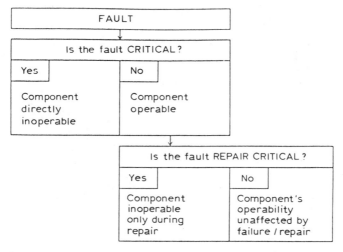

Fig. 5. Definition of fault and repair effects on stand-by component.

The definition of a critical failure is not always obvious. One boundary case is an internal leakage. Valve tightnesses are tested during revision outages with a specific leakage test. Limits for an allowed leakage are determined in technical specifications, and if the leak exceeds the limit a corrective action is undertaken. In this study, these leakages are classified as repair-critical failures.

Besides the criticality classification, the events are divided into monitored and latent failures. This division is needed for stand-by components in which existing failures are often not detected before a test or demand. Monitored failures are detected immediately, e.g. by control room monitoring, while latent failures are revealed in tests, maintenance or on demand.

Repair and Unavailability Times

In the failure reporting system, the reported time instants related to failure and corrective actions are date of failure detection, start of repair, and return to use. Also the amount of repair work done is expressed as man hours/number of men. In the MECA sheets, the time periods are

Table 1. Principal Failure Modes and Causes Related to Different Failure Effects on Valve Operability.

Failure effect	Failure mode	Failure cause
Does not close	Wrong operation of torque switch	Wrong adjustment, drifting Dirt, oxidation
	Mechanical stiffness of stem	Poor maintenance Wear
	Wrong positioning of limit switch	Wrong adjustment
	Voltage cut-off (switchgear eq.)	Dirt, oxidation
Does not open	Wrong operation of torque switch	Wrong adjustment, drifting Dirt, oxidation
	Mechanical stiffness of stem	Poor maintenance Wear
	Voltage cut-off (switchgear eq.)	Dirt, oxidation
External leakage	Leakage from bonnet or packings	Wear Poor maintenance Material deficiency
Internal leakage	Leakage from sealings	Wear Dirt Foreign objects Material deficiency

presented as follows:

(1) Undetected unavailability time
(2) Waiting time from failure detection to start of repair
(3) Man hours/number of men
(4) Repair time
(5) Total unavailability time

For non-critical failures there is no unavailability time and for repair-critical failures it is the same as repair time. For latent critical failures, the unavailability time cannot be exactly determined, because the failure occurrence instant is not detected. Thus, the undetected unavailability is approximated by half of the time from earlier activation (demand or test). Total unavailability time of a critical failure is obtained by summing the undetected unavailability time, waiting time and repair time. The unavailability times and time instants related to failure detection and corrective actions are presented in Fig. 6.

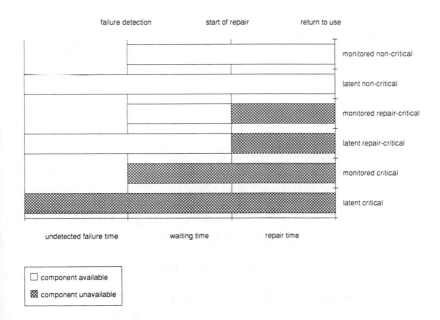

Fig. 6. Definitions of time periods related to corrective maintenance.

RESULTS OF ANALYSES

Failed Subcomponents

As described in the previous section, the valve has been divided into 12 parts. The number of failures in each subcomponent is presented in Fig. 7. The failures detected in shut-down cooling system (321) valves are shown separately because of the differing operational conditions (continuous water-flow) of the shut-down cooling system (321).

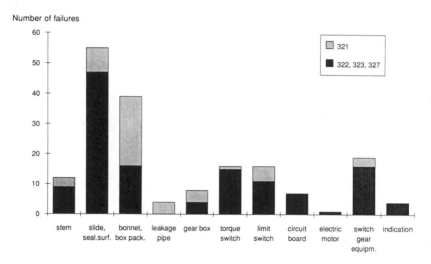

Fig. 7. Failed subcomponents.

The number of failures in system 321 covers 30% of all reported events, although less than 10% of the studied valves are situated in system 321. A majority of all reported failure events are caused by deficiencies in packings and sealing surfaces. Most of the bonnet and stem packing failures and all leakage pipe failures have occurred in system 321. In other stand-by systems the dominating items are sealing surfaces and slide. On the electromechanical side torque switches, switchgear equipment and limit switches are the main contributors to failures.

Means of Detection of Failure Modes

The means of detection of different failure modes are illustrated in Fig. 8. Failure detection in periodic test situations covers 65% of reported

Number of failures

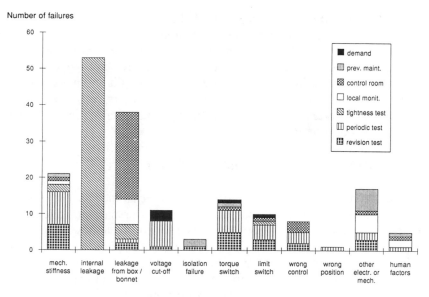

Fig. 8. Detection of failure modes.

events. In tightness tests mainly internal leakages are revealed, but also some external leakages. Although revision tests represent only 10% of all periodical tests, 40% of failures detected in tests (tightness tests excluded) appear during revisions. Most of these failures are such that they can be revealed mainly in revision tests, like recalibrations of torque and limit switches and stiffness of stem. External leakages are detected mostly by control-room monitoring. Visual inspections reveal some external leakages and mechanical damage. Five failures were detected in real demand situations.

Failure Effect on Valve Operability

As Fig. 8 shows, leakages represent 50% of all failures. Internal leakages in leakage tests have been observed in all systems, but most of the external leakages have occurred in system 321. In fact, almost 50% of all external leakages have occurred in two individual valves (at TVO 1). Both of these valves were replaced in 1987 and since then no failures have occurred in mechanical items of these new valves.

The valve operability has not been affected by 42 failure events. These failures are mostly detected in electromechanical components.

Failures to open or close are classified as critical failures because they have prevented the correct function of the valve. The number of such failures is 46, about equally divided between opening and closing failures. While in the case of all failures the dominant failed subcomponents were sealing surfaces and packings, the critical failures are governed by incorrect torque switch functions and contactor failures in switchgear equipment. The critical failures are detected mainly in tests. Twenty-six critical failures were detected during the operating period, four of these on demands outside tests.

Repair Actions and Unavailability Times

The corrective maintenance actions were not classified in the MECA sheets. However, we give here an overview of repair activities. The corrective actions can be roughly divided into the following groups: replacement, repair, other maintenance (e.g. lubrication, cleaning) and adjustment. In some cases (e.g. some failures to open because of stuck stem), no actions are needed and only the valve motioning is enough. Most corrective actions have been component repairs (e.g. slide and sealing grinding). Adjustment is generally needed in the case of incorrect limit and torque switch settings. Failed subcomponents were replaced in 30 cases; additionally two valves were replaced because of material deficiency. In 20 cases, the maintenance actions were not reported.

The repair time of a failure depends on several factors. In addition to the type of failure, the failure criticality affects the repair times. Non-critical failures do not require isolation of the repair object from the operable system and do not cause unavailability of the valve and thus their repair duration has little importance. These failures are often easy to repair and thus repair times are short. Critical failures are usually repaired as soon as possible and thus the waiting time for repair is short, although approximated total unavailability time is long due to the undetected unavailability period. The repair-critical failures contribute to the component unavailability during the repair time. Thus the repair of such failures is often postponed to revision outages, if possible.

The repairs of primary interest are those performed during plant operation, i.e. critical failures detected during the operating period and such repair-critical failures that for some reason have not been postponed to the next revision. The estimated Weibull distributions of repair times for these two groups are presented in Fig. 9. In the case of critical failures, the waiting time is included in the total repair time. The repair times are significantly shorter (average values 45 h for critical failures and 13 h for

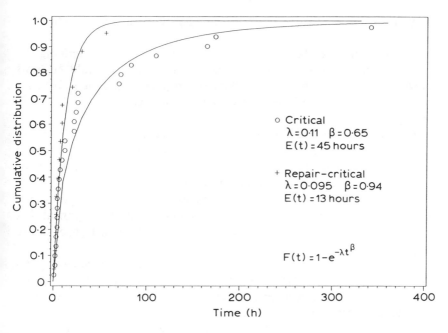

Fig. 9. Distributions of component unavailability times caused by repairs during plant operation.

repair-critical failures) than the allowed repair time defined in technical specifications (720 h for single failure and 72 h for double failures).

Time Dependency in Failure Occurrence and Component Ageing

Qualitative analysis of ageing-related failures can be based on examination of root causes. In theory, the failures could be divided into time-independent and ageing-related ones according to the root causes. In practice, however, the incompletely and in some cases erroneously described or coded failure causes cannot be analysed reliably. Here we have divided the failure causes roughly, considering normal wear, oxidation and corrosion as ageing failures apart from other failures. These causes represent together 52% of failures reported during the observation period. The annual fraction of these failures has been nearly constant during this period. Other failures (e.g. drifting of torque switch position) may also be ageing-related but their time-dependence is more difficult to identify.

Failure trends can be analysed quantitatively without examining the failure causes in detail. A computerized trend analysis would be most powerful in connection with the plant failure reporting system. It could be a practical tool to follow the trends in failure occurrence and identify changes in failure rate.

The trends in reported failures have been analysed with the computer code ENHPP (Estimation of Non-Homogeneous Poisson Process) (Huovinen, 1989). In the Weibull model used it is assumed that the repair of a component returns the component to the condition it was just before the failure occurrence ('as bad as old' behaviour). This assumption may not be adequate, especially in the case of replacement of component, but the model is useful in identification of trends and prediction of future behaviour.

Trend analyses are performed separately for electromechanical parts and mechanical valve parts. Failures of stem, bonnet and stem packings, slide and sealing surfaces, and leakage pipe were grouped together as mechanical parts while other subcomponents were included in electromechanical parts. The internal leakages are detected only in the specific tightness tests performed annually during the revision outage and thus these failures are treated apart from the other failures.

According to the results of trend analyses the failure rate of electromechanical components is almost constant (or slightly decreasing). Also the mechanical valve parts have a nearly constant failure rate. As an example of trend analyses the failure trend of electromechanical components is presented when the failures of both plants are pooled together (Fig. 10). The annual number of internal leakages was found to have an increasing trend. The annual number of internal leakages in TVO 1 is generally higher than in TVO 2.

CONCLUSIONS

Analysis of operating experience using FMEA and MECA methods has been demonstrated. Motor operated closing valve failure data from TVO 1 and 2 failure data collection systems have been studied, classified and stored on FMEA and MECA sheets according to a classification developed for MOVs. A majority of failures are caused by internal leakages detected in tightness tests or external leakages from packings. Failure

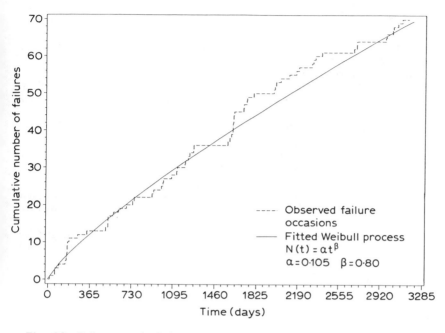

Fig. 10. Failure trend of electromechanical components in TVO 1 and 2.

detection in periodic situations covers 60% of reported events. More than 50% of all failures are detected during revisions and nearly half of critical failures have occurred in revisions. Results indicate a potential problem of incorrect torque switch settings due to possible drifting or degradation, incorrect calibration or incorrect design specifications. These critical failures are also indicative of a very complex interaction of these faults with diverse mechanical failure modes, e.g. mechanical stiffness of stem, of an electrically and mechanically integrated valve function. The above problem has been recognized and a new testing system for MOVs is under consideration. Also the overhaul of the actuators has been expanded.

REFERENCES

Ekberg et al., (1985). The ATV-system and its use. In *Proc. Int. Topical Meeting on Probabilistic Safety Methods and Applications*, San Francisco, 24 February–

1 March 1985. EPRI NP-3912, Electric Power Research Institute, Palo Alto, CA.

Eriksen, L. & Knochenhauer, M. (1988). *Impact of differences in testing conditions and anticipated real demand conditions on reliability data for motor actuated valves.* ABB Atom Report RPC 88-44.

Huovinen, T.K. (1989). *Estimation of some stochastic models used in reliability engineering.* Technical Research Centre of Finland, Research Report 598, Espoo, Finland.

IEC Standard 812 (1985). *Analysis Techniques for System Reliability—Procedure for Failure Mode and Effects Analysis (FMEA).*

Laakso, K.J. (ed.) (1990). *Optimization of technical specifications by use of probabilistic methods—a Nordic perspective.* Final Report of the NKA project RAS-450, Nord 1990–93.

Laakso, K.J. & Burns, D.J. (1985). A systematic maintainability review for plant design. Paper presented at *2nd European Logistics Symposium*, Växjö, Sweden, 11–12 June.

T-boken (1985). *T-boken—Reliability Data for Mechanical and Electrical Components in Swedish BWR's*, 2nd edition. Nuclear Safety Board of the Swedish Utilities and Swedish Nuclear Power Inspectorate.

PART 3

Condition monitoring

3.1

On the Selection of Condition Based Maintenance for Mechanical Systems

BASIM AL-NAJJAR

*Linköping University, Department of Mechanical Engineering,
Division of Quality Technology,
S-581 83 Linköping, Sweden*

ABSTRACT

In this chapter some problems regarding the selection of a condition based maintenance technique for mechanical components of dangerous and/or costly failures are discussed. A sequential method for the selection of a cost-effective technique when several policies are available is presented. In order to reduce false alarms and to identify a replacement time, a cumulative sum chart is proposed. A graphical method for the selection of a cost-effective technique and another graphical method for the estimation of the threshold level for that technique are suggested. These two methods are based on the concept of the Total Time on Test, TTT-plot.

INTRODUCTION

The requirements for increased plant productivity and safety, and reduced maintenance costs, have led to an increasing interest in methods for condition monitoring of mechanical systems. In the literature on Reliability-Centred Maintenance, RCM, the selection of a maintenance technique is mainly carried out on the level of system failure modes. Also, distinguishing criteria such as the long run average cost per unit time are not modelled; see, for example, Nowlan *et al.* (1978). In the present study, a summary of three papers, Al-Najjar (1990*a*, *b*, *c*), component failure causes and failure mechanisms are involved in the selection problem, and a long run average cost per unit time is modelled. In the next four sections, the identification of significant components is described, state-changes of a component are discussed, new classifications of failures, monitoring parameters and monitoring techniques are proposed, data sampling and analysis are discussed, the cumulative sum chart is proposed as a technique to reduce the fluctuation in monitoring parameter value, and the selection of a cost-effective policy is carried out based on economical and non-economical distinguishing criteria. These sections summarize Al-Najjar (1990a). The section on the modelling of a condition dependent failure rate function is a summary of Al-Najjar (1990b). The final section addresses the problem of selecting a cost-effective monitoring technique based on observational data. To carry out the selection, we suggest the use of a generalization of a method, related to the Total Time on Test, TTT-plot, introduced by Bergman (1977). Also, a graphical method to estimate the threshold level of a monitoring parameter when using a cost-effective technique is proposed; see also Al-Najjar (1990c).

FAILURES OF MECHANICAL COMPONENTS

A failure is defined in the British Standard Maintenance Glossary as 'the termination of the ability of an item to perform its required function', and in Reliability-Centred Maintenance, RCM (see Nowlan et al., 1978), as 'an unsatisfactory condition'.

Only components having considerable failure consequences and a non-negligible failure frequency should be considered for actions of condition based maintenance.

In order to select a cost-effective maintenance technique, more attention should be paid to the study of failure progression in connection with replacement policies.

Figure 1 shows the proposed sequential method for the selection of a

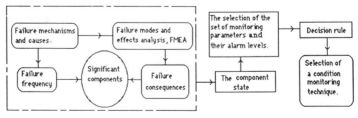

Fig. 1. A sequential method for the selection of a condition monitoring technique.

condition monitoring technique. The method is confined to failures of conventional mechanical components, where a component is assumed to be the smallest part in a mechanical system.

Mechanisms of General Failure Causes

Failures in mechanical components occur due to three major causes: inherent weakness, misuse and gradual deterioration. Only mechanical failures according to gradual deterioration lend themselves to condition monitoring. Failures of this type experienced most frequently in mechanical systems are caused by fatigue, wear, corrosion or excessive deformation.

General causes of fatigue are, for example, surface and subsurface cracks. Cracks start according to different mechanisms, which in general include stress raisers, like notches, fretting corrosion, inclusions, internal stress with alternating stresses. Important factors, when monitoring fatigue failure development of a component, are the propagation rate of a crack, the fatigue limit, and surface mechanical properties.

Wear may occur by means of different mechanisms, for example weld junction due to local heating and cold welding. The wear-mechanism map is discussed in Chapter 1.2 of this book. General causes of wear are, for example, abrasive wear and scuffing. Important factors when monitoring wear failure development are the characteristic thickness of a component or the clearance between two parts in a kinematic pair, and wear rate.

Failure Consequences

Some important factors to be considered while assessing failure consequences are component functional nature, failure nature, operating environments, failure effect on machine operational safety and economical losses.

In general, failures may be divided into two groups, non-hidden and hidden. Non-hidden failures are those which have a direct impact on machine performance. They may be called safety failures if they affect machine or human being safety, and operational failures if they interrupt or disturb machine operational capability. But, failures resulting in only increased maintenance costs are called non-operational failures.

Hidden failures are those which have no direct effect on machine performance. In general, a functional failure may be either potential or actual. The potential failure is an identifiable physical condition which indicates that an actual failure is imminent; see Nowlan *et al.* (1978). The actual failure is an identifiable physical condition which indicates that a functional failure has occurred. Actual failures may be either partial or total functional failures. These failures arise as gradual or sudden failures, which may occur either as a permanent or as an intermittent failure; for more details see Al-Najjar (1990*a*).

Significant Components

Failure modes, effects and criticality analysis, FMECA, is an FMEA diagram including not only failure criticality but also failure intensity and fault detection probability.

A component is considered significant only if its risk priority number, RPN, exceeds a predetermined value in a particular scale, where, for example,

$$RPN = FI \times FC \times FDP$$

where FI is the failure intensity, FC is the failure criticality and FDP is the probability that a failure is not detected. The main advantage of this procedure is that it allows us to focus intensive attention on few components rather than on many. In Al-Najjar (1990*a*) a modified version of the usual FMECA is shown.

THE COMPONENT STATE

In this study the condition of a component, denoted at age t by $x(t)$, is evaluated by the current value of a monitored parameter, called the parameter value. The component state is often considered as random in time.

Parameter values such as vibration level, rms, and wear rate, are usually considered constant during the interval prior to the initiation of a potential failure, i.e. during the normal operating interval. But in the wear out region they may often be assumed to be increasing exponentially in operating time; see Collacott (1977). However, during the wear out interval, a parameter value may sometimes decrease temporarily.

Thus, the most interesting interval in the component life length is the wear out region, i.e. the interval following the discovery of a potential failure.

Define the parameter value, $x(t)$, of a component at age t by the maximum value of the monitoring parameter during the interval $(0, t)$ for $t > 0$. Suppose that the parameter value of a component is monitored continuously, where $x(t) \geqslant 0$ for $t \geqslant 0$.

The ability of a parameter value in predicting failures can be described as a probability of failure in a future time interval conditional on the current value of the parameter. Formally, this may be described as follows. Let ζ be the random time to failure, then

$$P[\zeta \in (t, t + \Delta t), \quad \text{given } \zeta > t \text{ and } x(t) = x, \ t \geqslant 0] = h(x) \, dt + O(\Delta t)$$

where as usual $O(\Delta t) \to 0$ as $t \to 0$. It is clear that the condition of the component, $x(t)$, influences the time to failure. In many cases, when this condition dependent function h exists, it is assumed to be non-decreasing.

CONDITION MONITORING

A monitoring parameter may be defined as a measurable variable able to display information concerning the component condition. Only some of the monitoring parameters in each process are significant indicators of the occurrence and development of potential failures. The difference in the intrinsic information carried by these parameters may be explained by their correlations with the deterioration process and their sensitivities to disturbing factors.

A set of suitable parameters is a set of measurable variables which can reflect the information about the component condition at any moment. Factors of importance for the selection of this set are knowledge concerning failure mechanisms and causes, component failure modes, measuring equipment, and the accuracy in detecting the initiation of a potential failure and in predicting time to failure.

Monitoring parameters may be classified according to the type of their intrinsic information into direct and indirect parameters. A direct parameter is a parameter, like thickness, whose value is directly measured by a particular sensor in a way so that the effect of disturbing factors may be assumed negligible. Indirect parameters are divided here into four categories which are the primary performance trend parameters, like pressure or efficiency, the secondary performance trend parameters, like vibration, and cumulative stress parameters which are usually employed in geriometry. Geriometry may be defined as a measure of the accumulated stress causing component or system degradation; see Salter (1978).

Values of parameters in the fourth category, time scaled parameters, are measured along the time axis, for example age or calendar time.

A similar classification can be made for condition monitoring techniques; see Al-Najjar (1990*a*).

Sampling and Data Analysis

In order to select a data sampling method, factors such as failure mechanisms, failure causes, failure consequences, rate of decay, cost and properties of sampling equipment should be considered.

Along the component life there are two interesting events to be detected as early as possible, which are potential failure intiation and when the parameter value exceeds the threshold level, x_{th}. The estimation of the threshold level is often based on practical experience, published standards or the manufacturer's recommendations.

We denote by x_0 the mean value of the monitored parameter of a component during the normal operating interval. The level x_0 can be treated as a component characteristic. Its variation is due to, for example, differences in material, design or manufacture.

Manufacturer's recommendations, past data and published standards should be kept in mind when estimating x_0. In general, 20–40 observations are usually considered necessary to estimate a variable like x_0; see Bergman and Klefsjö (1990). The component is assumed to be in a normal condition if the mean of its parameter value is less than or equal to x_0.

Let x_p and x_{th} be warning and action levels, respectively, so that when a parameter value reaches x_p a potential failure is assumed to have been initiated, where $x_0 < x_p < x_{th}$. If it exceeds x_p, more care should be paid to the failure development to figure out its trend and to identify, approximately, active failure mechanisms and causes, while at the second level, x_{th}, immediate corrective action should be taken.

It may take a relatively long time before a potential failure develops into an actual failure. Thus, monitoring the wear out region provides lead time which enables the maintenance engineer to maintain the machine when all costs are low, and to use almost all of the useful life of a component. That is, monitoring this region may reduce life cycle cost.

In most cases we have a random fluctuation in the parameter value, $x(t)$. Only if a real change has occurred in the parameter value should action be taken. In order to sort out a systematic change based on randomly fluctuating parameter values, a Shewhard control chart can be used. A more sensitive chart is the cumulative sum chart, cusum-chart;

see, for example, Wetherill (1986). Using this chart, changes in the mean of the observations are detected by keeping a cumulative total of deviations from a reference value. When the mean of the observations is equal to the reference value, the cumulative sum fluctuates about zero, but as soon as the mean differs from the reference value, the cumulative sum begins to increase or decrease. Thus, the cumulative sum chart can be utilized to detect whether and when a deviation from a prescribed level has occurred, and to estimate the amount of the change.

Al-Najjar (1990a) presents two examples of how to utilize the cusum technique to identify a potential failure and to find a replacement time.

STRATEGY SELECTION

Consider a component subject to random failure. Upon failure the component is replaced by a new one, or repaired to an as-new condition, and the process repeats. Denote the time to failure of the component by the random variable ζ. Let the time to replacement, T_x, be defined on the parameter value, $x(t)$. That is, T_x is the time moment when $x(t)$ first reaches x_{th}. Let the replacement rule be as follows: replace at failure or at T_x whichever occurs first.

Define the probability of failure by $P(\zeta \leqslant T_x)$, where T_x can be considered as a given time, i.e. age replacement, or as a random variable when condition based replacements are used. Assume that the time is measured along operating time. Let the replacement cost be equal to c while at failure an additional cost K is suffered. Denote by $N_\pi^c(t)$ the number of replacements due to failed components, i.e. corrective actions, when policy π is adopted. Denote by $N_F(t)$ the total number of repairs or replacements when using failure replacement policy, FRP. Assume that the monitoring system will not add new failures. Denote by B_π the long run average cost per unit time. This cost could be written as the average cost of one cycle per average cycle length, see Cox (1967). Thus

$$B_\pi = \frac{c + KP(\zeta \leqslant T_{x,\pi})}{E[\min(\zeta, T_{x,\pi})]} \tag{1}$$

The cost equation is usually written without a term representing separately the invested capital required to establish a monitoring technique, see eqn (1). For example, the comparisons between age and condition based replacements, and between different condition based replacement strategies, demand clear definition of this capital.

The invested capital per unit time, I, may be estimated in advance. It is assumed to cover the costs per unit time of all activities required to carry out the monitoring job, for example, costs of measuring instruments, buildings, and man-hours. Then

$$B_\pi = \frac{c + KP(\zeta \leqslant T_{x,\pi})}{E\left[\min(\zeta, T_{x,\pi})\right]} + I_\pi \qquad (2)$$

The cost c would be paid each time a non-failed component is replaced independent of the policy involved. Optimization of eqn (2) can be achieved through optimizing only its first term. The rule for making an optimal choice between different maintenance policies is to select the maintenance policy which yields the least B.

The Efficiency of a Monitoring Technique

In this section, two quantities for the determination of monitoring technique efficiency are considered: effectiveness, $e_\pi(t)$, and accuracy, $a_\pi(t)$. The effectiveness, $e_\pi(t)$, may be defined as the proportion of the expected number of failures avoidable by technique π relative to the total expected number of failures under FRP, $E(N_F(t))$; while the accuracy, $a_\pi(t)$, of the same strategy may be defined as the proportion of $E(N_F(t))$ to the expected number of the total removals, $E(N_\pi(t))$. Assume that $a_\pi(t)$ and $e_\pi(t)$ converge to a_π and e_π as $t \to \infty$, then for the long run they may be written

$$e_\pi = 1 - \frac{\mu P(\zeta \leqslant T_{x,\pi})}{E\left[\min(\zeta, T_{x,\pi})\right]} \qquad (3)$$

$$a_\pi = E\left[\min(\zeta, T_{x,\pi})\right]/\mu \qquad (4)$$

where $\mu = E(\zeta)$. For more details see Al-Najjar (1990a). Ideally, both a_π and e_π are equal to 1, i.e. the replacements occur close to but just before failures. When adopting FRP, i.e.

$$E(N_\pi(t)) = E(N_\pi^c(t)) = E(N_F(t))$$

e_π and a_π are equal to 0 and 1, respectively. Let

$$B_\pi = b_\pi + I_\pi$$

where

$$b_\pi = \frac{c + KP(\zeta \leqslant T_{x,\pi})}{E\left[\min(\zeta, T_{x,\pi})\right]} \qquad (5)$$

Substitute eqns (3) and (4) in eqn (5) to yield, after simplification,

$$b_\pi = \frac{c + K(1 - e_\pi)a_\pi}{\mu a_\pi} \qquad (6)$$

The cost equation (6) is illustrated in Figs 2a and 2b in a special case.

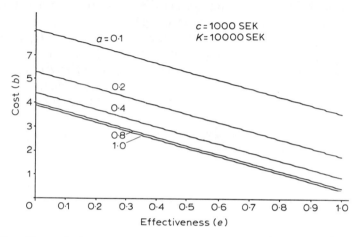

Fig. 2a. Plots of the cost per unit time, *b*, expressed by eqn (6), versus effectiveness, *e*, for given values of accuracy, *a*, and the average costs *c* and *K*.

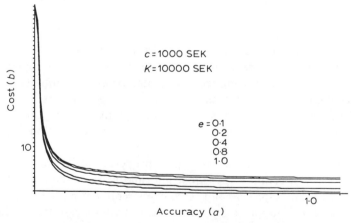

Fig. 2b. Plots of the same cost, *b*, versus accuracy, *a*, for given values of effectiveness, *e*, and the average costs *c* and *K*.

The cost b may be reduced through increasing effectiveness, e, or accuracy, a, for a given accuracy or a given effectiveness respectively, or through increasing both, see Fig. 2a. From Fig. 2b, the rate of reduction in b reduces in accuracy for a given effectiveness, while it is constant for all effectiveness and independent of accuracy, as illustrated in Fig. 2a.

Now, suppose that the conditions of n components are monitored until failure using k different techniques. Let the failure times, ordered due to their size, i.e. $\zeta_1 \leqslant \zeta_2 \leqslant \cdots \leqslant \zeta_n$, be given. Then at each failure time the probability of failure, $P(\zeta \leqslant T_{x,\pi})$, and the expected time to replacement, $E[\min(\zeta \leqslant T_{x,\pi})]$, for each component, can be estimated using observational data; see Bergman (1977). Then the pair effectiveness, e, and accuracy, a, which yields the least cost b for each technique may be determined using a figure which illlustrates eqn (6), i.e. Fig. 2a for this special case. By comparing k invested capitals per unit time and k pairs of effectiveness and accuracy, a cost-effective policy can be determined. More discussion about effectiveness can be found in Al-Najjar (1990a).

Selecting a Monitoring Parameter Based on Its Intrinsic Information

In general, loss or confusion in the received information occurs due to disturbing factors, data manipulation or errors in measuring instruments. For a well-selected direct parameter, disturbing factors and data manipulation, may have a negligible effect on its value, but they may have an appreciable effect on the other parameters.

The spectrum of a sound or a vibration signal is able to describe a number of failure causes while other parameters cannot. Note that a vibration signal is more easily interpreted than a sound signal, while different vibration measuring techniques are usually not equally sensitive in following failure development. Further, some parameters, for example SPM and temperature, respond to the change in the component condition during machinery running, but they are not equally fast in displaying these changes.

Implementation of these and other properties of monitoring parameters for the selection of the most informative parameter is illustrated by a figure in Al-Najjar (1990a). Two cases representing the difference in the information supplied by monitoring parameters are studied in Chapter 3.2 of this book.

Decision Rule Tree

According to Nowlan *et al.* (1978), a maintenance technique is often assumed to be cost-effective unless by application it can be proved otherwise.

The most interesting information concerning the component condition is that regarding potential failure initiation and development. It is obvious that some techniques are not able to display such information or are not cost-effective.

In the suggested decision rule tree, correlated parameters and the corresponding techniques should be identified. The level, i.e. failure mechanisms, failure causes or failure modes level, of a correlated parameter can be determined by means of the factors stated in the section on condition monitoring.

Then the first criterion is the applicability of the suggested techniques, which can be determined by specialist engineers. The second criterion is the cost-effectiveness. This criterion is the optimum long run average cost per unit time, B.

The procedure for making decisions is the same for all failures. But for those of hidden consequences, before identifying the correlated parameters it is valuable to determine whether the occurrence of failure is associated with physical evidence, see Fig. 3. Practical information from the implementation of the selected technique may be utilized to improve the decision.

ON THE CONDITION DEPENDENT FAILURE RATE FUNCTION IN MECHANICAL SYSTEMS

This section is confined to the cases where the assessment of the replacement moment is determined by the condition dependent failure rate function rather than by the component condition.

The major reason behind using the failure rate function in this connection is that it is easier to identify normal operating and wear out intervals by inspection of the failure rate curve than by the appearance of a probability density function. This property is important in following the development of a potential failure.

Now, if high and unexpected stress cycles are ignored, the component has no chance to fail during the normal operating interval as long as the

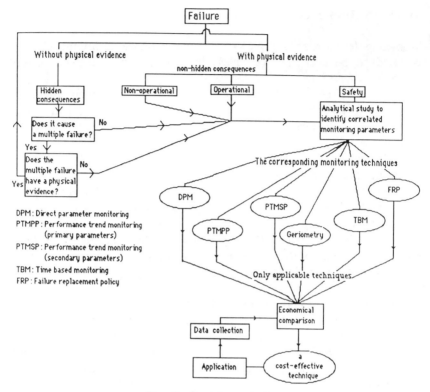

Fig. 3. Decision rule tree.

parameter value, $x(t)$, is non-increasing. Thus, $h(x(t))$ may be assumed equal to zero during that interval, while it is non-decreasing in the wear out region.

Since $x(t)$ is random in time, then the probability of failure in $(t, t + \Delta t)$, given that it was functioning at time t and it was in condition $x(t)$, $t \geqslant 0$, may give a better picture of the remaining component life than observing only $x(t)$. Based on the failure rate a replacement rule may be defined as follows: replace at failure or as soon as the condition dependent failure rate, $h(x(t))$, first approaches a prescribed level.

The use of $h(x(t))$ for determining a replacement time may be illustrated by the cost equation. Denote by the random variables ζ_p and ζ_w the time to a potential failure and the wear out interval, respectively. Then, the random time to failure is

$$\zeta = \zeta_p + \zeta_w$$

The stopping time is

$$T = \zeta_p + T_x$$

where as before

$$T_x = \inf\{t;\ x(s) \geqslant x\}, \quad \text{for } 0 \leqslant s \leqslant t$$

Then, the cycle length between two replacements is

$$E(\xi_p) + E[\min(\zeta_w, T_x)]$$

When the distributions of the variables ζ_w and T_x, and $E[\min(\zeta_w, T_x)]$ are known, the long run average cost per unit time, B, when the policy π is adopted, could be written

$$B_\pi = \frac{c + KE\left[1 - \exp\left(-\int_0^{T_{x,\pi}} h_\pi(x_\pi(s))\,\mathrm{d}s\right)\right]}{E(\zeta_{p,\pi}) + E[\min(\zeta_w, T_{x,\pi})]} + I_\pi \tag{7}$$

where $E(\zeta_p)$ may not be the same for all techniques, and

$$E\left[\exp\left(-\int_0^{T_x} h(x(t))\,\mathrm{d}t\right)\right] = \int_0^\infty \exp\left(-\int_0^{T_x} h(x(t))\,\mathrm{d}t\right)\mathrm{d}F(T_x)$$

where $F(T_x)$ is the cumulative distribution function of T_x.

Modelling of a Condition Dependent Failure Rate Function

Phenomenologically, three regions of material losses may be distinguished in a wear process; see, for example, Chapter 1.2 of this book. These are run in, normal operating and wear out regions. Denote by D^M the amount of the material loss. In the wear out region, large increments of wear in one interval of time cause even larger increments in the next time interval. It follows that

$$\mathrm{d}D^M/\mathrm{d}\delta = bD^M$$

(see Czichos, 1978). Thus the wear rate of a component at time t may be written as

$$\mathrm{d}D^M(t)/\mathrm{d}t = b\exp(bt)$$

where b is constant.

It is known that the Paris law,

$$\mathrm{d}a/\mathrm{d}N = c(\Delta K)^m$$

provides a reasonable description of the growth rate of a macrocrack in a mechanical component, where da/dN is the crack growth rate per cycle, and c and m are constants. The stress intensity factor, ΔK, is given by the difference between the maximum and the minimum stress intensities in the fatigue cycle, i.e.

$$\Delta K = K_{max} - K_{min}$$

In general, the stress intensity factor

$$\Delta K = \alpha \Delta \sigma \sqrt{(\pi a)}$$
$$= q a^{\frac{1}{2}} \tag{8}$$

see Suresh and Ritchie, 1984; McEvily, 1983, where a is the crack length, $\Delta \sigma$ is the stress range, and π and α are constants. Substitute eqn (8) in the Paris law; after some simplification this yields

$$a = \exp(wt)$$

In the Canadian Navy, it has been indicated from observed data that the mean vibration level of a signature component as a function of time is a straight line, with slight positive slope for 75% of a machine useful life at which point it starts an exponential rise to the point of failure; see Glew and Watson (1968).

The increment in the vibration level of, for example, the second multiple of the shaft speed in the axial direction, is usually used to monitor the growth of cracks in a shaft. Then the increment in the level of this second multiple and in the wear rate of a component, under specified operating conditions and during the wear out region, can be described by a positive exponential function of time.

In Al-Najjar (1990b), these and similar arguments are used for modelling a condition dependent failure rate function. Also, for the selection of a cost-effective technique a modified version of a proportional hazards model, PHM, is proposed.

A GRAPHICAL METHOD FOR THE SELECTION OF A MAINTENANCE TECHNIQUE

In Al-Najjar (1990c) a graphical method for the selection of a maintenance technique is discussed. Suppose we are given n observations $t_1, t_2, \ldots, t_n$ from a particular life distribution $F(.)$. Let these observations be ordered according to their sizes, i.e. $t_1 \leqslant t_2 \leqslant \cdots \leqslant t_n$. Let T_i denote the total time generated in ages less than or equal to t_i, i.e.

$$T_1 = nt_1$$

and generally

$$T_i = \sum_{j=1}^{i} (n-j+1)(t_j - t_{j-1})$$

for $i = 1, \ldots, n$ where $t_0 = 0$. Also, let

$$u_i = T_i / T_n$$

Then the Total Time on Test, TTT-plot, is drawn by plotting u_i against i/n. Its application will be explained by way of an example. The plot can be used to check whether the plotted data have an exponential distribution, and whether the failure rate function is increasing or decreasing. If it is an increasing function of the component age, then the TTT-plot approaches a concave curve for a large number of observations, see Fig. 4, while it approaches a convex curve if the failure rate is decreasing.

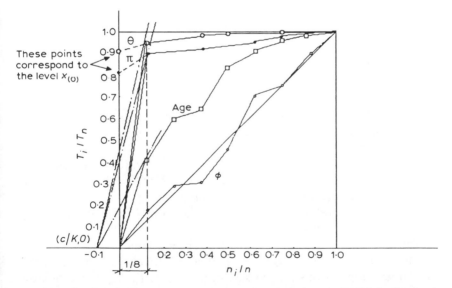

Fig. 4. The GTTT-plot of policy age, π, θ and ϕ, where $T_i(T_n)$ is the total time generated on test by all components before their parameter values exceed the ith level (the nth level); n_i/n is the proportion of failures which have occurred at the ith level to the total number of failures.

Generalized TTT-Plots and
Condition Dependent Replacement

Suppose that the vibration levels or the wear rates of n components are monitored until respective failure times $\zeta_1, \ldots, \zeta_n$. Then the empirical distribution function, F_n, may be defined as

$$F_n(t) = (1/n) \times (\text{number of } \zeta_j \text{ such that } \zeta_j \leqslant t)$$

where $j = 1, \ldots, n$, and n is the total number of observed failures. Let

$$x_j = \sup_{t \leqslant \zeta_j} x_j(t)$$

Now let us order the indices so that $x_{(i)}$ corresponds to that x_j which is ith in size. Then the ordered indices are $x_{(1)} \leqslant x_{(2)} \leqslant \cdots \leqslant x_{(n)}$. Define $S_j(x)$ as the total time on test generated by the jth component before its parameter value exceeds x for the first time, i.e.

$$S_j(x) = \inf\{t; \, x_j(t) \geqslant x\}$$

Let

$$S(x) = \sum_{j=1}^{n} S_j(x)$$

Now, define

$$T_i = S(x_{(i)})$$

which is the total time accumulated by all components while their parameter values are less than or equal to $x_{(i)}, i = 1, \ldots, n$. Then the TTT-plot can be obtained.

In order to estimate B we replace $P(\zeta \leqslant T_x)$ in eqn (2) by its estimator $F_n(t)$. It was proved by Ingram and Scheaffer (1976) that the time interval minimizing the cost equation may be found among $\zeta_1, \ldots, \zeta_n$. Thus, to estimate this interval it is enough to find the index i_0 minimizing B. If i_0 is equal to n, replacements occur at failure.

The index i_0 may also be estimated graphically from the TTT-plot. To do this, draw the line through $(-c/K, 0)$ which touches the plot and has the largest slope. If this line passes through $(i_0/n, T_{i0}/T_n)$, our estimator is the optimum replacement interval equal to t_{i0}; see Fig. 4. The estimated replacement interval is close to the optimum if the number of observations is large enough; see Bergman (1977). Thus, the estimate of the minimum long run average cost per unit time when the technique π is used, can be written

$$B_\pi^* = \frac{c + K\dfrac{i_{0,\pi}}{n}}{\dfrac{1}{n}T_{i0,\pi}} + I_\pi \qquad (9)$$

Comparison of Maintenance Techniques

We have defined x_j as the maximum value of a monitoring parameter during a time $t \leqslant \zeta_j$, which is reasonable theoretically. But, to be conservative, one could define x_j as the level of the monitoring parameter at failure. Also, define $S_j(x_{(i)})$ as the total time on test generated by the jth component before its parameter value exceeds the level of the ith failure, $x_{(i)}$. We assume that the failure is always associated with a physical evidence, for example fracture. Thus, the indices for each technique could be recorded, so that $x_{(1)} \leqslant x_{(2)} \leqslant \cdots \leqslant x_{(n)}$ which are the levels of a monitoring parameter at n failures.

In Bergman (1977), only one monitoring parameter was considered. Here, we are mainly concerned with the comparison of many techniques. Denote by n_i the number of failures which have occurred before the parameter value exceeds the level $x_{(i)}$, $i = 1, \ldots, n$. The use of the generalized, GTTT-plots is illustrated in the following example.

Example

Assume that eight components are monitored by means of the age replacement technique and the condition dependent techniques π, θ and ϕ until respective failure times $\zeta_1, \ldots, \zeta_8$. The condition dependent technique ϕ is supposed to use a new monitoring parameter whose relation with the deterioration process under consideration is not well understood.

Note that the number of components used in this example may not be enough to estimate the long run average cost per unit time, B, with high precision.

For each monitoring parameter, select six levels, $x_{(0)}, \ldots, x_{(5)}$, so that the first level is arbitrary while the other five levels represent the parameter values at failures of the components.

Graphically, the optimum values of i_0/n for the age replacement policy and for condition replacement policies π and θ are the same and equal to $\frac{1}{8}$. Failure times and calculations for policy π are given in Table 1 and the GTTT-plots for all policies are shown in Fig. 4.

Table 1. Failure Times and Calculated Quantities of the TTT-plot of Technique π which is Shown in Fig. 4.

| Time (hour) | Component | | | | | | | | $\sum_j$ | $T_i = \sum_i n_i$ | n_i | $\dfrac{n_i}{n}$ | $\dfrac{T_i}{T_n}$ |
	1	2	3	4	5	6	7	8					
$S_j(x_{(0)})$	1 700	3 530	2 100	3 800	700	2 780	1 450	2 360	$\sum S_j(x_{(0)}) = 18\,420$	18 420	0	0	0.81
$S_j(x_{(1)})$	1 750	3 600	2 700	4 300	930	2 950	1 600	2 500	$\Sigma[S_j(x_{(1)}) - S_j(x_{(0)})] = 1910$	20 330	1	0.13	0.9
$S_j(x_{(1)}) - S_j(x_{(0)})$	50	70	600	500	230	170	150	140					
$S_j(x_{(2)})$	1 750	3 600	2 800	4 400	950	3 100	1 600	2 590	$\Sigma[S_j(x_{(2)}) - S_j(x_{(1)})] = 460$	20 790	3	0.38	0.92
$S_j(x_{(2)}) - S_j(x_{(1)})$	0	0	100	100	20	150	0	90					
$S_j(x_{(3)})$	1 750	3 600	2 800	4 400	1 130	3 230	1 750	2 900	$\Sigma[S_j(x_{(3)}) - S_j(x_{(2)})] = 770$	21 560	5	0.63	0.95
$S_j(x_{(3)}) - S_j(x_{(2)})$	0	0	0	0	180	130	150	310					
$S_j(x_{(4)})$	1 750	3 600	2 800	4 400	1 130	3 230	1 950	3 200	$\Sigma[S_j(x_{(4)}) - S_j(x_{(3)})] = 500$	22 060	6	0.75	0.97
$S_j(x_{(4)}) - S_j(x_{(3)})$	0	0	0	0	0	0	200	300					
$S_j(x_{(5)})$	1 750	3 600	2 800	4 400	1 130	3 230	1 950	3 800	$\Sigma[S_j(x_{(5)}) - S_j(x_{(4)})] = 600$	20 660	8	1.0	1.0
$S_j(x_{(5)}) - S_j(x_{(4)})$	0	0	0	0	0	0	0	600					
Total time									22 660				

Assume that $I_\pi = 1 \cdot 22$, $I_\theta = 2 \cdot 4$ and $I_{\text{age}} = 0 \cdot 4$ SEK/time unit; also assume that $c = 1000$ and $K = 10\ 000$ SEK. Then, by applying eqn (9), the minimum values of B for these policies are $2 \cdot 1$, $3 \cdot 20$ and $2 \cdot 4$ SEK/time unit, respectively. Trivially, the cost-effective policy is that which yields less B, i.e. the policy π.

In this example, it is seen that the failure rate increases dramatically when $x_\pi(t)$ or $x_\theta(t)$ increases. For the same techniques and when n is large, it is easy to verify by looking at Fig. 4 that the failure rate is approximately equal to zero before the parameter value exceeds the level $x_{(0)}$.

Both condition monitoring techniques π and θ have large explanatory power while technique ϕ does not. On the other hand, if the information supplied by a monitoring parameter is uncorrelated or weakly correlated with the deterioration process under consideration, then its TTT-plot fluctuates about the diagonal. This means that the failure rate when using this technique should be approximately constant. Thus, the TTT-plot corresponding to a technique ϕ reveals a very weak relation between the monitored parameter and the actual component condition.

Then, using the GTTT-plot, we can determine the optimum replacement interval, distinguish a cost-effective technique and discover weakly correlated or uncorrelated monitoring parameters, for example the comparison between plots of policies π and ϕ; see Fig. 4.

In Al-Najjar (1990c), the situation in which some failures cannot be avoided by using a particular technique for monitoring a machine is discussed and illustrated by an example.

Estimation of the Threshold Level

The threshold level is often assessed without regard to the cost, B. Here, we defined it as the replacement level which leads to the minimum long run average cost per unit time, B. Let the levels $x_{(0)}, \ldots, x_{(5)}$ of the parameter value stated in the example be $1 \cdot 75$, $2 \cdot 25$, $2 \cdot 5$, $3 \cdot 25$, $3 \cdot 75$, and $4 \cdot 5$ mm/s, overall level rms, respectively. Assume that six additional levels are stated below $x_{(0)}$ at $0 \cdot 15$, $0 \cdot 3$, $0 \cdot 6$, $0 \cdot 9$, $1 \cdot 2$ and $1 \cdot 45$ mm/s. Denote these levels by $x_{(06)}, \ldots, x_{(01)}$, respectively. Also, denote by $T_{x(r)}$ the total time generated by the components before their parameter values exceed the level $x_{(r)}$, for $r = 06, \ldots, 01, 0, \ldots, 5$.

The plot of $T_{x(r)}/T_n$ versus the parameter value is shown in Fig. 5. For the components of increasing failure rate function, like those used in the example, the rate of increment in $T_{x(r)}/T_n$ and in the failure rate may be considered constant in $x(t) \leqslant x_{(1)}$ and decreasing in $x(t) > x_{(1)}$. The opti-

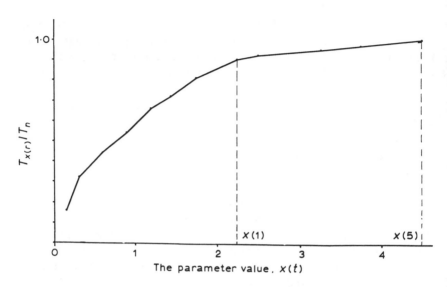

Fig. 5. $T_{x(r)}/T_n$ versus the parameter value, $x(t)$.

mum $T_{x(r)}/T_n$ can be determined graphically by usng the GTTT-plots for $r = 0, \ldots, 5$. Then the corresponding threshold level which in this example is equal to $x_{(0)}$ may be determined from Fig. 5.

CONCLUSIONS

From previous discussions, significant components can be identified on the bases of failure mechanisms and failure causes using the modified version of the Failure Modes, Effects and Criticality Analysis, FMECA, diagram. Using the cumulative sum technique, false alarms which may arise due to random fluctuations of parameter value measurements can be greatly reduced; the technique is also applicable to the identification of a replacement time.

Considering the invested capital per unit time in the cost equation makes the comparison between maintenance techniques possible and independent of the monitoring parameter used. Further, Generalized Total Time on Test (GTTT) plots can be utilized for the selection of a cost-effective technique and for the estimation of the monitoring parameter threshold level of the selected technique, as well as for the identification of monitoring parameters which are weakly correlated with the deterioration process under consideration.

ACKNOWLEDGEMENTS

The author wishes to thank Professor Bo Bergman for many helpful discussions, comments and suggestions, and Associate Professor Karl-Edward Johansson and Dr Min Xie for helpful discussions.

REFERENCES

Al-Najjar, B. (1990a). *Condition based maintenance for mechanical systems.* Licentiate Thesis No. 248, Paper I, Linköping University, Sweden.

Al-Najjar, B. (1990b). *On the modelling of condition dependent failure rates in mechanical systems.* Licentiate Thesis No. 248, Paper II, Linköping University, Sweden.

Al-Najjar, B. (1990c). *On a graphical method for the selection of a cost-effective technique.* Licentiate Thesis No. 248, Paper III, Linköping University, Sweden.

Bergman, B. (1977). Some graphical methods for maintenance planning. *Annual Reliability and Maintainability Symposium,* IEEE Philadelphia, 467–71.

Bergman, B. & Klefsjö, B. (1990). *Kvalitet från Behov till Användning,* chapter 12. Institute of Technology, Department of Mechanical Engineering, Linköping University, Sweden.

Collacott, R.A. (1977). *Mechanical Fault Diagnosis and Condition Monitoring.* Chapman & Hall, London.

Cox, D.R. (1967). *Renewal Theory,* chapter 11. Barnes & Noble, London.

Czichos, H. (1978). *Tribology: A System Approach to the Science and Technology of Friction, Lubrication and Wear.* Elsevier, Amsterdam.

Glew, A.W. & Watson, D.C. (1968). Vibration analysis as a maintenance tool. *Trans. I. Mar. E.* (Canadian Division), Supplement 32.

Ingram, C.R. & Scheaffer, R.L. (1976). On consistent estimation of age replacement intervals. *Technometrics,* **18,** 213–19.

McEvily, A.J. (1983). *On the quantitative analysis of fatigue crack propagation.* ASTM STP 811, American Society for Testing and Materials.

Nowlan, F.S., *et al.* (1978). *Reliability-Centered Maintenance.* AD-A066 579, US Department of Commerce, National Technical Information Service, NTIS.

Salter, R.G. (1978). Improving vehicle life-cycle reliability by prognostic maintenance management through geriometry. *Diagnosis and Prognosis, MFPG, 28th meeting.* The Rand Corporation, Santa Monica, CA.

Suresh, S. & Ritchie, R.O. (1984). Propagation of short fatigue cracks, *International Metals Review,* **29**(6), 445–76.

Wetherill, G.B. (1986). *Sampling Inspection and Quality Control,* chapters 2 and 4. Chapman & Hall, London.

3.2

Condition Monitoring Methods for Rotating Machinery

R.J. Kuoppala,* E.O. Jantunen and P.A. Enwald

Technical Research Centre of Finland, Laboratory of Production Engineering, PO Box 111, SF-02151 Espoo, Finland

ABSTRACT

A short description of the commonly used condition monitoring methods for rotating machinery is given. Some of these methods, such as cepstrum analysis, synchronized time domain signal analysis, frequency analysis and various oil analysis methods are discussed in greater detail. The measurement results from two laboratory case studies performed at the Technical Research Centre of Finland are presented. The first case study was carried out with a one-step gearbox and the measurements consisted of overall vibration level measurements, synchronized time domain signal analysis, spectrum analysis, cepstrum analysis, acoustic emission measurements, automatic wear particle counting, wear particle analysis and spectrometric oil analysis. Cepstrum analysis was a very efficient tool in monitoring the condition of the gearbox. The synchronized time domain signal analysis was also found to be a promising method. This method makes it possible to detect even the faults of an individual tooth of a gear. The second case study carried out with a rolling bearing was aimed at testing a new on-line wear particle sensor, and for comparison also other monitoring techniques were used. The on-line sensor worked very well and failure in the bearing could be predicted well in advance.

* Present address: The Finnish Defence Forces, General Headquarters, Electro-technical Section, PO Box 919, SR-00101 Helsinki, Finland.

INTRODUCTION

In order to minimize labour costs and to be more competitive, the introduction of automation has attracted increasing interest in industry. Consequently, the increased use of automation has made the production processes more vulnerable to various kinds of faults. In automated production processes an unexpected breakdown can cause a lot of damage. Possibly the whole production process has to be stopped, with perhaps a great deal of unusable product having been produced in the meantime, and unfortunately in some cases personal injury may be the result. This again has led to the growing need for effective and reliable condition monitoring methods in order to achieve maximum availability and to minimize unscheduled shutdowns of production. Instead of regular shutdowns for maintenance, the tendency today is to use condition monitoring in order to follow the trends of behaviour in the production machinery so that it is possible to predict beforehand the need for maintenance and to do the work without interrupting the production process. We can say that the goal of run-time condition monitoring of rotating machinery is to increase the reliability of production processes in the industry and to schedule the maintenance actions as economically as possible.

Today there exists a great variety of different kinds of condition monitoring methods and techniques for rotating machinery. In some cases it is sufficient to use simple methods, which are only capable of fault detection, but very often there is also the need for diagnosis of the nature of the failure. We have to know which specific part is suffering from failure. We must define the expected lifetime of the part in question so that we can decide whether the manufacturing process should be stopped for maintenance or whether it could be possible to continue until a more suitable moment for shutdown.

The question of selecting the optimum condition monitoring method for every individual part of machinery is not solely a technical task. In fact the choice of condition monitoring policy and methods has to be based on economic facts which makes decision making more difficult. These basic questions related to the selection of the condition monitoring technique based on both economic and technical aspects are discussed in Chapter 3.1 of this book, and in this chapter we concentrate mainly on the technical aspects of condition monitoring methods for rotating machinery.

It is by no means an easy task to predict the future development of the condition of machinery and we have to have a lot of reliable statistical data on which we can base our decisions and diagnosis. This statistical data can be collected by trending fault developments, which very often involves the use of computers because of the huge amount of data to be gathered.

Different methods of condition monitoring for rotating machinery such as pumps, compressors, fans and gears have been studied at the Technical Research Centre of Finland for a number of years using laboratory and field tests. It is the aim of this chapter to give both an overview of the whole field and a more detailed description of some specific condition monitoring methods for rotating machinery which we have studied.

In this chapter we concentrate mainly on vibration measurement, because it is the most commonly used method in condition monitoring of rotating machinery. In over 90% of the cases of failure a change in the vibratory behaviour of the machinery takes place. Another condition monitoring technique, which is described in greater detail, is oil analysis of various kinds. At first the various vibration-measurement and oil-analysis techniques are discussed briefly and after that the use of some of these methods is described in the light of two case studies, namely a one-step gearbox and a rolling bearing.

CONDITION MONITORING METHODS

The condition monitoring methods can be divided into four different main categories, namely vibration measurements, oil analyses, sound measurements and other methods. Sound measurements are not very often used as a condition monitoring method, if the human method of listening to the sound of running machines is not taken into account. There are certain advantages in making sound measurements; for example, the necessary measuring equipment is cheaper and easier to use than those aimed for vibration measurements. The disadvantages of sound measurements are apparent. The measuring process takes place further away from the measuring object than in the case with vibration measurements, and consequently sound measurements are more vulnerable to disturbances from other sources than vibration measurements are.

There also exist a great number of other methods, such as endoscope, stroboscope, microscope, distance, laser, strain, humidity, temperature and pressure measurements, which all have their specific fields of application in condition monitoring of rotating machinery. These other methods, as well as sound measurement techniques, are not discussed in detail and we concentrate on vibration measurement and oil analysis techniques. Table 1 contains a short summary of some of the most commonly used condition monitoring methods and also shows their fields of application (Kuoppala et al., 1986a).

Very often in practice it is better to use a combination of various condition monitoring methods than just one method. The reason for this is simply that the use of a number of methods gives more information

Table 1. Various Methods for Condition Monitoring of Rotating Machinery and Their Fields of Application.

	Overall vibration level	Frequency analysis	Acoustic emission	Kurtosis	Crest factor	SPM	Cepstrum analysis	Spectrometric oil analysis	Wear particle analysis	Particle counting	Magnetic plugs	Temperature measurements	Shaft alignment	Stroboscope	Ultrasonic measurements	Sound measurements
Unbalance	1	1	–	–	–	–	–	–	–	–	–	–	–	x	–	–
Misalignment fault	1	1	–	–	–	–	–	–	–	–	–	–	x	x	–	–
Rolling bearing	x	x	o	x	x	1	x	x	x	x	x	x	–	–	x	x
Sliding bearing	x	x	x	–	–	–	–	x	x	x	x	x	1	–	x	–
Gears	x	1	o	o	o	x	1	x	x	x	x	–	–	–	x	x
Resonance	x	1	–	–	–	–	–	–	–	–	–	–	x	x	–	x
Cavitation	x	x	x	o	o	x	–	–	–	–	–	–	–	–	x	x
Mechanical tolerances	x	x	–	–	–	–	–	–	–	–	–	–	x	x	–	–
Bent shaft	1	1	–	–	–	–	–	–	–	–	–	–	–	x	–	–
Electrical unbalance	1	1	–	–	–	–	–	–	–	–	–	–	–	–	–	–
Oil whirl	x	1	–	–	–	–	–	o	–	–	–	–	1	–	–	–
Friction	x	x	x	–	–	x	–	–	–	–	–	x	x	–	x	x
Faulty driving belts	x	x	–	–	–	–	–	–	–	–	–	–	–	1	–	–
Dirt	1	1	–	–	–	–	–	–	–	–	–	–	x	x	–	–
Contamination of oil	–	–	–	–	–	–	–	1	x	x	x	–	–	–	–	–
Speed of wear	–	–	–	–	–	–	–	x	1	x	x	–	–	–	–	–
Insufficient lubrication	x	x	x	–	o	1	–	x	x	–	–	x	x	–	x	x

1 = Normally applicable.
x = Applicable with limitations.
o = Requires a case-to-case study.
– = Not normally used.

and makes the drawing of conclusions on the severity of the situation much easier, as can also be seen from Table 1. In some cases it is, of course, also possible that one individual measurement technique could give misleading results due to difficulties in measurement instrumentation.

Today it is common in large production plants to use hundreds of transducers of various kinds connected to the machinery. The huge amount of information that they produce is collected by computers, which also analyse the data and prepare outputs as drawings, listings and in some cases work orders for the personnel who are responsible for the actual maintenance work.

Depending on the amount of intelligence in such a large condition monitoring system, we can also talk about artificial intelligence (AI) condition monitoring systems, which are capable of decision making to a certain degree. The development of AI condition monitoring systems has been closely related to the increase in processing power of computers together with the development of programming tools for this special purpose. The Technical Research Centre of Finland together with nine other Scandinavian participants has developed an expert system tool (ROTA) for diagnosing rotating machinery. The Finnish part of the joint project (DIXPERT) is described in Holmberg et al. (1989).

The main advantage of such an intelligent diagnosis system is the help that it provides in interpreting the vast amount of data that the conventional condition monitoring systems (CMS) provide to the maintenance personnel. Instead of studying the results of traditional condition monitoring systems and decision making, which normally would have to be done by highly skilled personnel, a lot of time and money can be saved by immediately taking the maintenance steps provided by the ROTA system.

Vibration Measurements

Today a great number of various kinds of vibration measurement techniques and analysis methods are available. The selection of a suitable method for a particular case can be based on economic and technical considerations (this book, Chapter 3.1). In many cases the vibration level of critical machinery is monitored on a continuous basis using a simple method, and compared against preset limits. If an excessive level is detected more sophisticated methods are used to determine the severity and nature of the problem.

Overall Vibration Level Measurements

The measurement of the overall vibration level is probably the most commonly used method for monitoring rotating machinery. In overall vibration level measurements the bandwidth is broad, e.g. 10–1000 Hz, and because of that the term 'broadband measurement' is also used in the literature. It has been observed in various studies (Kuoppala & Kuusisto, 1985) that this frequency band covers in most cases the vibration in machinery due to various faults. The measured parameter is normally the root-mean-square value of the vibration velocity, v_{rms}.

International standards, such as VDI 2056 and ISO 2372, give guidance on the criteria for classifying the condition of machines as a function of the measured vibration levels. It is easy to compare the measured values with those given in the standards and to evaluate the condition of the machinery. In some cases the manufacturer of the machinery has given his own limits to the machinery in question, which of course then give a more accurate basis for evaluation.

It is also possible to use overall level measurements for higher frequencies, for example in the case of rolling bearings and gearboxes (Kuoppala et al., 1986a). The measurement technique of the overall vibration level has been widely covered in the literature (Broch, 1980). The main advantage of overall vibration measurements is that they are easy to perform, the necessary equipment being cheap and small so that it can be carried around the factory. Overall vibration level measurements are a suitable tool for the indication of a fault in machinery, but if the machinery is not simple, it is not possible by means of overall vibration measurements alone to diagnose the location and cause of the fault, and more sophisticated means of analysing the data are needed.

Crest Factor

The crest factor is defined as the relation between the peak value and the root-mean-square value of the vibration signal, and it gives some indication of the waveshape of the vibration signal being studied (Broch, 1980). For pure harmonic motion, the crest factor is the square root of 2. When a machine is in normal working condition, the crest factor varies from 2 to about 6. In the case of failure, for example in a rolling bearing, the crest factor increases above 6 and can become as high as 20. The crest factor has most often been used in the case of rolling bearings, because in the case of, for example, gears and pumps it does not give a reliable indication of possible faults (Kuoppala et al., 1986a).

Frequency Analysis

Frequency analysis is a means of dividing the vibration signal into frequency components, and this can be done in a number of ways (Randall, 1977). Today, frequency analysis is probably most often carried out by using a spectrum analyser, which performs a Fast Fourier Transform (FFT). The theory of FFT can also be found in Randal (1977). By analysing the origin of the frequency components in the frequency spectrum and the trends in the change of the spectrum as a function of time, it is very often possible to define the cause of vibration and to locate the faulty component (Collacot, 1979). Typical examples of this would be the failure of a gear tooth and faults in rolling bearings.

If the spectrum analyser is equipped with two or more channels, a number of possibilities for further analysis arise. One signal is used as input and the other as output, and the relationship between them can be calculated. This calculated relationship, which is a function of the frequency, describes the dynamic behaviour of the machinery, assuming it is linear (Herlufsen, 1984).

The relationship can be described, for example, by such functions as the frequency response, which is the transfer function between input and output signals, and the coherence function, which gives a measure of the validity of the frequency response function (Randall, 1977). Performing a frequency analysis is a more demanding job than measuring overall vibration level signals, and also the necessary equipment is more expensive even though its price has been decreasing.

Cepstrum Analysis

The use of cepstrum analysis for condition monitoring of rotating machinery is mainly based on its ability to detect periodicity in the spectrum, e.g. families of harmonics and uniformly spaced sidebands, while being insensitive to the transmission path of the vibration signal from its origin to the external measuring point (Randall & Hee, 1981). Therefore cepstrum analysis is often used in order to define the origin of vibration. It makes it possible to study more closely the harmonic components of vibration, and also the possible sidebands are more clearly seen.

Cepstrum is defined as the Fourier Transform (=spectrum) of the (logarithmic amplitude) spectrum and it can be calculated with a similar spectrum analyser to that used for frequency analysis (Collacot, 1982). It is also possible to remove the harmonic components and sidebands from the cepstrum and after that to calculate a new spectrum from the cepstrum, which makes it easier to study the remaining frequencies. Cepstrum analysis is especially suitable for condition monitoring of gears, as it clearly indicates the harmonic components of a frequency and consequently shows, for example, the harmonics of the gear mesh frequency.

Synchronized Time Domain Signal Analysis

Instead of by frequency analysis or cepstrum analysis, the vibration signal, which is measured in the time domain, can also be manipulated in another way. It is possible to synchronize the measured signal with some other signal so that the sampling rate corresponds, for example, to the excitation frequency of that other measuring object. The synchronized time domain signal makes it possible to monitor, for example, the condition of an individual tooth of a gear by measuring the signal, when the tooth is in contact with another one. The principle of this method is that the vibration velocity signal is synchronized with the running speed of the shaft so that, after averaging, the signal of each individual tooth can be seen separately (Verkasalo, 1985).

Acoustic Emission

Measurement of acoustic emission, which is sometimes also called Stress Wave Emission, is a method in which very high frequencies of vibration are measured so that the lower frequency limit could be defined at about 40 kHz. A typical frequency range in acoustic emission measurement is from 80 to 120 kHz. Acoustic emission is widely used in the field of structural and material testing under loading (Randall, 1977). In that type of measurement the cracks in the material are localized using the time lag between the signals from various transducers. In condition monitoring, instead of the translation time, it is usually the actual contents of the signal that are being studied, for example the number of signals that are above a certain limit or the root-mean-square value of the signal (Kuoppala et al., 1986a).

The main advantage of acoustic emission measurements is that the normal vibration caused by the running machinery does not disturb the measured signal because it takes place at much lower frequencies. The use of acoustic emission for condition monitoring is still very limited. The reason for this could be that it has not been studied very much. There are also some practical problems related to measuring acoustic emission. The connection of the transducer to the measuring object has an effect on the measurement results. Acoustic emission is also rather sensitive to such factors that cause a damping effect at higher frequencies, for example lubricating oil layers and connection surfaces between various parts of the structure of the machinery. Also if there are fluids in the production process being monitored that are streaming with high velocity, they could disturb the acoustic emission signal dramatically. However, acoustic emission has been proved to be a promising method in laboratory tests with rolling bearings (Kuoppala et al., 1986b).

Shock Pulse Measurement

Rolling bearings introduce rather high frequency vibrations if there happens to be a failure. That type of vibration consists of impulses, because it is caused by either the rolling elements hitting faults in the bearing race or the failure in rolling elements hitting the bearing race. At that position the acceleration levels get high, depending of course on the size, running speed, etc., of the rolling bearing. In shock pulse measurement (SPM) techniques these impulses are recorded by taking advantage of the resonance frequency of the accelerometer, which typically is in the order of about 32 kHz (Kuoppala et al., 1986a). The signal from the transducer is amplified and transformed into a shock pulse. These values are compared to the reference values of the meter, after the inner diameter and running speed have been given as input to the meter. In order to be able to evaluate these recordings, there are three different categories in the meter: green = normal condition, yellow = starting failure, and red = damaged bearing. It is essential to the use of the SPM measurement technique that it is used frequently, so that the trend of fault developments can be found and thus the reliability of the measurements improved.

Kurtosis Method

The Kurtosis method is a statistical means of studying the time domain signal. The idea is to take samples in a suitable frequency range. After that the signals are manipulated using the following formula:

$$K = \frac{1}{\delta^4} \sum_{i=1}^{N} \frac{(x_i - \bar{X})^4}{N}$$

where δ^2 is the variance, N the number of samples, $\bar{X}$ the mean value of samples, and x_i an individual sample.

The use of Kurtosis analysis in condition monitoring of rotating machinery is based on the fact that for a rolling bearing in normal condition the Kurtosis value is about 3 (Rush, 1979). In the case of failure, the Kurtosis value increases rapidly. The advantage of the Kurtosis analysis is that it is not very sensitive to the loading or running speed of the machinery in question. Although special measuring equipment has been manufactured in order to enable the measurement of Kurtosis value, it has not been very much used in everyday condition monitoring in industry.

Modal Analysis

Modal analysis is a new method, which during the last few years has become more popular and has stimulated great interest in various forums (Schmidtberg & Pal, 1986). The term modal analysis, used in a very wide sense, could be defined as analysing the vibration modes of a structure. This has sometimes led to confusion as the same term is also used in the case of rotating machinery, when the vibration characteristics of the machinery are defined during normal operation and without any outside excitation such as an electrically driven vibration exciter. In such a case it would be better to use the term operational deflection shapes. The same measuring and analysis equipment (multichannel) that enables the use of modal analysis in the case of structures also enables very easily the definition of the vibration modes of a rotating machinery excited by itself. It should be noted that modal analysis excited with an outside exciter is seldom used in condition monitoring of rotating machinery when the machinery is running. However, in some cases this kind of technique is being used during the design and testing phase of the machinery, because these mode shapes and natural frequencies of the machinery are affected by the change of internal inertia forces caused by the running of the machine.

Oil Analyses

The oil analyses discussed in this study concentrate mainly on detecting solid particles in lubricating or hydraulic oils. The analyses of chemical properties of oils are not covered.

Spectrometric Oil Analysis

The concentration of different elements present in oil can be measured by spectrometric analysis (Burrows et al., 1965; Golden, 1971). The most common elements to be analysed are copper, chromium, nickel, iron, aluminium, lead, magnesium, silicon, titanium and silver. In the analysis the oil sample is burned and the wavelengths of light characteristic of the element are detected. Because of the improper burning, particles larger than 10 µm are not detectable (Bensch *et al.*, 1978; Välttilä, 1988). Spectrometric oil analysis (SOAP) is used in quite a wide field of applications. It is the most usual oil analysis method because of its rapidity and versatility.

Particle Counting

There are many kinds of particle counters based on different techniques such as optical, sedimentation, Coulter principle, etc. In this study only optical methods are covered.

The size distribution of debris in a fluid can be qualified with an automatic optical particle counter. The size range of particles to be analysed varies according to the size range of the sensor. The usual particle size range is 2·5–150 µm (Kerkkänen & Kuoppala, 1990). In the analysis the oil sample is led through a small channel in the sensor. There is a light source and a photodiode placed on opposite sides of the channel. When a particle passes through the channel it partially blocks the light beam and generates a pulse proportional to the particle size in the photodiode. The process is thus based on the assumption that particles pass through the channel one at a time. This assumption establishes the maximum concentrations that can be used. The typical upper limit of concentration is 4000 particles/ml (Kerkkänen, 1987). The size distribution of particles can be determined by separating them into various size categories. Automatic particle counters are mostly used in oil analyses of hydraulic machines. They function best with fairly clean oils which have low viscosity. The classification level of hydraulic fluid can be specified on the grounds of particle populations counted. The commonly used classification bases are ISO 4406, NAS 1638 and SAE 749D standards and the CETOP RP 70 H recommendation.

Wear Particle Analysis

Most wear particles from machine parts are ferromagnetic. Wear particle analysis uses the magnetism of the particles to separate them from the oil sample, and therefore wear particle analysis is a suitable method for condition monitoring of almost all oil-lubricated machines. In the analysis the oil sample is led over a glass plate placed in a strong non-homogenous magnetic field. The wear particles are fixed on the glass plate according to the particle size. The glass plate can then be analysed using an optical microscope and wear particle analyser (Ronkainen, 1986). By using a wear particle analyser, the severity indexes of the wear can also be defined. They give information on the wear particle concentration and the proportion of small and large particles. These factors effectively indicate the severity of the wear. Information on the wear mechanism, material and morphology of the particles can be studied with the aid of a microscope. Different metal particles can be identified on the basis of their colours. Colour change may be introduced by some gases or chemical vapours and reagents (Anderson *et al.*, 1979).

On-line Sensors

There has been much development in the sector of continuous monitoring of wear particles (Chambers *et al.*, 1988). Most of the published sensors are still prototypes. Some commercial products already exist, but irrespective of the great variety of potential machinery to be monitored they are used only in very few applications. Machines on big production lines and other machines where a rapid indication of failure is very important (aeroplanes, etc.) are especially suitable objects for using on-line sensors in wear particle analysis. Chapter 3.3 of this book presents results of new studies of on-line monitoring of contamination level in hydraulic oils.

The general principle of sensors is commonly magnetism or wear effect caused by wear particles. Magnetism is used for collecting debris in many of the on-line sensors, because the wear particles are usually magnetic. The amount of particles can be measured by coil or Hall-sensor. The prototype of a wear particle sensor constructed at the Technical Research Centre of Finland is based on the principle shown in Fig. 1. The changes in the magnetic circuit induced by wear particles are measured with a Hall-sensor (S1). Another Hall-sensor (S2) is used to compensate for the effect of temperature variations. With the coil (L) it is possible to estimate

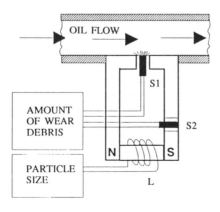

Fig. 1. The prototype of a wear particle sensor constructed at the Technical Research Centre of Finland.

the size of larger wear particles. Also in this sensor the changes in flow rate have an influence on the results as is the case with other sensors.

CASE STUDY 1. ONE-STEP GEARBOX

The aim of the study was to observe the wear and failure of a one-step gearbox in the laboratory by using vibration measurements and oil analyses (Kerkkänen & Kuoppala, 1990). In this study two separate tests were run. During the tests the gear was overloaded by about 50% in order to accelerate the wear. (Chambers *et al.*, 1988).

Testing Arrangement

The testing arrangement and measuring points are shown in Fig. 2. The power of the gearbox was rated at 17·9 kW, and the number of teeth of the input and output gears were 23 and 101, respectively, with a gear ratio of 4·3913. The gearbox was assembled with a circulation lubrication system, using SAE 80/90 type oil as the lubricant. The electric driving motor ran at a constant speed of 1500 rpm (25 Hz) and consequently the speed of the output gear was about 342 rpm (5·7 Hz).

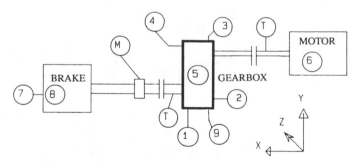

Fig. 2. Gearbox test arrangement and measuring points. (1)–(8): vibration and temperature; (9): acoustic emission; M: driving torque; T: tachometer.

Vibration Measurements

Vibration measurements consisted of overall level measurements, synchronized time domain signal analysis, spectrum analysis, cepstrum analysis and acoustic emission measurements. Oil analyses consisted of automatic particle counting, wear particle analysis and spectrometric oil analysis. The temperatures of the oil, the surfaces of the gearbox, the brake and the air were also recorded.

The overall vibration level measurements did not show any remarkable effect until during the last few minutes of the test runs (Aatola et al., 1989). Therefore this method may not be regarded as a predictive condition monitoring method in this specific case.

The synchronized time domain signal did show the failure of the gear very clearly (Kerkkänen & Kuoppala, 1990). With the signal of revolution from a tachometer at the input shaft the time domain signal was averaged, and in this way was formed a signal which shows the vibration of every individual tooth. Figure 3 shows the time domain signal at the beginning of the test and Fig. 4 shows the signal at the end of the test. In Fig. 4 the high level of vibration at the twelfth tooth, which eventually broke down, can be seen.

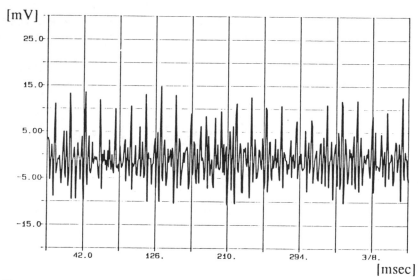

Fig. 3. Synchronized time domain signal at the beginning of the gearbox test (measuring point 3).

Cepstrum analysis also showed the failure quite clearly. The cepstral component corresponding to the input shaft speed increased by 19 dB 10 min before the failure during the second test run (Aatola & Leskinen, 1990). This increase began with a slight increase of about 3 dB over the

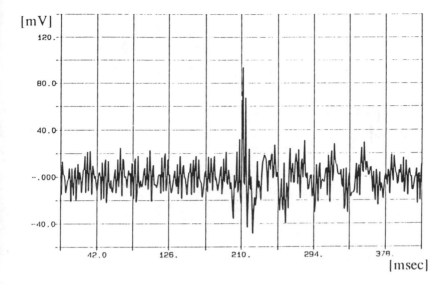

Fig. 4. Synchronized time domain signal at the end of the gearbox test (measuring point 3).

4-h period before the failure. It was also possible to locate the failure with cepstrum analysis, because the corresponding component for the output shaft was nearly constant throughout the whole test. The changes in the cepstral parameters are easily seen at 40 and 80 ms between the cepstra plotted at the beginning of the test (Fig. 5) and at the end of the test (Fig. 6). The synchronized cepstrum analysis was more sensitive than the ordinary cepstrum analysis. The synchronized cepstrum analysis of the signal picked up from a long distance also gave information on the oncoming failure, when no sign was seen with ordinary cepstrum analysis (Aatola & Leskinen, 1990).

Frequency analysis used in a broad frequency band such as from 0 to 10 000 Hz is not very efficient because of the limitations in resolution of ordinary spectrum analysers. When the spectrum is zoomed more closely in the proximity of the gear mesh frequency, it is possible to notice the failure during the test. The actual gear mesh frequency did not show any remarkable change until 10 min before failure, when a decrease of nearly 6 dB was noticed (Aatola & Leskinen, 1990). The spectral sideband around the gear mesh frequency corresponding to the input shaft increased by about 3 dB during the 4-h period before failure and dramati-

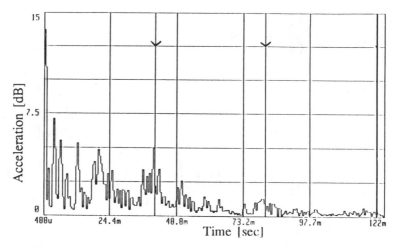

Fig. 5. Cepstrum at the beginning of the gearbox test (measuring point 3).

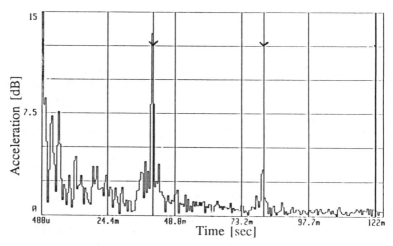

Fig. 6. Cepstrum at the end of the gearbox test (measuring point 3).

cally just before the failure (Fig. 7). The corresponding component of the output shaft increased only 10 min before failure.

There were no remarkable changes in acoustic emission signals during the entire test runs. At the end of the operation the root-mean-square values of the acoustic emission signals were increased but no dramatic

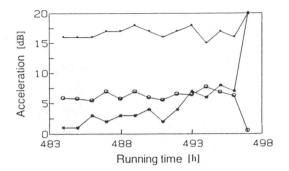

Fig. 7. Spectral sideband component corresponding to input (—•—) and output (—·—) shafts and gear mesh component (—o—) (measuring point 3).

change was seen (Aatola *et al.*, 1989). Unfortunately the amplification used was too low, resulting in a high level of noise in the measuring signal.

Wear Particle Analysis

An increase in the amount of wear particles, caused by breaking-in wear, was detected quite early in results of the oil analyses. The oil refills after sampling lowered the impurity level of the oil and so had a negative effect on the resolutions of the oil analysis methods. After 340 h running, the wear particle concentration increased drastically. The reason was that the gearbox was temporarily running without lubrication. The oil volume in circulation was small and supervision of the oil level was difficult. In addition there was a cumulative error in the amount of the refilled oil. These factors caused a decrease in the oil level during the test runs. The endoscopical inspection made afterwards showed that there was some material extricated from the teeth of the input gear. Despite the different measuring principles, the results correlated quite well and the changes in the particle level were detected with all methods.

A wear particle sensor was used for three time periods during the second gearbox test run. The first period was run at the beginning of the test and it lasted about 40 days, the second was run after the middle of the test and lasted for about 17 days, and the third was run at the end of the test until the failure, lasting less than 1 day. The sensor was cleaned between the test periods, because it had reached its saturation point. The

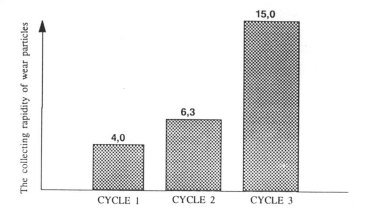

Fig. 8. The output slopes of the time periods (cycles 1–3) measured from the beginning of the cycles. Gearbox test 2.

slopes of the output signal of the sensor are shown as histograms in Fig. 8 for all three periods. It can be seen that the sensor gave an indication of severe wear for almost 1 day before the failure occurred.

CASE STUDY 2. ROLLING BEARING

The aim of tests with the rolling bearing was to test the new wear particle sensor developed at the Technical Research Centre of Finland. Altogether six independent test runs were made using the rolling bearing test bench (Kerkkänen & Kuoppala, 1990).

Testing Arrangement

The test bench is shown in Fig. 9. The electric motor had a power rating of 1.5 kW and was running at a speed of about 600 rpm. The motor was

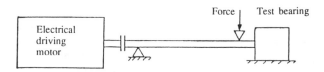

Fig. 9. Rolling bearing test bench.

connected to the shaft with a flexible coupling and there were two bearings supporting the shaft. At the other end of the shaft was the rolling bearing to be tested. A force was transmitted to the supporting bearing next to the bearing under test using a hydraulic cylinder. This force acted in a radial direction. The rolling bearing to be tested was fixed in the axial direction at its outer ring and the inner ring was on top of a conical tube mounted above the shaft. The rolling bearing under test was an SKF-filled notch ball bearing number 61810. The lubrication was circulatory using a pump to feed the oil to the upper part of the bearing. The oil flowed from the housing through a discharge tube to a tank and from there again to the pump.

In the rolling bearing tests, temperature, acoustic emission and vibration acceleration levels were measured in two orthogonal directions both radial to the shaft. From the signal of the vertical accelerometer transducer the root-mean-square value of the vibration velocity was calculated in the frequency range from 10 to 1000 Hz. The outside temperature was measured. In addition to the above, an on-line wear particle sensor was connected to the oil circulation and was used to measure the amount of wear particles in the lubricating oil. The rotational speed of the shaft was measured with a tachometer. The overall level of vibration, temperature and output voltage of the wear particle transducer were recorded with a plotter. An instrumentation tape recorder was used once per hour for recording the acceleration signals, the acoustic emission signals, the tachometer signal and the output signal of the wear particle sensor. Samples were taken from the circulating oil for wear particle analysis and SOAP-analysis. The output from the overall vibration level measurement and the temperature signal output of the bearing were connected to an automatic condition monitoring system, which could shut down the whole testing apparatus from the mains current if critical signal levels were likely to be exceeded.

Wear Particle Analysis

The changes in the amount of ferromagnetic particles could be detected with the aid of wear particle analysis. The development of the amount of wear particles as a function of time in bearing test 2 is shown in Fig. 10. It can be seen that the relative amount of large particles (the upper end of the plate) increased during the test, indicating an increase in the severity of wear.

The development of the severity indexes of wear in bearing test 2 is

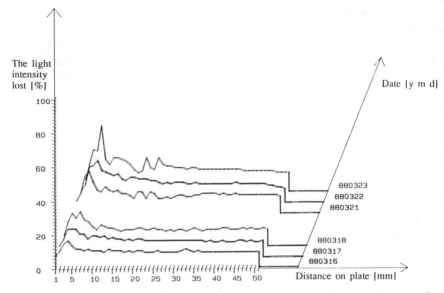

Fig. 10. The development of wear particle distribution during bearing test 2.

shown in Fig. 11. The curves show that at the end of the test severe wear took place as a major wear mechanism and therefore especially the amount of large particles increased drastically. The failure shown in Fig. 12 was generated on the outer surface of the bearing. A microscopic examination showed hundreds of particles about 5 μm in size found on

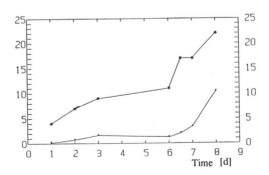

Fig. 11. The development of the severity indexes I0 (— ∗ —) and I1 (— · —) in bearing test 2.

Fig. 12. Photograph of the outer surface of the bearing after tests.

the plate dated 21.3.88. This was regarded as detection of fatigue wear in the bearing.

On-line Wear Particle Sensor

The wear particle sensor developed at the Technical Research Centre of Finland worked well as an indicator of changes in particle concentration during the tests (Fig. 13). Breaking in, mild and severe wear can all be

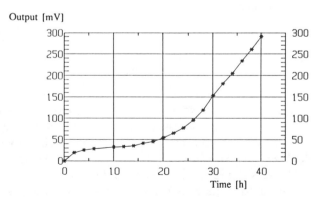

Fig. 13. The signal of the wear particle sensor during bearing test 5.

distinguished from the sensor signal. The total particle amount during tests was about 10 mg. The wear particle sensor only measures the actual wear in the machine, because the changes in the functional parameters of the machine do not have an influence on the results. The vibration measurements do not have this advantage.

Vibration Measurements

The measurements of the root-mean-square value of the overall vibration velocity showed tendencies similar to wear particle analysis, although with some variation between different test runs. In particular, the overall vibration level did not show any clear indication of failure during the fourth and fifth test runs. During the second test run the wear particle sensor showed a remarkable increase after 110 running hours and an even more remarkable increase after 122 running hours. The root-mean-square value of the overall vibration level increased after 105 and 116 running hours. The acoustic emission measurement results in these tests were also similar to those reported earlier (Kuoppala et al., 1986b), giving a clear indication of the failure at about the same time as the overall vibration measurements did.

For the rolling bearing used in the tests, the frequencies that indicate failure were calculated as 102·4 Hz for the outer ring, 117·6 Hz for the inner ring and 144·2 Hz for the rolling elements. During the second test run, a frequency analysis was carried out in order to locate the failure in the bearing; the result was that the failure took place in the outer ring of the bearing, because the increase of amplitudes could be seen at the second (205 Hz) and fourth (410 Hz) harmonic components of the 102·4 Hz base frequency.

CONCLUSION

Cepstrum analysis turned out to be a very efficient tool in monitoring the condition of gearboxes. The synchronized time domain signal was also found to be a promising method. In the case study of the rolling bearing, the advantages of oil analysis methods were shown. The novel on-line sensor worked very well and failure in the bearing could be predicted well in advance. The sensor gives an immediate indication of the condition of the machine. In addition, its construction is both electrically and mechanically quite simple. During the tests it has been shown that it is important to use several condition monitoring methods at the same time, because they almost always complement one another.

REFERENCES

Aatola, S. & Leskinen, R. (1990). Cepstrum analysis predicts gearbox failure. *Noise Control Eng. J.*, **2**, 53–9.

Aatola, S., Kerkkänen, K., Leskinen, R. & Linjama, J. (1989). Methods of monitoring gearbox condition under lifetime testing (Mittaavan kunnossapidon menetelmät vaihdelaatikon kunnonvalvonnassa) (in Finnish). *Technical Research Centre of Finland, Research Reports*, No. **596**.

Anderson, D.P., Bowen, E.R. & Bowen, J.P. (1979). Advances in wear particle analysis. In *Temper Colors*, Office of Naval Research, Arlington, VA, pp. 1–20.

Bensch, L.E., Fitch, E.C. & Tessman, R.K. (1978). *Contamination Control for the Fluid Power Industry*. Pacific Scientific Company, Oklahoma.

Broch, J.T. (1980). Mechanical vibration and shock measurements. In *Brüel & Kjær*, Nærum, Denmark. 370 pp.

Burrows, J.A., Heerdt, J.C. & Willis, J.B. (1965). The determination of wear metals in used lubrication oils by atomic absorption spectroscopy. *Anal. Chem.*, **37**, 579.

Chambers, K.W., Arneson, M.C. & Waggoner, C.A. (1988). An on-line ferromagnetic wear debris sensor for machinery condition monitoring and failure detection, *Wear*, **128**, 325–37.

Collacot, R.A. (1979). *Vibration Monitoring and Diagnosis*. Godwin, London.

Collacot, R.A. (1982). *Mechanical Fault Diagnosis and Condition Monitoring*. Chapman & Hall, London.

Golden, G.S. (1971). Determination of iron in used lubrication oil. *Applied Spectroscopy*, **25**, 668.

Herlufsen, H. (1984). Dual channel FFT analysis (Part I). *Brüel & Kjær Technical Review*, **1**, 3–56.

Holmberg, K., Kuoppala, R. & Vuoti, A. (1989). Expert system for wear failure prediction. Paper presented at *5th Int. Cong. on Tribology, EUROTRIB 89 Helsinki*, Helsinki University of Technology, Espoo, Finland, 12–15, June.

Kerkkänen, K. (1987). The use of particle counting in oil analyses (Hiukkaslaskennan käyttö öljyjen epäpuhtausanalyyseissä) (in Finnish). MSc Thesis, Helsinki University of Technology.

Kerkkänen, K. & Kuoppala, R. (1990). Methods of machine failure diagnostics (Koneiden vikadiagnostisoinnin menetelmiä) (in Finnish). *Technical Research Centre of Finland, Research Reports*, No. **700**.

Kuoppala, R. & Kuusisto, E. (1985). Prediction of machine failures by wear particle and vibration analyses. Paper presented at *Eurotest Conference*, Brussels 19–21, March.

Kuoppala, R., Leskinen, R. & Leppämäki, E. (1986a). Condition monitoring of rotating machinery (Pyörivien koneiden käynninaikainen kunnonvalvonta) (in Finnish). *Technical Research Centre of Finland, Research Notes*, No. **596**.

Kuoppala, R., Leskinen, R. & Leppämäki, E. (1986b). Applications of methods to condition monitoring of machinery (Mittausmenetelmien sovelluksia koneiden kunnon valvonnassa) (in Finnish). *Technical Research Centre of Finland, Research Reports*, No. **418**.

Randall, R.B. (1977). Application of B & K equipment to frequency analysis. In *Brüel & Kjær*, Nærum, Denmark. 239 pp.

Randall, R.B. & Hee, J. (1981). Cepstrum analysis. *Brüel & Kjær Technical Review*, **3**, 3–40.

Ronkainen, H. (1986). The use of wear particle analysis in condition monitoring of machinery (Kulumishiukkasanalyysin käyttö koneiden kunnonseurannassa) (in Finnish). MSc Thesis, Helsinki University of Technology.

Rush, A.A. (1979). Kurtosis—a crystal ball for maintenance engineers. *Iron & Steel International*, February 1979, 23–7.

Schmidtberg, R. & Pal, T. (1986). Solving vibration problems using modal analysis. *Sound & Vibration*, March, 16–21.

Välttilä, J. (1988). The contamination analysis of lubrication oils and hydraulic oils (Voitelu- ja hydrauliöljyjen epäpuhtausanalyysit) (in Finnish). *Technical Research Centre of Finland, Research Notes*, No. **911**.

Verkasalo, L. (1985). Condition monitoring of gears based on vibration measurements (Värähtelymittauksiin perustuva hammasvaihteiden kunnonvalvonta) (in Finnish). MSc Thesis, Oulu University.

3.3

On-line Monitoring of Contamination Level in Hydraulic Oils

Pawel Radzikowski

Royal Institute of Technology, Department of Fluid Technology, S-100 44 Stockholm, Sweden

ABSTRACT

The main purpose of this investigation was to find suitable methods for on-line monitoring of the contamination level in hydraulic oils in order to avoid costly breakdowns for both industrial plants and mobile machines. Three on-line sensors, available on the market, based on different methods have been investigated. These are light obscuration, filter mesh obscuration and electrical resistance increase.

The sensors have been tested in a test rig, which was specially designed to avoid particle sedimentation. Two kinds of contaminations have been used: sand powder and iron powder. Additionally, in some tests, particles were generated by severe overloading of the pump. Several mass concentrations have been used to test the sensitivity and linearity of each method. The linearity was acceptable in most cases. The sensitivity is different for each method, though also acceptable. It has been found that sand powder is much more abrasive than iron power and easier to indicate with the electrical resistance increase method. Some field tests have been performed which showed that a large mistake can be made while taking a bottle sample because of the particle sedimentation. This can be eliminated by on-line monitoring.

INTRODUCTION

Monitoring in General

The main purpose of machine monitoring, whatever form it takes, is to avoid unexpected failures and costly breakdown time. The latter cannot be eliminated but it can be minimized. One early way of monitoring was to check the machine parts regularly (Neale, 1987) or to record statistics concerning the components that failed, how often, the kind of damage, etc. This way, which at one time was the only way possible, has some disadvantages:

(1) it requires experienced personnel to check if some parts could still be used;
(2) machines must be stopped often; the time could be used for production;
(3) even checking machine parts at regular time intervals does not guarantee that a failure can be indicated in time, as machines do not tend to fail regularly.

Modern techniques make it more and more possible to monitor machines on-line. However, the decision to adopt on-line monitoring depends on the following factors.

(1) The cost of monitoring should be lower than the average cost of unexpected down times.
(2) It may not be easy to determine which of the system components should be monitored. If there are many components, a critical one should be defined. This implies that some study of the system function should be done.
(3) The kind of consequences an eventual failure can imply should be examined, e.g. a chain reaction resulting in damage of other components, total failure, etc.
(4) On-line monitoring is not suitable for components which give no warning before failure.
(5) There is always a possibility of a false alarm.

There are certain on-line monitoring methods whose suitability depends on the kind of systems to be monitored and the kind of information which can be obtained.

(1) Measurement of the system performance—power, flow rate, temperature, pressure, efficiency (thermodynamic measurement). This can be seen as additional monitoring because some of the these parameters are measured anyway.
(2) Measurement of vibrations (this book, Chapter 3.2), specially suitable for rotating machinery.
(3) For hydraulic and lubricating systems, measurement of contamination level in the oil. It has been mentioned that one problem is to find

the critical component to be monitored on-line as it is impossible to monitor all of them. In the case of a hydraulic system this problem is minimized, because the oil being monitored contains information about all the components. If something wrong is happening, resulting, for example, in a large amount of suspended particles, the next step could be to find from which component it comes. This means that some kind of scanning is required.

Monitoring of Contamination Level in Oil

Definitions:

(1) ACFTD: Air Cleaner Fine Test Dust—sand powder commonly used in contamination tests because of the well defined particle distribution.
(2) ISO Solid Contamination Code, ISO 4406; see Table 1.

The ISO contaminant code is constructed from the combination of two range numbers. The first represents the number of particles in a 100 ml sample of the fluid that are larger than 5 μm, and the second the number of particles that are larger than 15 μm. For example, code ISO 19/15 indicates that there are between 250 000 and 500 000 particles > 5 μm and between 16 000 and 32 000 particles > 15 μm.

In a normally working hydraulic system there is a balance between the number of particles being generated in the system and those being filtered. However, if the filter function has failed, the number of particles can increase drastically. More particles in the oil cause even more particles to be generated (Radzikowski, 1988). This, if not discovered and stopped in time, can cause severe wear and finally failure. Another possible source of particle generation occurs when a component, e.g. a hydraulic pump, is exposed to abnormal wear. Particles being generated in this way contaminate the oil and can cause wear in other components before they get trapped by a properly working filter. Contamination can also come into the hydraulic system from a dirty environment, e.g. if there is a vent hole in the oil reservoir, etc. Combinations of those reasons are also possible. The most dangerous particles, in terms of dimension, are those as large as the clearances in the hydraulic component, because they can wear out the surface of the component while passing through the clearance, while the smaller particles can pass easily and the larger ones cannot normally pass at all (Fig. 1).

This means that from the reliability point of view the admissible size

Table 1. ISO Range Numbers from the ISO Solid Contamination Code (ISO 4406)

Number of particles per 100 ml		Range number
More than	Up to and including	
8×10^6	18×10^6	24
4×10^6	8×10^6	23
2×10^6	4×10^6	22
1×10^6	2×10^6	21
500×10^3	1×10^6	20
250×10^3	500×10^3	19
130×10^3	250×10^3	18
64×10^3	130×10^3	17
32×10^3	64×10^3	16
16×10^3	32×10^3	15
8×10^3	16×10^3	14
4×10^3	8×10^3	13
2×10^3	4×10^3	12
1×10^3	2×10^3	11
500	1×10^3	10
250	500	9
130	250	8
64	130	7
32	64	6
16	32	5
8	16	4
4	8	3
2	4	2
1	2	1

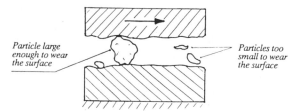

Particle large enough to wear the surface

Particles too small to wear the surface

Fig. 1. The most dangerous particles are those as large as the clearance, because they can wear the surface.

of solid particles in the oil should be smaller than the smallest clearance in the hydraulic component. This can be achieved by using a filter element of a proper pore size. In modern high pressure components the clearances are made smaller and smaller in order to reduce oil leakage.

This means that finer filter elements should be used, which seems not to be fully appreciated by many users of hydraulic systems. But even a large amount of very small particles can cause problems, e.g. by blocking very sensitive components such as servo valves, etc.

Monitoring of some hydraulic systems has shown (Day, 1987) that about 70% of failures were caused by too high contamination levels. In many other cases the failures were preceded by an increased contamination level. On the other hand, testing of about 120 different hydraulic systems (see *Guidelines to Contamination Control in Hydraulic Fluid Power Systems*) has provided values of contamination levels experienced in different hydraulic systems that are acceptable from the reliability point of view. For example, for mobile machines it is ISO 18/11, which means that if the contamination level, all the time, is kept at ISO 18/11, or lower, the probability of a failure is minimized. Some other tests (see the two references on Ferrography) have shown that, in the case of hydraulic systems, monitoring of the contamination level was the first method to indicate that there was something wrong, long before the measurement of vibrations could indicate anything. The explanation is easy. Vibrations can appear in a hydraulic component when the clearances between the moving parts become too large, making a gap. This happens when material has been removed as a result of wear. It results normally in a large amount of particles in the oil even long before the gap is large enough to cause any vibrations. Generally, it can be mentioned that the oil in hydraulic systems is like the blood in a human being. It contains much information about the system's 'health' but the problem is to be able to read and explain it. This requires suitable equipment and experience. It is obvious that the hardness of the particle material is a very important factor. Many soft particles are not as dangerous as a few particles of a hard material such as sand. Having that in mind, we can try to define what kind of information a method for on-line contamination level indication should be able to supply.

(1) Number of particles and their size distribution.
(2) Material of the particles. Having found that many particles in the oil are of, e.g., aluminium, the components they may come from can be traced; or a large number of sand particles can indicate that the air breathing filter does not work and dust comes in. It should be able to indicate the abrasivity of the particles.
(3) The method should be sensitive enough to be able to indicate an increasing contamination level early enough.

(4) It should be able to withstand vibration and generally a hard environment.

Unfortunately, an on-line method to fulfil all of this at the same time does not exist. It would be acceptable, however, if a sensor for on-line monitoring could give a first warning easily understood by inexperienced personnel. Such a sensor could be fitted in a strategic place in order to get the most information. For a hydraulic system such a place is just before the filter. Another possible solution is to fit oil taps in many places and to scan the system regularly. It must be pointed out here that 'on-line' does not necessarily mean continuous. It would be enough to measure, for example, once a day or generally at any time deemed necessary. The first possible reason for a high contamination level is that the filter has failed or has been blocked and should be replaced. This can be checked by measurement of the contamination level before and after the filter. If the filter works well, the possible source of the high contamination level can be found by checking the contamination level after each component such as a pump or motor. When the source of the high contamination level is located the next step would be to take a bottle sample and use some more advanced laboratory methods such as microscopy or analytic ferrography to more precisely identify the contaminant. This way all the components can be scanned by means of one sensor only. Moreover the same sensor can be used to scan other systems also.

Why Monitor On-line?

A commonly used method for monitoring contamination level has been to extract bottle samples and send them to a laboratory, where advanced test methods could be used. This method, which may sometimes be essential if the contaminants must be examined in order to explain their origin and character, has some disadvantages.

(1) Even taking bottle samples regularly can 'miss' a failure indication in time, simply because machines do not tend to fail regularly.
(2) In monitoring contamination level, we need to get a representative oil sample carrying the latest information about the system's 'health'. However, getting such a sample can often be a difficult task using bottle sampling. If the environment is very dirty, the number of particles coming from it into the bottle can sometimes be higher than the number entering from the oil itself.

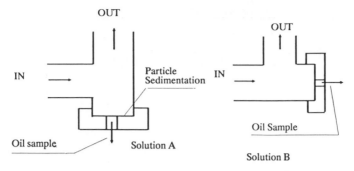

Fig. 2. Different oil taps.

(3) The tap, from which the oil sample is extracted, is a place where the solid contaminants normally settle down; see Fig. 2.

Solution A in Fig. 2, though used very often, is vulnerable to particle sedimentation and is not recommended. In solution B, which is recommended, the tap is flushed all the time, which minimizes particle sedimentation.

The first oil sample extracted from the tap is not representative, because the sediments are being flushed with the oil. The size of the flushing volume before the oil sample can be considered as representative can vary a lot depending on the hydraulic system, the environment and above all the oil tap. However, it seems that the 0·2 litres recommended by ISO 4021 is definitely too little. The problem of particle sedimentation can be illustrated by some field tests; see Fig. 3 which shows results from an ironworks with a very dirty environment. After about 2 litres of oil had been flushed from the tap, the particle counter was connected to it and on-line monitoring of the contamination level begun. The contamination level registered stabilized after about 15 litres of oil had been flushed. This means that the stabilized stage represents the real contamination level in the system while the first stage represents the combined effect of the real contamination level and the particle sedimentation in the oil tap. The difference obtained in this case is too large and not acceptable. A test performed at another ironworks showed almost the same tendency; however, the volume flushed before the contamination level stabilized was even higher.

In practice, the problem was found to be less serious, as the initial contamination levels in all the cases were indicated as too high, which

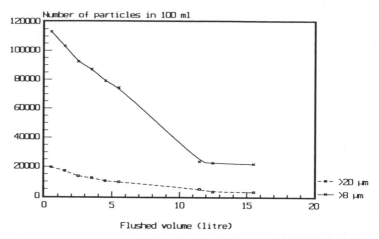

Fig. 3. On-line monitoring by particle counting: field test 1, performed at an ironworks.

means that steps to avoid a potential failure would be undertaken rather too early than too late. This is not always the case because the information obtained from such an oil sample is not representative. Severe wear may already have taken place in one of the components while the sediments in the oil sample could contain e.g. a large amount of rubber particles from a sealing that had failed and been replaced some time ago. On-line monitoring of contamination level eliminates this kind of problem, supplying the actual information about the system's condition.

Another advantage with on-line monitoring of a slightly different character is illustrated in Fig. 4. This test was performed at a paper mill, where a radial piston hydraulic motor had been monitored. The oil tap was first flushed with about 15 litres of oil in order to remove the sedimentation. The particle counter was then connected to the tap and the contamination level was monitored on-line for several hours. The hydraulic motor was loaded about every seventh minute, which resulted in an increased contamination level. Every load cycle was followed by an increased contamination level. It is not fully established whether this was the result of particle generation or if the vibrations during each load cycle shook the particles that had settled down. Probably the reasons were combined, with the second as the main one.

In this case the contamination level, both during every load cycle and between load cycles, was very low. However, if it had been higher a large

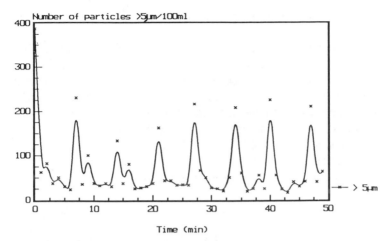

Fig. 4. On-line monitoring by particle counting: field test 3, performed at a paper mill.

mistake could have been made by bottle sampling depending on whether the sample was taken just after a load cycle or between two of them. On-line monitoring in such a case enables the estimation of an average value and can even indicate what is actually happening in the system.

According to the Seminar on Contamination Measurement in Oil Hydraulics (1990), the volume flushed before a bottle sample could be taken should be between 3 and 5 litres, if the tap is formed like B, Fig. 2. With another kind of tap it should be much higher. However, at least two oil samples should be taken with at least 2 to 3 litres of oil flushed in between. If the contamination level indicated in both of them is similar, which means the flushing stage is over, the samples can be acceptable.

TEST OBJECTS

On the basis of a literature study, three sensors available on the market for use in on-line indication of contamination level have been chosen for more thorough testing. The measurement bases for the three sensors are:

— Light obscuration, particle counting
— Filter mesh obscuration
— Electrical resistance increase

A short description of each method follows.

Light Obscuration, Particle Counting

A narrow transparent passage through which oil can flow is situated between a light source and a photocell. A passing particle causes an obscuration of the light source proportional to the area of the particle. This can be converted into an electrical signal, the strength of which is directly proportional to the particle size. If the flow rate through the sensor is known, the number of particles per unit volume and their size distribution can be obtained. This method is a basic one, because almost all the experience we have today about contaminations, including the ISO code, is mainly based on particle counting.

Filter Mesh Obscuration

We assume a fully characterized filter mesh with a defined number of pores of known size, e.g. 5 μm and constant known laminar flow rate through it. If the fluid is not contaminated, the pressure drop across the mesh is directly proportional to the dynamic viscosity of the fluid, but if it is contaminated, the particles larger than the pore size will be trapped on the mesh. More particles trapped on the mesh reduce the available open area and the pressure drop across the mesh will increase. Assuming constant flow rate and constant oil viscosity, and having measured the pressure drop across the mesh, the degree of the mesh obscuration and the number of particles greater than the pore size can be estimated per unit volume.

Electrical Resistance Increase

A thin metallic film is placed on a ceramic bolt. The film has an electrical resistance which, if the temperature is constant, is inversely proportional to the cross-sectional area of the film. It is exposed to an oil jet and if there are solid particles in the oil, they will erode the film surface while hitting it. The cross-sectional area will be reduced and the electrical resistance will increase. This, if measured with the same time interval, can indicate the degree of oil contamination, e.g. as an absolute increase of the resistance per time unit. The output unit is defined by the manufacturer as 1 Ab = 0·1 ohm/hour, i.e. if the resistance increased by 0·1 ohm during 1 hour, the output unit is 1 Ab. How fast the film is eroded depends not only on the number of solid particles in the oil, but also on their abrasiveness and shape, assuming a constant velocity in the oil jet.

TEST RIG

A special test rig (Fig. 5) with the following features has been designed. The number of pipe connections and other possible particle traps has been minimized, and the oil reservoir was made with a cone-shaped bottom, with the return flow pipe orifices directed on it in order to obtain flushing. Oil taps have been supplied with specially designed plugs in order to get representative oil directly from the middle of the stream. The pipe flow was turbulent.

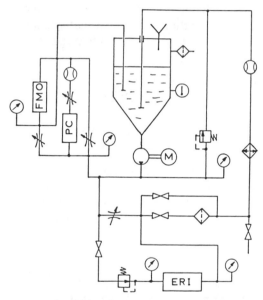

Fig. 5. Test rig. PC: Particle counter; FMO: Filter mesh obscuration sensor; ERI: Electrical resistance increase sensor.

All these steps were undertaken in order to reduce the particle sedimentation and to get the contamination level in the rig as constant as possible. The results indicated by all the methods can only be compared if they are exposed to the same contamination level. The rate of change of the contamination level in the rig was tested according to ISO 4572, which says that the contamination level measured with the particle counter should not vary by more than 10% during 1 hour; in this case the variation was less than 3%.

TEST PERFORMANCE

Test Conditions

Shell T32 hydraulic oil was used in the test rig (32 cSt at 40°C). The oil temperature was 40°C during all the tests. The main flow was always turbulent and the pressure was 40 bar. The filter was disconnected during the tests.

Contaminations in real hydraulic systems consist of many different materials, such as iron, sand, rubber, dust, etc. Before exposing the sensors to the real, undefined contaminations, it seemed prudent to test them with some contaminations of known material and defined particle distribution. As a result, two different kinds of particles have been used in the tests:

— ACFTD: sand powder, commonly used in contamination tests mostly because of the well defined particle distribution;
— iron powder with undefined particle distribution;
— additionally, in some tests, iron particles were generated by overloading the pump. This kind of test was started only.

Several tests with different mass concentrations of ACFTD and iron powder have been performed, so that the sensitivity and linearity of each method could be tested. A double mass concentration should, at least theoretically, cause each sensor to indicate a double contamination level.

Oil temperature, system pressure and system flow rate were measured during the tests. In addition, the following quantities defining the particles in the oil were measured: with the particle counter the number of particles larger than 5, 10, 15, 25, and 40 μm in 100 ml oil; with filter mesh obscuration the number of particles larger than 5, 15, and 25 μm, also in 100 ml oil; and with the electrical resistance increase sensor the abrasivity of the particles, with output unit of 1 Ab.

RESULTS AND DISCUSSION

The results are presented in the Appendix and Figs 6–19. Simultaneous on-line measurement of contamination level with several sensors based on different methods supplies much more information on the 'behaviour' of the solid contaminant particles in hydraulic oils, than if only one method is used. Considering wear, a very important factor is the

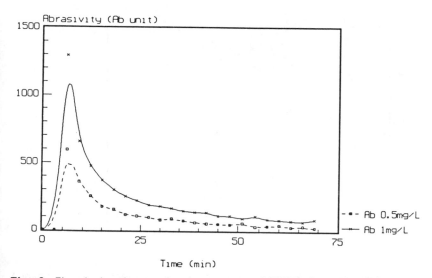

Fig. 6. Electrical resistance increase sensor. ACFTD abrasivity change as a function of time for two mass concentrations: 0·5 mg/litre (ISO 16/13) and 1 mg/litre (ISO 17/14).

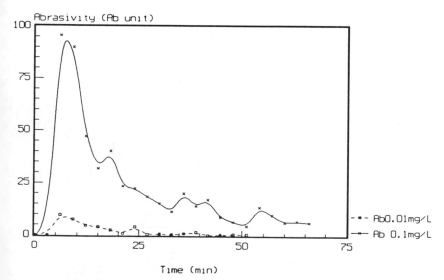

Fig. 7. Electrical resistance increase sensor. ACFTD abrasivity change as a function of time for two mass concentrations: 0·01 mg/litre (ISO 11/8) and 0·1 mg/litre (ISO 14/11).

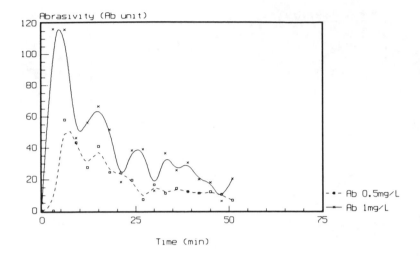

Fig. 8. Electrical resistance increase sensor. Iron powder abrasivity change as a function of time for two mass concentrations: 0·5 mg/litre (ISO 14/10) and 1 mg/litre (ISO 15/11).

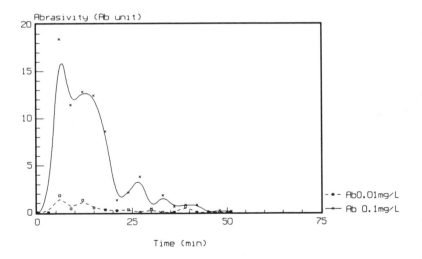

Fig. 9. Electrical resistance increase sensor. Iron powder abrasivity change as a function of time, for two mass concentrations: 0·1 mg/litre (ISO 11/8) and 0·01 mg/litre (ISO 10/7).

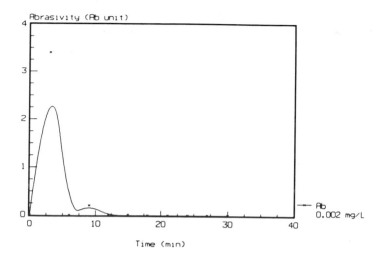

Fig. 10. Electrical resistance increase sensor. ACFTD abrasivity change as a function of time, for 0·002 mg/litre (ISO 10/7).

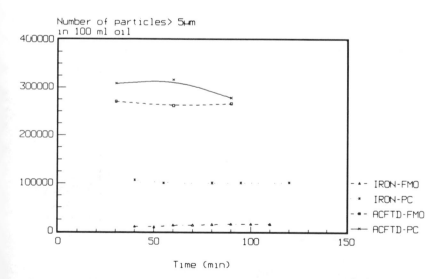

Fig. 11. Number of particles >5 μm measured with particle counter and filter mesh obscuration sensor. Two different contaminations: 5 mg/litre ACFTD (ISO 19/15) and 5 mg/litre iron powder (ISO 17/13).

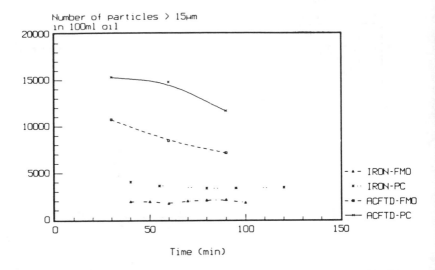

Fig. 12. Number of particles >15 µm measured with particle counter and filter mesh obscuration sensor. Two different contaminations: 5 mg/litre ACFTD (ISO 19/15) and 5 mg/litre iron powder (ISO 17/13).

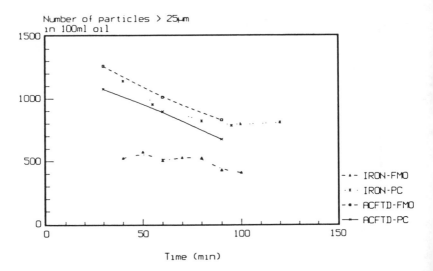

Fig. 13. Number of particles >25 µm measured with particle counter and filter mesh obscuration sensor. Two different contaminations: 5 mg/litre ACFTD (ISO 19/15) and 5 mg/litre iron powder (ISO 17/13).

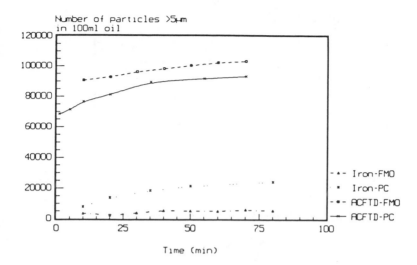

Fig. 14. Number of particles >5 µm measured with particle counter and filter mesh obscuration sensor. Two different contaminations: 1 mg/litre ACFTD (ISO 17/14) and 1 mg/litre iron powder (ISO 15/11).

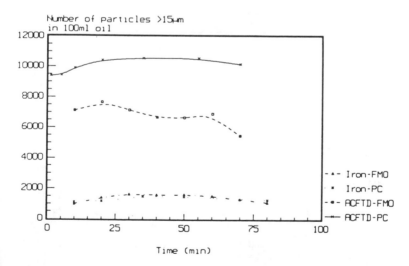

Fig. 15. Number of particles >15 µm measured with particle counter and filter mesh obscuration sensor. Two different contaminations: 1 mg/litre ACFTD (ISO 17/14) and 1 mg/litre iron powder (ISO 15/11).

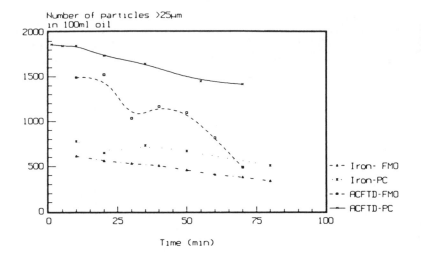

Fig. 16. Number of particles > 25 μm measured with particle counter and filter mesh obscuration sensor. Two different contaminations: 1 mg/litre ACFTD (ISO 17/14) and 1 mg/litre iron powder (ISO 15/11).

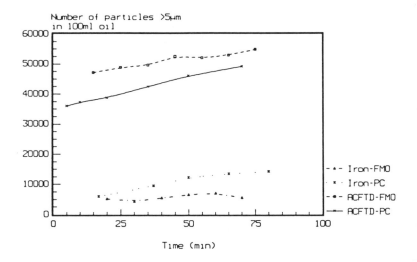

Fig. 17. Number of particles > 5 μm measured with particle counter and filter mesh obscuration sensor. Two different contaminations: 0·5 mg/litre ACFTD (ISO 16/13) and 0·5 mg/litre iron powder (ISO 14/11).

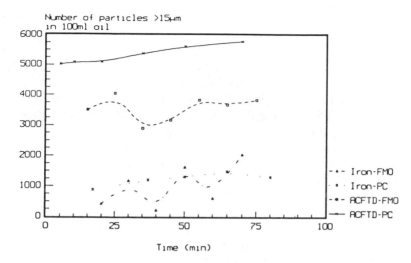

Fig. 18. Number of particles >15 µm measured with particle counter and filter mesh obscuration sensor. Two different contaminations: 0·5 mg/litre ACFTD (ISO 16/13) and 0·5 mg/litre iron powder (ISO 14/11).

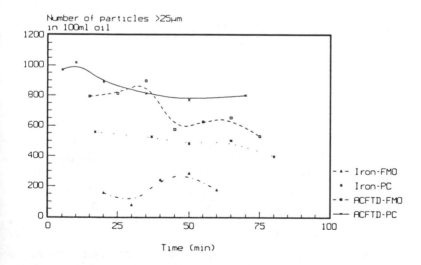

Fig. 19. Number of particles >25 µm measured with particle counter and filter mesh obscuration sensor. Two different contaminations: 0·5 mg/litre ACFTD (ISO 16/13) and 0·5 mg/litre iron powder (ISO 14/11).

abrasiveness of the particles, which was impossible to indicate using particle counting only.

Comparison of the abrasiveness values, Figs 6 and 7, shows a very distinct relationship with mass concentration. Immediately after ACFTD was injected into the oil, the abrasivity increased to a maximum value. If the abrasivity for 0·01 mg/litre is about 10 Ab units, the corresponding values for 0·1, 0·5 and 1 mg/litre should be about 10, 50, and 100 times higher. That is also the case; see other graphs in Figs 6 and 7. The way it changed seemed to be fully acceptable. The abrasivity decreased very quickly. The time when the abrasivity became reduced to about 20% is about 25 min and almost the same for each mass concentration. During 25 min the main volume has been circulated about 60 cycles. The abrasivity of the particles could only be reduced by hitting and wearing the material of the test rig. This is why some iron particles could be seen in the oil sample studied in the microscope. Very low concentrations, as low as 0·002 mg/litre, could also be indicated. However, while measuring such low concentrations, the pressure drop causing the oil jet should be higher. The abrasivity change for the iron powder showed a similar trend, but it was less than with ACFTD. Iron particles seem to be much less abrasive than ACFTD; compare values in Figs 6 and 8, 7 and 9. The abrasivity of the iron particles was reduced in a similar way to that of ACFTD, in most cases to about 20% after the main volume had been circulated about 60 cycles. This factor must be taken into consideration when trying to indicate hard wear.

Let us suppose that the iron particles have been generated in a failed component, e.g. a pump. These particles are very abrasive at the beginning and easy to indicate, but the abrasivity is quickly reduced and after some cycles it is much more difficult to indicate them by measurement of the abrasivity. If the wear is taking place continuously the sensor is supplied with 'new' abrasive particles all the time, but if the wear happens sporadically, e.g. in a failed component connected from time to time, its indication may easily be overlooked in this way. This kind of test has been performed when the abrasivity of the particles was very high, about 150 Ab units, while the contamination level was as low as ISO 11/8; however, the abrasivity decrease could not be indicated, because new particles were supplied all the time.

The possibility of indicating particles with the filter mesh obscuration method seems to be good; however, it is necessary to arrange a suitable by-pass flow, which varies depending on the material of the particles. For ACFTD, the results obtained with the by-pass flow rate of 1 litre/min were good, especially for 5 µm particles; see Figs 11, 14 and 17. For the other particle sizes, 15 and 25 µm, the differences were larger, but in most cases particle counting and filter mesh obscuration indicated the same ISO code; see the Appendix. Iron powder required a much higher by-pass flow rate, at least 3 litre/min, otherwise the repeatability was not acceptable. Generally, it was more difficult to indicate the same mass concentration of iron powder than of ACFTD. One of the reasons is that the former contains fewer particles. The results obtained for larger iron particle sizes were a little better as shown in Fig. 15 and 16. As the real contaminants consist of many different materials, the required by-pass flow rate should be chosen according to the highest possible density of the particle material, e.g. iron.

CONCLUSIONS

All the methods tested seem to be suitable for on-line monitoring of contamination level. The most sensitive of all is the particle counter, which could even indicate the lowest mass concentration. However, some oil additives and air bubbles can be indicated as particles because of the different refractive index. It must also be mentioned that 5 mg/litre of ACFTD is the highest particle concentration the particle counter can measure on-line, as higher concentrations would need dilution. The sensitivity of the filter mesh obscuration method varies depending on the material of the solid contaminant particles. The lowest indicatable mass concentration of ACFTD is about 0·1 mg/litre with the by-pass flow rate of about 1 litre/min. For iron powder it is about 0·5 mg/litre with the by-pass flow of at least 3 litre/min. This method has practically no upper concentration limit and is specially suitable for very contaminated oils. Some problems can be caused by oils with bad filterability.

The way the electrical resistance increase method reacts for doubled mass concentrations seems to be fully acceptable. The sensitivity can be increased by increasing the pressure drop causing the oil jet. Measured at 16 bar and 32 cSt, the lowest indicatable mass concentration of ACFTD was 0·002 mg/litre and for iron powder it was 0·01 mg/litre. This method is a very interesting one because it supplies information about the abrasivity of the solid contaminant particles. A standard value defining the abrasivity of the solid contaminant particles could in the future be a useful qualitative complement to the ISO code.

REFERENCES

Day, M.J. (1987). The use of particles counting techniques in the condition monitoring of fluid power systems. *Conference on Condition Monitoring*, University College of Swansea, UK.

Neale, M.J. (1987). Trends in maintenace and condition monitoring. *Conference on Condition Monitoring*, University College of Swansea, UK.

Radzikowski, P. (1988). Tillståndskontroll av hydraulvätskors renhet (On-line monitoring of contamination level in hydraulic oils) (in Swedish). *Rapport NR 88-02*, Department of Fluid Technology, Royal Institute of Technology, Stockholm, pp. 2.1–2.11.

ISO 4406. *Hydraulic fluid power–Fluids–Solid contaminant code*, pp. 1–2.

Guidelines to contamination control in hydraulic fluid power systems. The Association of Hydraulic Equipment Manufactures, London, p. 10.

Ferrography: a tool for wear particle analysis. *Hydraulic & Pneumatic*, November 1986.

Ferrography—history case. Standard Oil Eng. Materials, Solon, OH.

ISO 4021. *Hydraulic fluid power—Particulate contamination analysis— Extraction of fluid samples from lines of an operating system*, p. 2.

Seminarium om föroreningsmätning inom hydraulik (Seminar on contamination measurement in oil hydraulics), May 1990 (in Swedish). Department of Fluid Technology, Royal Institute of Technology, Stockholm, p. 26.

Hiac/Royco—Pacific Scientific, 141 Jefferson Dr., Menlo Park, CA 94025, USA.

Coulter Electronics Ltd, Northwell Dr., Luton, Beds LU3 3RH, UK.

Fulmer Systems Ltd, Hollybush Hill, Berksire SL2 4QD, UK.

ISO 4572. *Hydraulic fluid power—Filters—Multi-pass method for evaluating filtration performance*, pp. 1-9.

APPENDIX. TEST RESULTS

Mass concen-tration (mg/litre)	Contamination	ISO code[a]		ERI(16 bar 32 cSt)[d]	
		PC[b]	FMO[c]	Max. Ab[e]	Ab after 60 cycles
5	ACFTD	19/15/12	19/15/12	4 600	900
5	Iron p.	17/13	15/14	1 500	170
1	ACFTD	17/14/11	17/13/11	1 100	200
1	Iron p.	15/11/10	13/11/9	115	25
0·5	ACFTD	16/13/10	16/12/10	500	100
0·5	Iron p.	14/11/10	13/11/9	60	15
0·1	ACFTD	14/11/8	14/11/8	100	20
0·1	Iron p.	11/8	—	18	4
0·01	ACFTD	11/8	—	10	2
0·01	Iron p.	10/7	—	2	0·2
0·002	ACFTD	11/7	—	3	0
0·002	Iron p.	9/6	—	—	—
0·001	ACFTD	9/6	—	—	—
0·001	Iron p.	9/6	—	—	—

[a]The ISO code (ISO 4406) sometimes has appended a third value, which represents the number of particles > 25 µm, e.g. ISO 19/15/12.
[b]Particle counter.
[c]Filter mesh obscuration.
[d]Electrical resistance increase (Shell T32 hydraulic oil at 40°C).
[e]1 Ab $= 0·1$ ohm/hour.

As a comparison with the values in the table, it can be mentioned that, for example, for aircraft test stends the average experienced contamination level, which can be considered to be acceptable from a reliability point of view, is ISO 13/10, while for mobile machines it is ISO 18/11 (*Guidelines to Contamination Control in Hydraulic Fluid Power Systems*).

3.4

A Stochastic Model for Wear Prediction through Condition Monitoring

URHO PULKKINEN

Technical Research Centre of Finland,
Laboratory of Electrical and Automation Engineering,
PO Box 34, SF-02150 Espoo, Finland

ABSTRACT

The application of stochastic filtering for prediction of wear is described, applying the approach in the case of a simple wear model and determining the estimate for accumulated wear given the results of condition monitoring measurements. The estimate is formed by updating the distribution of a stochastic process, which describes the degree of wear. The updating procedure is based on the successive application of the Bayes formula. Although the analytical calculations are difficult, it is concluded that the approach is promising.

INTRODUCTION

The monitoring of the state of components is important in the planning of preventive maintenance and operation policies of a system. Some failures develop gradually and may be detected by suitable measurements. The most advanced techniques, based mainly on the measurement of vibration and the measurement of wear particles, are developed for wear diagnosis. However, these measurements are not often used in prediction of the lifetime of the component.

The wear propagates irregularly due to the inhomogeneity of the materials, varying environmental conditions and other factors. Thus, it is feasible to apply stochastic models in wear prediction. In that case it is possible to evaluate the remaining lifetime if the model parameters have been estimated from previous experiments with similar components. If the state of the component is monitored with measurements, the predicton of the time to failure can be improved by combining the measurement information with the stochastic failure model.

The condition monitoring measurements do not usually give exact information on the degree of the wear. The result of the measurement is related to the state of the component stochastically: the randomness of the relation is due to the measurement errors and to other uncontrollable factors. For example, if the state of the component is analysed by applying vibration measurement, then the result of the measurement may be disturbed by vibration of other components in the system. The statistical relation between the component state and the result of the condition monitoring measurement can be described with suitable probability models.

If we describe the wear propagation and the correlation between the degree of wear and the condition monitoring measurements by using stochastic models, it is obvious that the wear prediction problem reduces to a problem of stochastic filtering. The future state of the system is predicted by using the model describing the process dynamics and incomplete measurements from the system. The stochastic filtering models have been applied in the field of process control, where the best known model is the Kalman filter. The literature concerning Kalman filters and their applications is extensive; here we mention only an introductory textbook by Maybeck (1979). The general principles of stochastic filtering are also discussed in Liptser and Shiryaev (1978). It is also worth noticing that stochastic filtering is in fact a generalization of the Bayesian statistics.

The prediction of wear with stochastic filtering models is not a standard approach in practical engineering. Only a few articles have been published (see, for instance, Sarma et al., 1978).

The methods of condition monitoring or failure diagnostics are discussed widely in the literature. The basic methods are based on vibration measurements and oil analyses. In the vibration measurements the amplitude, power, and frequencies of the vibration are analysed with electrical devices and computers. The spectrum analysis in its various forms is a standard approach. Further, techniques based on acoustic emission are applied. The methods of condition monitoring are discussed in Chapters 3.1–3.3 of this book.

Oil analyses are based on the analysis of the wear particles from samples of the lubrication oil. The wear particles are analysed chemically, optically and electrically in order to identify the size distribution and chemical properties of the particles (see, for example, Aatola *et al.* (1989) and Chapters 3.1–3.3 of this book).

The aim of this chapter is to describe the mathematical background of wear prediction based on incomplete information from condition monitoring measurements. As an example we consider a simple wear model. Further, we discuss the problems connected to the wear prediction modelling and the possibilities of applying stochastic filtering models.

PRINCIPLES OF WEAR PREDICTION MODELS

Stochastic Modelling of Wear Evolution

The wear prediction based on condition monitoring measurements requires stochastic or statistical models for both the wear process and the measurements. The wear models describe how the component degrades and the measurement models relate the degree of wear of the results of condition monitoring. The prediction of wear is made possible by a combination of these models. This approach leads to stochastic filtering models.

We consider a single component which is subjected to wear. The degree of wear at time $t \geq 0$ is denoted by X_t. In principle, X_t may be a vector which describes the degrees of several types of wear of several parts of the component. Since the wear increases with time we must have:

$$X_{t+u} \geq X_t, \quad \forall t \geq 0, \quad u \geq 0 \tag{1}$$

The wear X_t may, for example, describe the total accumulated wear volume at the time t.

The evolution of the wear is stochastic and we have to describe it with a suitable stochastic process model. One approach is to relate X_t to another stochastic process, say Y_t, which is a solution of a stochastic differential equation:

$$dY_t = H(Y_t, t)\, dt + G(Y_t, t)\, d\beta_t \tag{2}$$

where

dY_t is the increment of Y_t at time $t(= Y_{t+dt} - Y_t)$,
$d\beta_t$ is the increment of a Brownian motion,
$H(Y_t, t)$, $G(Y_t, t)$ are functions satisfying some regularity conditions.

The solution of the above stochastic differential equation exists only in the sense of stochastic (Ito-)integrals (see Maybeck, 1979). Intuitively we may interpret eqn (2) as follows. The increment of Y_t depends on the present time t and the value of Y_t. However, the process is affected by a random disturbance, β_t. If the process is not disturbed, the evolution of Y_t follows an ordinary differential equation. In principle, given the statistical properties of the distrubance β_t, it is possible to determine the statistical properties of Y_t.

The solution of eqn (2) is not suitable for the description of the wear, since Y_t may be non-increasing. Because we assume eqn (1), the increments of the wear, dX_t, must be non-negative. In order to use Y_t in the modelling of the wear we have to relate it to X_t. One possibility is to model the wear rate by using Y_t. In that case:

$$X_t = \int_0^t \alpha(Y_t)\,dt \qquad (3)$$

where $\alpha(\cdot)$ is a non-negative function describing the wear rate.

In eqn (3) we may for example have

$$\alpha(Y_t) = a(Y_t - y_0)^2 \qquad (4)$$

where a is a positive constant. Y_t describes some physical phenomena, and according to eqn (4) the wear rate increases if Y_t deviates from the optimal conditions (y_0).

In the solution of eqn (2) the Ito-integral is evaluated over the Wiener measure. In many cases it may be feasible to evaluate the integral over a Poisson measure, which makes it possible to take into account some point process phenomena. In that case the wear rate may have jumps at some random time points.

In principle, we may deduce the probability distribution of X_t, $f_{X_t}(x)$, from the solution of eqn (2), and using eqn (3). In practice this may be very difficult. The formulation of the wear process through stochastic differential equation models is not necessary. Bogdanoff and Kozin (1985) have introduced so-called cumulative damage models, which can easily be modified for wear modelling purposes. In a later section of this chapter we apply a model which is in fact a simple cumulative damage model.

We can describe the wear process by writing directly the conditional probability distributions for X_{t+u} given X_t, $t \in [0, t]$, without using some other models:

$$f(X_{t+u}|X_t)\,dx = P(X_{t+u} \in dx|X_s, s \in [0, t]) \qquad (5)$$

The probability distributions of eqn (5) can be deduced from eqns (2) and (3), but it is also possible to construct them directly as we shall do in our example later in this chapter. If we assume that X_t is a Markov process, we may write eqn (5) in the form

$$P(X_{t+u} \in dx | X_s, s \in [0, t]) = P(X_{t+u} \in dx | X_t) \tag{6}$$

In eqns (5) and (6) we used the notation $X_t \in dx$ for $X_t \in (x, x + dx]$. The same notation will be used everywhere in this paper.

Given the initial wear, X_0, or its distribution, we can in principle determine the distribution for $X_t, t \geqslant 0$, by using the distributions of eqns (5) or (6).

The component fails when he wear exceeds some limit, i.e. the component is failed when $X_t \geqslant d$. The time to failure, T, is thus a random variable defined by

$$T = \inf\{t, X_t \geqslant d\} \tag{7}$$

If the wear is described with a vector variable, the definition of the failure conditions may be difficult. In that case the failure criteria may be constructed componentwise as follows. Let the components of X_t be X_{1t}, $X_{2t}, \ldots, X_{mt}$. The failure time T may be defined as the first time point where the largest component of X_t exceeds the wear limit:

$$T = \inf\{t, \max\{X_{it}, i = 1, \ldots, m\} \geqslant d\} \tag{8}$$

More generally, the failure time may be defined as the first time point where the (vector) wear process hits some set, $\mathscr{D}$, i.e.

$$T = \inf\{t, X_t \in \mathscr{D}\} \tag{9}$$

The distribution of T can be determined, for example, by using the conditional distributions of eqn (5) or (6). We denote the distribution of T, the lifetime distribution, with

$$G(t) = P(T \leqslant t) \tag{10}$$

If the component has not failed before time t, we can write the distribution of the remaining lifetime as the conditional distribution

$$P(T \leqslant s | t \geqslant t) = \frac{P(T \leqslant s)}{1 - P(T \leqslant t)}, \quad s \geqslant t \tag{11}$$

If the only information on the component state is that the component has not failed before some time point, we have to base our predictions of the remaining lifetime on the above distributions of eqns (10) and (11). If we have observed failure times of similar components, and if we make some mathematical assumptions on the observed failure times, we can base our predictions on those observations. In that case we must first construct a probability model for the past observations and use that model in predictions. This problem is discussed widely in the statistical literature.

The distributions given by eqns (10) and (11) may also be used in the optimization of preventive maintenance policies or replacement and repair of the component. In the literature there are many examples of this kind of optimization technique.

The probability models for X_t and T are the basic elements of the wear prediction models which must be combined with the models of the condition monitoring measurements in order to develop stochastic filtering models.

Stochastic Filtering Principle for Wear Prediction

The state of the component may be followed by making measurements which are in one way or another related to the degree of wear. The information obtained from the condition monitoring measurements can be used to predict the wear process more accurately than by applying directly the distributions given by eqns (10) and (11).

We assume that we can measure the value of a random variable, m_t, at any time point and that the value of m_t is related to the wear process X_t. We describe the relation between X_t and m_t with conditional probability distribution $h(\cdot|\cdot)$:

$$h(m_t|X_t = x_t)dm = P(m_t \in dm|X_t = x_t) \qquad (12)$$

We assume that

$$P(m_t \in dm|X_u, u \in [0, t]) = P(m_t \in dm|X_t) \qquad (13)$$

i.e., m_t does not depend on the earlier values of X_t.

Our basic problem is to say something about the past, present and future values of X_t after observing a series of measurements of the process $m_s, s \in [0, t]$. Mathematically, we have to determine the conditional probability distribution

$$f(X_s|m_u, u \in [0, t]) \, dx = P(X_s \in dx|m_u, u \in [0, t]) \qquad (14)$$

The process of determining the above distribution is called *estimation* of X_t if we are interested in the present value of X_t, *prediction* if we are interested in the future values of $X_s, s > t$, and *smoothing* if we are interested in the past values of $X_s, s \in [0, t)$.

In practice, the X_t may be predicted only on the basis of measurements made at discrete time points $0 \leqslant t_1 < t_2 < \cdots$. The continuous prediction requires the determination of the infinite-dimensional distributions of the processes m_t and X_t, which is also theoretically impossible,

We assume that X_t is a Markov process (for simplicity) with $X_0 = 0$, and that the first measurement is available at time point t_1. We may determine the distribution of X_t just before the time point t_1 given that the process starts from $X_0 = 0$ by using the wear process model: $P(X_{t_1 -} \in dx | X_0 = 0) = f(x_{t_1 -} | X_0 = 0) \, dx$. We use the measurement information at the time point in updating the distribution of X_{t_1} by applying the Bayes formula:

$$f(x_{t_1} | m_{t_1}) = \frac{h(m_{t_1} | x_{t_1 -}) f(x_{t_1 -} | X_0 = 0)}{\int h(m_{t_1} | x_{t_1 -}) f(x_{t_1 -} | X_0 = 0) \, dx_{t_1}} \tag{15}$$

The evolution of X_t in the time interval (t_1, t_2) may be determined using the above distribution and the wear process model:

$$f(x_t | m_{t_1}) = \int f(x_t | x_{t_1}, m_t) f(x_{t_1} | m_{t_1}) \, dx_{t_1}$$

$$= \int f(x_t | x_{t_1}) f(x_{t_1} | m_{t_1}) \, dx_{t_1}, \quad t \in (t_1, t_2) \tag{16}$$

in which we have assumed that the evolution of the wear does not depend on the measurements (i.e. $f(x_t | x_{t_1}, m_t) = f(x_t | x_{t_1})$ or equivalently X_t is independent of m_{t_1} given X_{t_1}). The distribution of X_t given m_{t_1} just before the second measurement at time point $t_2, f(x_{t_2 -} | m_{t_1})$, can be determined using eqn (16). When we substitute $f(x_{t_2 -} | m_{t_1})$ for $f(x_{t_1 -} | X_0 = 0)$, m_{t_2} for m_{t_1} in eqn (15), we obtain the distribution $f(x_{t_2} | m_{t_1}, m_{t_2})$. Continuing in a similar way we can update the distribution of X_t at any time point to solve the filtering problem.

Sometimes the observations m_t are related to the process Y_t upon which the wear process X_t depends. In that case we use eqn (2) to determine the transition probabilities for Y_t and use the same approach as above to predict Y_t. After that we use the predictions of Y_t to determine the distributions of the wear process X_t. This approach is applied in the following sections of this chapter where we discuss a simple wear prediction model.

A SIMPLE STOCHASTIC FILTERING MODEL FOR WEAR

Physical Background

In order to describe and predict wear it is useful to think of it developing gradually in several phases or regimes. Each phase of wear has its own wear rate and thus knowledge of the wear phase helps in evaluation of the future evolution of the wear process.

The wear regimes of mechanical components have been classified according to the mechanisms of particle formation, each associated with wear rate prognosis. Earlier it was customary to classify the wear rate merely as mild or severe, but the most recent classifications consist of several wear categories (Beerbower, 1980).

The wear rate has been generalized by means of the Archard wear equation,

$$V = KdW/P_m \qquad (17)$$

where K is the specific wear rate, d the distance travelled, W the load and P_m the penetration hardness of the softer material.

Most of the other tribological parameters have been included in the specific film thickness,

$$\Lambda = \xi/D \qquad (18)$$

where ξ is the elastohydrodynamic film thickness and D is the composite roughness of the surfaces, expressed as

$$D = \sqrt{D_1^2 + D_2^2} \qquad (19)$$

where D_1 and D_2 are the root-mean-square roughness of the two surfaces, or

$$D = 0.90(D_1 + D_2) \qquad (20)$$

where D_1 and D_2 are the centre-line-average values.

The elastohydrodynamic film thickness depends on many parameters, such as viscosity, velocity, pressure–viscosity coefficient, etc.

According to Beerbower (1974, 1976, 1980) any wear regime could be defined by characteristic values of K and Λ. Further (Beerbower, 1980), this is plausible, since eqn (13) provides a basis for estimating what fractions of the asperities are undergoing no strain, elastic strain and plastic strain under working conditions. At $\Lambda = 1$, about 50% of the asperities will be in plastic strain, while at $\Lambda = 4.5$ with ground surfaces only a minor proportion will undergo even elastic strain.

In the following we describe briefly the wear regimes discussed by
Beerbower (1980). Regime 1, named 'zero-wear' by Bayer *et al.* (1962) or
'elastohydrodynamic zero-wear prefatigue', consists of two parts. If
$\Lambda < 2\cdot5$, the duration of this regime is very short and it cannot even be
noticed in experiments; the transition is to regime 3. If, however, $\Lambda > 2\cdot5$
the prefatigue period may last for many years, and the transition is to
regime 2.

Regime 2, 'contact fatigue' or 'high-cycle fatigue', is generally recognized, but regime 3, 'adhesive wear', 'high-transfer', 'delamination' or
'low-cycle fatigue', is more controversial (see Beerbower, 1976). This
'low-cycle fatigue' regime refers to the kind of fatigue in which the cyclic
strain exceeds the elastic limit, so that cracks are initiated almost at once
and the time to failure depends on the propagation rate. The other
regimes, 4–6, are various kinds of corrosive wear, and the last regime is
'abrasive wear'.

Each of the wear regimes has its typical wear particles and typical
scars. Further, the wear rate is typical to each regime. By studying the
particle size distributions from the lubrication oil it is possible to give a
diagnosis on the state of wear of the component. Based on extensive data,
Beerbower (1980) presents the particle size distributions for the wear
regimes discussed above.

Beerbower (1980) suggests a simple method for the prognosis of wear.
First the wear regime is determined on the basis of wear particle
measurement. Then the appropriate specific wear rate is selected from
tabulated values and is used to estimate the remaining lifetime. This
approach is deterministic, and no stochastic features of wear are taken
into account.

In the following we shall discuss a stochastic model based on the 'wear
regime' thinking. Our model is a mathematical abstraction, and we
introduce it in order to study the possibility of applying stochastic
filtering models to the prediction of wear. The physical feasibility of the
model is not discussed. However, we believe that by modifying our
assumptions and by more careful analysis of experimental results, we can
also obtain practically significant results.

A Wear Model

We assume that the wear propagates in phases which are the counter-
parts of the wear regimes mentioned above. In the following we shall
speak of wear states instead of wear phases or regimes. The total number
of states is assumed to be n, and the process starts from state 1 and goes

through the states in a fixed order. We denote the state of the wear process at time point t by $\mathbf{s}_t$. The process $\mathbf{s}_t$ is in fact the counterpart of the process $\mathbf{Y}_t$ discussed earlier. We assume that the wear rate is specific to each state. The wear rate α_i in phase $i, i = 1, 2, \ldots, n$, is assumed to be a known constant.

The wear process, $\mathbf{s}_t$, is in state 1 over a random period of time, τ_1, and after that it jumps to state 2. The process goes through the states and stays in state i for a random time τ_i, until it reaches state n where it stays until the wear limit, X_{max}, is reached. The system may fail also in the earlier states, if the wear has been fast.

The wear volume, $\mathbf{X}_t$, at time t is a random variable, since the times spent in the states τ_i are random variables, $\mathbf{X}_t$ is related to the variables τ_i by the following equation:

$$\mathbf{X}_t = \sum_{i=1}^{j-1} \alpha_i \tau_i + \alpha_j \left(t - \sum_{i=1}^{j-1} \tau_i \right) \tag{21}$$

in which $j = $ largest 1 for which $\sum_{i=1}^{j-1} \tau_i < t$.

Figure 1 illustrates the evolution of wear and the process $\mathbf{s}_t$.

If we know the joint distribution of the random variables $\tau_1, \tau_2, \ldots, \tau_{n-1}$, we can determine the distribution of $\mathbf{X}_t$. In the following we shall assume that the τ_i's are independent random variables with exponential distributions

$$\tau_i \sim \exp(\lambda_i); \quad f_{\tau_i}(\tau) = \lambda_i\, e^{-\lambda_i \tau} \tag{22}$$

With this assumption $\mathbf{s}_t$ is a time-homogeneous Markov process with the state space $S = \{1, 2, \ldots, n\}$. The probabilities that the process is in state i given that it is in state 1 at time point $t = 0$, $P(\mathbf{s}_t = i | \mathbf{s}_0 = 1) = P_i(t)$, can be determined from the following equations:

$$\begin{aligned}
\dot{P}_1(t) &= -\lambda_1 P_1(t) \\
\dot{P}_2(t) &= \lambda_1 P_1(t) - \lambda_2 P_2(t) \\
&\;\;\vdots \\
\dot{P}_i(t) &= \lambda_{i-1} P_{i-1}(t) - \lambda_i P_i(t) \\
&\;\;\vdots \\
\dot{P}_n(t) &= \lambda_{n-1} P_{n-1}(t)
\end{aligned} \tag{23}$$

with $\sum_{i=1}^{n} P_i(t) = 1$, $P_1(0) = 1$.

Since the process is time-homogeneous, we can solve the transition probabilities $P(\mathbf{s}_{t+u} = j | \mathbf{s}_t = i) = P_{ij}(u, t) = P_{ij}(u)$ from the same differential equation simply by modifying the initial conditions and setting $P_i(0) = 1$. Analytical expressions for $P_{ij}(u)$ are easily found. If the λ_i's are distinct,

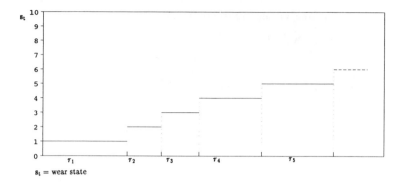

s_t = wear state

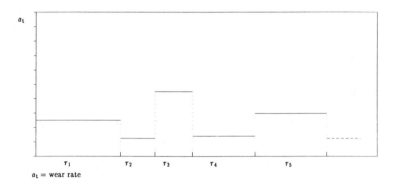

a_t = wear rate

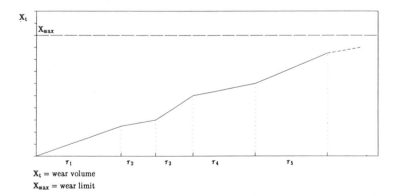

X_t = wear volume
X_{max} = wear limit

Fig. 1. The evolution of the wear process.

the transition probabilities are of the form

$$P_{ii}(u) = e^{-\lambda_i u}, \quad \text{for } i = 1, \ldots, n-1$$

$$P_{ik}(u) = \left(\prod_{j=i}^{k-1} \lambda_j\right) \sum_{j=i}^{k} \left(\prod_{\substack{l=i \\ l \neq j}}^{k} \frac{1}{\lambda_l - \lambda_j}\right) e^{-\lambda_j u}, \quad \text{for } k \neq i, \, k \leqslant n-1$$

(24)

$$P_{in}(u) = 1 - \sum_{j=i}^{n-1} P_{ij}(u)$$

$$P_{nn}(u) = 1$$

$$P_{ik}(u) = 0, \quad i > k$$

The transition probabilities can be determined by solving the differential equation (23) also when the λ_i's are not distinct. In that case they are not as simple as those given by eqns (24). Given the transition probabilities we can determine the probability distribution of s_t at any time point.

Filtering of the Wear Process

The condition monitoring measurements may, in the best case, give exact information on the state of the wear process, s_t, and by using the above transition probabilities we can give predictions on the future behaviour of the process. However, knowledge on the state of the process s_t does not reveal the lengths of the time periods over which the process occupies the earlier states, i.e. the exact values of the random variables τ_i are still unknown. Thus the measurements do not give exact information on the wear volume, X_t, at the present time and its future values.

The information that 'the wear process s_t is in state i at time point t' (= 'the wear has reached regime i') is denoted by $\{s_t = i\}$. By our assumptions the event $\{s_t = i\}$ can be expressed in terms of the random variables $\tau_j, j = 1, \ldots, n-1$:

$$\{s_t = i\} = \begin{cases} \left\{\sum_{j=1}^{i-1} \tau_j \leqslant t < \sum_{j=1}^{i} \tau_j\right\}, & \text{if } i > 1 \\ \{t < \tau_1\}, & \text{if } i = 1 \end{cases}$$

(25)

We use the information $\{s_t = i\}$ to update the joint distribution of the τ_i's. We assume first that the information $\{s_t = 1\}$ is obtained when the first condition monitoring measurement is made at time point t. The conditional joint distribution of interest is

$$f(\bar{\tau}|\{\mathbf{s}_t=i\})=\frac{P(\{\mathbf{s}_t=i\}|\bar{\tau})f_0(\bar{\tau})}{\displaystyle\int P(\{\mathbf{s}_t=i\}|\bar{\tau})f_0(\bar{\tau})\,\mathrm{d}\bar{\tau}} \tag{26}$$

where $\bar{\tau}=(\tau_1,\tau_2,\ldots,\tau_{n-1})$ and $f_0(\bar{\tau})$ is the joint (prior) distribution of $\bar{\tau}$ before the first condition monitoring measurement.

We can determine the distribution given by eqn (26) relatively easily for the first measurement. Since we assumed the independence and exponentiality of the τ_i's, their joint *a priori* distribution is

$$f_0(\bar{\tau})=\prod_{i=1}^{n-1}\lambda_i\,\mathrm{e}^{-\lambda_i\tau_i} \tag{27}$$

Combining eqns (26) and (27), and assuming that $i=1$, we have

$$f(\bar{\tau}|\{\mathbf{s}_t=1\})=f(\tau_1,\tau_2,\ldots,\tau_{n-1}|\{\mathbf{s}_t=1\})=0 \tag{28}$$

for $\tau_1<t$, and

$$f(\bar{\tau}|\{\mathbf{s}_t=1\})=f(\tau_1,\tau_2,\cdots,\tau_{n-1}|\{\mathbf{s}_t=1\})$$

$$=\frac{\displaystyle\prod_{i=1}^{n-1}\lambda_i\,\mathrm{e}^{-\lambda_i\tau_i}}{\displaystyle\int_0^\infty\int_0^\infty\cdots\int_t^\infty\prod_{i=1}^{n-1}\lambda_i\,\mathrm{e}^{-\lambda_i\tau_i}\,\mathrm{d}\tau_i}=\lambda_1\mathrm{e}^{-\lambda_1(\tau_1-t)}\prod_{i=2}^{n-1}\lambda_i\,\mathrm{e}^{-\lambda_i\tau_i}$$

$$=C_1(t)f_0(\bar{\tau}) \tag{29}$$

where

$$C_1(t)=\lambda_1\mathrm{e}^{\lambda_1 t} \tag{30}$$

The posterior distribution of $\bar{\tau}$ given $\{\mathbf{s}_t=1\}$ is of the above form due to the properties of the exponential distribution. The respective distributions given $\{\mathbf{s}_t=i\}$, $i\neq1$, are more difficult to determine. The event $\{\mathbf{s}_t=i\}$ restricts the domain of the random variables $\tau_1,\ldots,\tau_{n-1}$, as we can see from eqn (25). Thus the posterior distribution is the restriction of the prior distribution on the domain given in eqn (25).

The conditional distribution of $\bar{\tau}$ given $\{\mathbf{s}_t = i\}$ is

$$f(\bar{\tau}|\{\mathbf{s}_t = i\}) = \begin{cases} 0, & \text{if } \bar{\tau} \notin \mathcal{S}_i(t) \\ C_i(t)f_0(\bar{\tau}), & \text{if } \bar{\tau} \in \mathcal{S}_i(t) \end{cases} \tag{31}$$

where

$$\mathcal{S}_i(t) = \left\{ \bar{\tau} \left| \sum_{j=1}^{i-1} \tau_j \leqslant t < \sum_{j=1}^{i} \tau_j, \quad i > 1 \right. \right\} \tag{32}$$

and

$$C_i(t)^{-1} = \int_{\mathcal{S}_i(t)} \prod_{j=1}^{n-1} (\lambda_j e^{-\lambda_j \tau_j}) \, d\tau_1 \, d\tau_2 \ldots d\tau_{n-1} \tag{33}$$

The posterior distribution of $\bar{\tau}$ is the restriction of the prior distribution over the domain of integration in eqn (33). The integral in eqn (33) can be evaluated as follows. First we note that it is equal to the probability that the random variable $\xi_i = \tau_1 + \cdots + \tau_{i-1}$ is smaller than or equal to t and the random variable τ_i is larger than $t - \xi_i$, i.e.

$$\int_{\mathcal{S}_i(t)} \prod_{i=1}^{n-1} (\lambda_i e^{-\lambda_i \tau_i}) \, d\tau_1 \, d\tau_2 \ldots d\tau_{n-1} = P(\{\xi_i \leqslant t\} \cap \{\tau_i > t - \xi_i\}) \tag{34}$$

The density function of the random variable ξ_i can be determined as a convolution of the densities of $\tau_1, \ldots, \tau_{i-1}$. Thus we obtain

$$P(\{\xi_i \leqslant t\} \cap \{\tau_i > t - \xi_i\}) = \int_0^t g_{\xi_i}(\xi_i) e^{-\lambda_i(t - \xi_i)} \, d\xi_i \tag{35}$$

where $g_{\xi_i}(\xi_i)$ is the probability density of ξ_i.

The above distribution of $\bar{\tau}$ is based on the information obtained in the first condition monitoring measurement at time point t. Next we assume that a new measurement is made at a time point $v > t$.

The posterior distribution is given by

$$f(\bar{\tau}|\{\mathbf{s}_v = \mathbf{i}_v\}, \{\mathbf{s}_t = i\}) = \begin{cases} 0 & \text{if } \bar{\tau} \notin \mathcal{S}_{i_v}(v) \cap \mathcal{S}_i(t) \\ C(v, t, i, i_v)f_0(\bar{\tau}), & \text{if } \bar{\tau} \in \mathcal{S}_{i_v}(v) \cap \mathcal{S}_i(t) \end{cases} \tag{36}$$

where

$$C(v, t, i, i_v)^{-1} = \int_{\mathcal{S}_{i_v}(v) \cap \mathcal{S}_i(t)} f_0(\bar{\tau}) \, d\bar{\tau} \tag{37}$$

The posterior distributions given the results of several measurements can be evaluated respectively and we obtain the distribution

$$f(\bar{\tau}|\{s_{t_i}=i_1\},\ldots,\{s_{t_k}=i_k\})=\begin{cases}0 & \text{if } \bar{\tau}\notin \mathscr{S}(k)\\C(t_1,\ldots,t_k,i_1,\ldots,i_k)f_0(\bar{\tau}), & \text{if } \bar{\tau}\in \mathscr{S}(k)\end{cases} \tag{38}$$

where

$$\mathscr{S}(k)=\bigcap_{j=1}^{k}\mathscr{S}_{t_j}(i_j) \tag{39}$$

and

$$C(t_1,\ldots,t_k,i_1,\ldots,i_k)^{-1}=\int_{\mathscr{S}(k)}f_0(\bar{\tau})\,d\bar{\tau} \tag{40}$$

Depending on the number of the states of the wear process s_t, the evaluation of the posterior distribution given by eqn (40) may be rather difficult. However, the calculations are based on elementary calculus. The posterior distribution can be used in determining the distribution of accumulated wear, X_t, according to eqn (16), and thus a prediction of wear volume is obtained.

In many practical cases the measurement information is not exact, i.e. it is not possible to know the state of the wear process s_t exactly after obtaining the result of the condition monitoring measurement. This uncertainty can be modelled with a random variable m_t, which is correlated with the state of the wear process, s_t. In order to describe this we must postulate a set of conditional distributions for m_t given the state s_t. Accordingly, the measurement information is modelled by writing the conditional distributions, the measurement models, $h(m_t|s_t=i)$, $\forall i, t$.

In the following we assume that the distributions $h(m_t|s_t)$ do not depend on time t. This is a reasonable assumption, since the measurement methods are 'constant in time'. However, it is possible to assume that the distributions $h(m_t|s_t)$ depend on some unknown parameters which have a prior distribution. The prior distribution may be updated in the course of time by using the Bayes rule. In that case the distributions $h(m_t|s_t)$ are, in a way, time dependent, due to the gain of information. We shall not discuss this case here.

As described in the second section of this paper, we are interested in the conditional distribution of the state of the process s_t given the measurement information from the time interval $[0,t]$, $P(s_t=i|m_s, s\in[0,t])$. In the following we assume that the measurements are available at discrete time points $t_1, t_2, \ldots$ We obtain the conditional distribution of s_t given the measurement history by applying sequentially the transition probabilities of eqns (24), the measurement models and the Bayes rule.

The distribution of the wear process state $\mathbf{s}_t$ in the time interval $[0, t_1)$ can be determined using the transition probabilities of eqns (24). At time point t_1 we obtain the measurement value $\mathbf{m}_{t_1}$. We may use the measurement models, $g(\mathbf{m}_t|\mathbf{s}_t = i)$, in updating the distribution of $\mathbf{s}_{t_1}$ by using the Bayes rule, i.e. we may determine the conditional distribution of $\mathbf{s}_{t_1}$ given the measurement at time point t_1:

$$P(\mathbf{s}_{t_1} = i|\mathbf{m}_{t_1}) = \frac{h(\mathbf{m}_{t_1}|\mathbf{s}_{t_1-} = 1)P(\mathbf{s}_{t_1-} = i)}{\sum_{i=1}^{n} h(\mathbf{m}_{t_1}|\mathbf{s}_{t_1-} = i)P(\mathbf{s}_{t_1-} = i)} \qquad (41)$$

where $\mathbf{s}_{t_1-}$ is the state of the wear process just before time point t_1 and $P(\mathbf{s}_{t_1-} = i)$ is the corresponding probability. Because $\mathbf{s}_0 = 1$ with probability one, we can determine $P(\mathbf{s}_{t_1-} = i)$ using the transition probabilities of eqns (24):

$$P(\mathbf{s}_{t_1-} = i) = P_{1i}(t_1) \qquad (42)$$

The conditional distribution of $\mathbf{s}_t$ given $\mathbf{m}_{t_1}$ at any time point on the interval (t_1, t_2) is

$$P(\mathbf{s}_t = i|\mathbf{m}_{t_1}) = \sum_{j=1}^{i} P(\mathbf{s}_{t_1} = j|\mathbf{m}_{t_1})P_{ji}(t - t_1) \qquad (43)$$

At point t_2 we make another measurement, and using the distribution $P(\mathbf{s}_{t_2}|\mathbf{m}_{t_1})$ based on eqn (43) as a prior distribution we may determine the distribution $P(\mathbf{s}_{t_2}|\mathbf{m}_{t_1}, \mathbf{m}_{t_2})$. Continuing in this way we can update the distribution of $\mathbf{s}_t$ at any time point.

In order to estimate or predict the accumulated wear, $\mathbf{X}_t$, we must update also the joint distribution of $\tau_1, \tau_2, \ldots, \tau_{n-1}$ given the measurement history, i.e. we must evaluate the conditional distribution

$$f(\bar{\tau}|\mathbf{m}_{t_1}, \mathbf{m}_{t_2}, \ldots, \mathbf{m}_{t_m}) = f(\bar{\tau}|\bar{\mathbf{m}}_{t_m}) \qquad (44)$$

We cannot determine the distribution given by eqn (44) without making some further assumptions. If we have made only one measurement we may write, on the basis of the total probability

$$f(\bar{\tau}|\mathbf{m}_{t_1}) = \sum_{i=1}^{n} f(\bar{\tau}|\{\mathbf{s}_{t_i} = i\}, \mathbf{m}_{t_1})P(\{\mathbf{s}_{t_i} = i\}|\mathbf{m}_{t_1}) \qquad (45)$$

The difficulty in eqn (45) is the distribution $f(\bar{\tau}|\{\mathbf{s}_{t_i} = i\}, \mathbf{m}_{t_1})$. If we assume that $\bar{\tau}$ and $\mathbf{m}_{t_1}$ are independent given $\{\mathbf{s}_{t_i} = i\}$, or

$$f(\bar{\tau}|\{\mathbf{s}_{t_i} = i\}, \mathbf{m}_{t_1}) = f(\bar{\tau}|\{\mathbf{s}_{t_i} = i\}) \qquad (46)$$

we obtain

$$f(\bar{\tau}|\mathbf{m}_{t_1}) = \sum_{i=1}^{n} f(\bar{\tau}|\{\mathbf{s}_{t_i}=i\}) P(\{\mathbf{s}_{t_1}=i\}|\mathbf{m}_{t_1}) \qquad (47)$$

The distribution $f(\bar{\tau}|\{\mathbf{s}_{t_i}=i\})$ has the form given in eqns (31)–(35) and the conditional distribution of $\bar{\tau}$ given $\mathbf{m}_{t_1}$ can be evaluated.

The assumption given by eqn (46) has a practical interpretation. It means that the result of a measurement is independent of the time points where the wear process jumps from one state to another (given $\mathbf{s}_t$), and vice versa. In other words, the measurement does not disturb the wear process, which is a reasonable assumption.

Now our main interest is to determine the distribution given by eqn (44), Since we have determined the distributions of $f(\bar{\tau}|\mathbf{s}_{t_1}, \ldots, \mathbf{s}_{t_m})$ (see eqns (38)–(40)), we can calculate the distribution given by eqn (45), if we have a joint distribution for $(\mathbf{s}_{t_1}, \ldots, \mathbf{s}_{t_m})$ given the measurement history $(\mathbf{m}_{t_1}, \ldots, \mathbf{m}_{t_m})$. We determine this multidimensional distribution as follows.

The joint distribution of $(\mathbf{s}_{t_1}, \ldots, \mathbf{s}_{t_m}, \mathbf{m}_{t_1}, \ldots, \mathbf{m}_{t_m})$ is

$$P(\mathbf{s}_{t_1}, \ldots, \mathbf{s}_{t_m}, \mathbf{m}_{t_1}, \ldots, \mathbf{m}_{t_m})$$

$$= P(\mathbf{m}_{t_m}|\mathbf{s}_{t_1}, \ldots, \mathbf{s}_{t_m}, \mathbf{m}_{t_1}, \ldots, \mathbf{m}_{t_{m-1}}) \ldots P(\mathbf{s}_{t_2}|\mathbf{s}_{t_1}) P(m_{t_1}|\mathbf{s}_{t_1}) P(\mathbf{s}_{t_1}) \qquad (48)$$

$$= P(\mathbf{s}_{t_1}) P(\mathbf{m}_{t_1}|\mathbf{s}_{t_1}) \prod_{i=2}^{m} P(\mathbf{m}_{t_i}|\mathbf{s}_{t_i}) P(\mathbf{s}_{t_i}|\mathbf{s}_{t_{i-1}})$$

where we have assumed that $\mathbf{s}_{t_{i+1}}$ and $\mathbf{m}_{t_i}$ are independent given $\mathbf{s}_{t_i}$ (in other words that the measurement does not disturb the wear process). In eqns (48) $P(\mathbf{s}_{t_{i+1}}|\mathbf{s}_{t_i})$ is in fact the transition probability given in eqns (24). The probabilities $P(\mathbf{m}_{t_i}|\mathbf{s}_{t_i})$ are the measurement models $P(\mathbf{m}_{t_i}|\mathbf{s}_{t_i}) = h(\mathbf{m}_{t_i}|\mathbf{s}_{t_i})$.

The conditional distribution of $(\mathbf{s}_{t_1}, \ldots, \mathbf{s}_{t_m})$ given $(\mathbf{m}_{t_1}, \ldots, \mathbf{m}_{t_m})$ is

$$P(\mathbf{s}_{t_1}, \ldots, \mathbf{s}_{t_m}|\mathbf{m}_{t_1}, \ldots, \mathbf{m}_{t_m})$$

$$= C_{sm}(t_1, \ldots, t_m) P(\mathbf{s}_{t_1}) P(\mathbf{m}_{t_1}|\mathbf{s}_{t_1}) \prod_{i=2}^{m} P(\mathbf{m}_{t_i}|\mathbf{s}_{t_i}) P(\mathbf{s}_{t_i}|\mathbf{s}_{t_{i-1}}) \qquad (49)$$

where

$$C_{sm}(t_1, \ldots, t_m)^{-1}$$

$$= \sum_{\{\mathbf{s}_{t_1}, \ldots, \mathbf{s}_{t_m}\} \in \{1, \ldots, n\}} P(\mathbf{s}_{t_1}) P(\mathbf{m}_{t_1}|\mathbf{s}_{t_1}) \prod_{i=2}^{m} P(\mathbf{m}_{t_i}|\mathbf{s}_{t_i}) P(\mathbf{s}_{t_i}|\mathbf{s}_{t_{i-1}}) \qquad (50)$$

Using the rule of total probability we may now write the distribution $f(\bar{\tau}|\mathbf{m}_{t_1}, \mathbf{m}_{t_2}, \ldots, \mathbf{m}_{t_m}) = f(\bar{\tau}|\bar{\mathbf{m}}_{t_m})$ in the form

$$f(\bar{\tau}|\bar{\mathbf{m}}_{t_m}) = \sum_{s_{t_1}, \ldots, s_{t_m} \in \{1, \ldots, n\}} f(\bar{\tau}|s_{t_1}, \ldots, s_{t_m}) P(s_{t_1}, \ldots, s_{t_m}|\mathbf{m}_{t_1}, \ldots, \mathbf{m}_{t_m}) \quad (51)$$

In order to determine the distribution given by eqn (51) we had to construct the distribution $P(s_{t_1}, \ldots, s_{t_m}|\mathbf{m}_{t_1}, \ldots, \mathbf{m}_{t_m})$, i.e. we had to smooth the process s_t on the basis of the information from the measurements. This was possible because of the simplifying assumptions. In general cases the calculations would have been very complicated.

Prediction of Accumulated Wear

In the last section we determined some conditional distributions which are needed in the estimation or prediction of the accumulated wear. In practice we are not necessarily interested in the distribution of the wear volume. Suitable point estimates may be more useful. A suitable point estimate for the wear volume at some point is the conditional expectation of $\mathbf{X}_t$, given the measurements

$$\hat{\mathbf{X}}_{t_m} = E(\mathbf{X}_{t_m}|\bar{\mathbf{m}}_{t_m}) = \int S(\boldsymbol{\alpha}, j) f(\bar{\tau}|\bar{\mathbf{m}}_{t_m}) \, d\bar{\tau} \quad (52)$$

where

$$S(\boldsymbol{\alpha}, j) = \sum_{i=1}^{j-1} \alpha_i \tau_i + \alpha_j \left(t_m - \sum_{i=1}^{j-1} \tau_i \right) \quad (53)$$

The above expected value describes the wear volume at time point t_m, where the most recent condition monitoring measurement is made. It does not describe the future evolution of wear. The future accumulation of wear depends on the state of the wear process, s_{t_m}. We have constructed the conditional distribution of s_{t_m} given the measurements (see eqns (42) and (43)), and we apply it in the evaluation of the expected wear volume $\mathbf{X}_{t_m+u}, u \geqslant 0$.

We write the conditional expected value of $\mathbf{X}_{t_m+u}$ as

$$E(\mathbf{X}_{t_m+u}|\bar{\mathbf{m}}_{t_m}) = E(\mathbf{X}_{t_m}|\bar{\mathbf{m}}_{t_m}) + E(\mathbf{X}_{t_m+u} - \mathbf{X}_{t_m}|\bar{\mathbf{m}}_{t_m}) \quad (54)$$

The first expected value in the right-hand side of eqn (54) is given in eqns (52) and (53). The second expected value describes the increment of wear during the period $(t_m, t_m + u]$ and we write it as

$$E(\mathbf{X}_{t_m+u} - \mathbf{X}_{t_m}|\bar{\mathbf{m}}_{t_m}) = \sum_{i=1}^{n} E(\mathbf{X}_{t_m+u} - \mathbf{X}_{t_m}|\mathbf{s}_{t_m} = i)P(\mathbf{s}_{t_m} = i|\bar{\mathbf{m}}_{t_m}) \quad (55)$$

We may evaluate the expectation $E(\mathbf{X}_{t_m+u} - \mathbf{X}_{t_m}|\mathbf{s}_{t_m} = i)$ by applying the probability model of $\mathbf{s}_t$ and the relationship between $\mathbf{X}_t$ and $\mathbf{s}_t$. The expected value $E(\mathbf{X}_{t_m+u} - \mathbf{X}_{t_m}|\mathbf{s}_{t_m} = i)$ has a very complicated expression which is not given here.

Validation of the Stochastic Wear Model

The assumptions behind our wear model seem to be feasible. However, in order to apply the model in practical situations, the validity of the assumptions should be analysed. This requires a lot of experimental studies, which may be rather expensive. Until now no experiments seem to be suitable for the validation of the assumptions. This is due to the structure of earlier models which are not predictive in the same sense as our model. Another reason for the lack of suitable experimental data is the impossibility of doing measurements which give both the actual state of the wear and the value of the condition monitoring signal. This is needed when we want to establish the correlation between the measurement signal $(\mathbf{m}_t)$ and the state of the wear process ($\mathbf{s}_t$ or $\mathbf{X}_t$), i.e. the distribution $h(\mathbf{m}_t|\mathbf{s}_t)$ in our model.

The basic assumption of our model is that wear propagates in a phased way, and in each phase the wear rate is constant. The validity of this assumption can be questioned, but if we increase the number of wear phases we can describe almost any kind of wear process exactly enough. The length of time which the wear process spends in each phase cannot be measured or evaluated directly. Thus it is feasible to model it as a random variable, the distribution of which should be determined on the basis of experimental data.

In our model we assumed exponential distributions for the lengths of the wear phases. This assumption is probably unrealistic, and our other assumption, the independence of those random variables, is very questionable. We may abandon these assumptions, but only at the expense of the model complexity. Another possibility is to model directly the phase transition probabilities and use them in the estimation of the posterior distributions of the change points.

On the basis of our model it is possible to plan experiments, which help in evaluation of the validity of the model assumptions. The planning of the experiments is a very difficult task. The experiments should be economically optimal and they should yield the estimates of the model parameters and identify the possible flaws of the model assumptions.

POSSIBLE APPLICATIONS OF THE MODEL

The basic aim of our model is to give a better estimate for the component's residual life on the basis of measurements. The principles of this estimation are described above. Depending on the propagation of the wear process this prediction may be efficient or inefficient. The efficiency of prediction based on different monitoring principles can be compared with the model.

The conditional distribution of residual life can be used in economically optimal replacement of the component. This optimization problem can be solved with standard approaches of stochastic optimization. A similar approach can be used in the optimization of the maintenance of the component.

Usually it is not possible to monitor the component continuously and the measurements must be done at selected time points. In some cases the measurements may be expensive and thus the scheduling of measurements leads to an optimization problem. Our model is simple enough to make this kind of optimization possible.

The behaviour of the wear process determines whether the condition monitoring measurements will give any useful information for decision making. If the observed information is not strongly correlated to the state of the component it is of no use applying the condition monitoring system. Using our model it is possible to compare theoretically the usefulness of different condition monitoring measurements. Thus it is possible to optimize the monitoring principles also in this sense.

In practical applications we should be able to evaluate the essential distributions in parametric or closed forms, which may lead to complicated calculations. These problems can be avoided by discretizing the distributions. Although the discretized approximations are not exact, the results are still useful in practice.

In the above we have considered only a limited set of possible applications of our model. The applications depend on the task where the component is used and in every case the resulting optimization problems are different. The validity of the model determines the usefulness of the optimal policies derived from the model, and thus the first task before the applications is the validation of the model.

Usually the prediction of wear or residual lifetime of a component is not based on condition monitoring measurements. One reason for this has been the lack of suitable models. Here we have discussed the application of stochastic filtering for this purpose. Based on this limited study we find it a natural approach to link the condition monitoring with probabilistic reliability predictions. Our model here is based on a simplified probabilistic description of wear. The filtering formulae were extremely complicated even in this simple case. More realistic models would probably lead to mathematical difficulties. In order to make the models practical we have to develop both the models and effective computational algorithms.

REFERENCES

Aatola, S., Kerkkänen, K., Leskinen, R. & Linjama, J. (1989). Methods of monitoring gearbox condition under lifetime testing. *VTT Research Repots No. 596*, Technical Research Centre of Finland, Espoo (in Finnish).

Bayer, R.G. *et al.* (1962). Engineering model for wear. *Wear*, **32**, 239–49.

Beerbower, A. (1974). *Mechanical failure prognosis through oil debris monitoring.* USAAVLABS TR74-100, US Army Air Mobility Research and Development Laboratory, Fort Eustis, VA.

Beerbower, A. (1976). Spectrometry and other analysis tools for failure prognosis. *Lubr. Eng.*, **32**, 285–93.

Beerbower, A. (1980). Wear rate prognosis through particle size distribution. *35th Annual Meeting AISLE*, Anaheim, CA, 5–8 May, 1980.

Bogdanoff, J.L. & Kozin, F. (1985). *Probabilistic Models of Cumulative Damage.* John Wiley, New York.

Liptser, R.S. & Shiryaev, A.N. (1978). *Statistics of Random Processes*, Vols I–II. Springer–Verlag, New York, Heidelberg and Berlin.

Maybeck, P.S. (1979). *Stochastic Models Estimation and Control*, Vols. 1–2. Academic Press, New York, San Francisco and London.

Sarma, V.V.S., Kunhikrishnan, K.V. & Ramchand, K. (1978). A decision theory model for health monitoring of aeroengines. *J. Aircraft*, **16**(3), 222–4.

PART 4

Operational reliability

4.1

A Structure and Some Tools for Assurance of Industrial Availability Performance

REIDAR ØSTVIK

*SINTEF, The Foundation for Scientific and Industrial Research
at the Norwegian Institute of Technology, N-7034 Trondheim, Norway*

ABSTRACT

This chapter presents some background for, and the outline of, an industrial maintenance management tool developed for PC use in assessment and planning of maintenance programmes for production equipment. The basis for these programmes starts at the top management definition of company objectives, plans and needs, and ends at the ten-point logical steps analysis of the RCM reliability centred maintenance structure. The aim is to ensure high production quality and availability, together with safety, at a cost-efficient maintenance achievement.

INTRODUCTION

Establishing the optimum maintenance function for a technical system may be quite a complex task, because it very much depends on what is understood by the term 'maintenance function' for this particular application. This will vary for different technical cases of actual maintenance, and there will be different approaches to the same situation, both between companies and between managers.

The importance of this problem has lately been accentuated through an increase in attention, both from a practical, industrial management point of view, and through scientific involvement in development of models and structured approaches to the problem.

One contribution is presented by Moubray (1988), who has given an interesting overview over the last three 'generations' of industrial approach to the maintenance function. Chapter 4.4 of the present book describes an analytical tool for visualization of the management efforts put into the performance of maintenance tasks to be used for setting up a balanced and efficient maintenance strategy. Chapter 4.3 presents an approach to a decision support system for maintenance planning based upon the interaction between a reliability model and the strategies chosen for operation and maintenance.

The contents of the maintenance concept for an industrially oriented installation will, for example, depend upon

— The size and technical nature of the activity/installation
— Perspectives and demands set up by the top management
— Goals and strategies set by the maintenance management
— Special needs and demands defined for the installation

To exemplify the spectrum of variation in technical activities and installations for which maintenance has to be considered, one may mention the following relevant cases:

— An engineering industry making mechanical components in small series with machine tools, welding and manual work. In this case there will be only a minor difference between production and maintenance.
— A larger process production plant, fully automated, working with continuous 24-hour production, where local failures may seriously influence total production or safety. Keywords for maintenance will under such circumstances be production availability and safety.
— A car for public and private transport, made in large series for variable use by drivers with variable skills. For such large numbers of dissimilar units, maintainability and freedom from maintenance should be given serious consideration from the manufacturer during design and product development.
— A satellite, or a subsea oil production unit, given very high priority for reliability. Such installations usually have very limited availability for maintenance, and require the use of redundancy to satisfy reliability.
— An electronic instrument or apparatus, where functional capability depends on the coordinated function of a number of electronic circuits and components. Maintenance typically in this case is fault finding by procedure, and replacement of components.

To concentrate the scope of a model, the approach will mainly be related to production plants and systems with process type production.

Some examples of central tasks in a maintenance function are:

— Ensure capacity for production equipment
— Ensure availability for production equipment
— Ensure correct and stable production quality
— Ensure acceptable work environment safety
— Guarantee the function of stand-by equipment
— Minimize 'trouble' connected with use of equipment
— Satisfy hygienic and aesthetic norms and demands
— Keep maintenance costs within acceptable limits
— Minimize life cycle costs for equipment

The aim of this chapter is to present a model and the outline of a PC program for use in a maintenance function to assist in the design and reassessment of efficient maintenance programmmes for important production equipment. The objective is to ensure that individual demands and priorities are correctly taken care of in work tasks and frequencies, and with the proper methodology and competence. The model also gives good support for the identification of a cost-efficient spare parts storing programme, where the numbers of spares on stock should be based on an assessment of the cost of *not* keeping them in store versus the cost of keeping them.

LAYOUT OF MODEL

The model for a maintenance function has the layout shown in Fig. 1, which will be further detailed and discussed in the subsequent sections of this chapter.

SETTING GOALS FOR PRODUCTION EQUIPMENT AVAILABILITY

General

As illustrated in the introduction, the demands on the maintenance function will vary considerably from case to case and from time to time.

The disposition of the present model is that it is based on a defined

Fig. 1. The model for a maintenance function.

company structure of objectives, demands and plans. This structure starts with a definition of the position of the company in its external environment of markets, customers, and sales contracts and obligations, to prepare for the commercial situation. In addition, each company has its own characteristic internal situation influenced by restraints and limitations, facts and data for production resources.

To develop and to reconsider the company's overall objectives in due contact with the external and the internal situation is a work task for the top management in the company. In addition these objectives must be supplemented by a strategy to fulfil the intentions.

The management responsible for the function of the production equipment resources must enable the best possible utilization of these resources in order to fulfil the obligations. This utilization can be defined as the concept of availability performance assurance.

Superior Goals and Strategies

To identify the demands to be set on the production resources, some market related questions must be asked:

— Which markets are planned for the company for the next few years?
  - International
  - Domestic
— How will these markets develop?
  - Increase
  - Stay stable
  - Decrease
— Which are the plans for the company in these markets?
  - Keep its market share of X production units
  - Increase its market share from A to B
  - Decrease its market share from A to C
— Under which economic basis should these markets be served?
  - $X\%$ Profitability level
— Which demands must consequentially be set for the production resources?
  - Continuous production to an open market
  - Committed to concrete contracts of delivery
  - Reserve capacity, resources oversized
  - Hard-times situation, costs must be minimized
  - An annual production increase of $X\%$
  - Demands given for defined quality improvements

The answers to these questions may form the overall goals for markets, production targets and economic results.

The next task should be to form the company strategy for reaching these goals. Keywords for a strategy may be found in this list:

— Product price
— Product design
— Product quality
— Internal productivity
— Equipment availability
— Quality assurance
— Cost control

Goals for Availability Performance

A number of well-known terms, partly with minor interpretational differences between them, have been in use to describe long-term functions of production assets. Examples of terms are:

— Production equipment availability
— Production regularity
— Production capacity
— Production quality
— Technical safety
— Equipment function capability
— Time and resources used for maintenance
— Ratio of planned to unplanned maintenance
— Equipment maintainability
— Production losses/maintenance costs
— Life cycle costs

Most of these factors can, in a positive or negative version, be measured or calculated, and they will all be measures of the efficiency of a maintenance function. The best way to enable a comparison between such parameters is through a conversion of the parameters to economic losses and costs. Examples are:

Production loss costs:

— Loss through unavailability of production equipment
— Loss through broken delivery contracts
— Loss through reduced market share
— Loss through reduced price or scrapping due to inferior product quality

Maintenance costs:

— Time spent by in-house maintenance personnel
— Time spent by hired maintenance personnel
— Time spent on investigation of production problems
— Spare parts and equipment replacement
— Consumption and use of other maintenance resources

With the overall goals for market share, production targets and economic results defined, there is time for introduction of some new enquiries. These questions relate to probable availability performance and costs, consequences of the designated goals, and the actual strategy to fulfil them.

— What will be the capacity and availability needed for production equipment in future?
— Can particular demands regarding availability, capacity or quality assurance be identified for any equipment?
— Can any particular failure problems which must be avoided be foreseen?
— Which are the most important losses and costs connected to the function of production equipment with regard to fulfilment of the objectives?

The answers to these questions form a basis for the formulation of goals for equipment capacity, production quality, and availability, bearing in mind the need for quantitative values, which are important in the determination of production control and follow-up.

GOALS AND MAIN STRATEGIES FOR MAINTENANCE

The values stated as goals for the equipment availability, capacity and production quality form the basis for some major questions about maintenance, which are important for the tailoring of the maintenance function.

Consequences on the maintenace function of demands defined for equipment availability are as follows:

— Give details on the individual weight given to production loss and to maintenance cost
— Give details on individual importance and priority between production equipment units
— Which maintenance strategy should be chosen for an optimum solution for various equipment?
— How should mantainability be ensured in purchase and design of new production systems?
— Which organizational principles should be applied to reach a cost-efficient and dynamic maintenance function?
— Which are the general and special demands to be imposed on competence and training?
— Which are the technical hardware, instrumentation and analytical tools needed for maintenance?

The answers to these questions will be important contributions to the design of goals, strategies and technical support for the maintenance function.

NEED-BASED, RELIABILITY CENTRED MAINTENANCE

General Comments

The definition of goals and strategies for production and equipment availability and for the maintenance function should be a typical management work task to be performed in direct contact between production, maintenance and general management in a company. The identification of general resources for use in the maintenance function should, on the other hand, mainly be the responsibility of the maintenance management levels.

The contents of maintenance programmes for specific production equipment have traditionally been defined on the basis of a number of more or less structured methods.

One of the purposes of reliability centred maintenance is to reduce the amount of unplanned, acute maintenance for cases where this influences availability (Moss, 1985). A maintenance function built to handle high priority work tasks through planned actions will have a stabilizing effect on the work situation, without the frequent and acute variations, and with reduced time pressure.

The right level of action depends on the consequences of not performing any preventive action, as compared to the effects of possible achievements. The answers to these questions will not be obvious, and the solutions chosen should always be reassessed and adjusted after some time, when practical experience has been gained.

One criterion for optimization of programmes, methods and resources of the maintenance function should be that these are dynamically adjusted to the present situation and needs. Solutions to equipment problems through a rigid, static maintenance methodology usually give low value for money. This is equally important with regard to the profile and quality of human resources and competence available. One area of importance is, for instance, relevant competence in condition monitoring methodology and diagnosis of equipment failures.

The following sections give an outline of a computer based analysis programme developed for the design of need-based, reliability centred preventive maintenance for production equipment (Østvik & Thuestad, 1990). The programme is based on assessment of equipment priority, system reliability, actual failure modes for the present application, and relevant maintenance methodology available.

The main parts of this programme concern

— Goals and strategies as a basis for analysis
— Description of the system under analysis
— Assessment of failure problems
— Preventive maintenance programme analysis

DECISION BASIS

Goals and Strategies as a Basis for Analysis

Definitions and specifications should, depending on the actual situation under analysis, be given for the following topics:

— General objectives for the production system
— Goals for production availability performance
— Goals for the maintenance function
— Strategy to be applied for reaching maintenance goals
— Reliability, availability for the production equipment
— Maintainability for the production equipment
— Maintenance support for the production equipment

Goals and demands should, if possible, be given in quantitative terms to enable follow-up and control to ensure that the development satisfies the given objectives.

An analysis as described can be performed at different stages during the life of a technical system. If it is in the startup of a plant, it may be necessary to give definitions of all parameters listed above. If the analysis is performed at a later stage, and is limited to a new piece of equipment, or is a repetition of an earlier analysis to include additional data from practical experience with a system, the last three parameters on the list will be the most important terms for evaluation. In many cases, however, technical organizations have not paid very much attention to any detailed clarification of their overall goals and demands, which are an important basis for management and planning of practical day-to-day activities.

Technical System Description and Structuring

The system description involves the following possible activities:

— Definition of system limits
— System hierarchy
— System network

If the unit which is under analysis is of a complex nature, it is important to define the limits of the system under consideration. This definition includes a description both of physical details to be included in the system, and of significant factors influencing the performance, introduced, for example, through operation or maloperation, and through maintenance.

The hierarchical way of describing a system into subsystems, units, components and parts may be useful in many ways. The hierarchy forms a tree structure of the whole system, developed by breaking the product down into successively lower-level assemblies, until all parts have been included. For the build-up of the hierarchy tree, general advice is to give more weight to functional connections than to mechanical bonds.

A system network is another tool for system description which gives a practical picture of systems built by multiple elements in a series/parallel type of structure, where system availability is very much influenced by the criticality of the positions of possible failing components. This will naturally influence the priority to be given to the individual components with regard to maintenance power offered for system function.

Investigation of Failure Problems

The process of defining and structuring a system itself provides valuable knowledge about system effects of possible failures. Usually the following methods and resources are used for drawing a picture of the reliability situation:

— Preliminary hazards analysis on system level
— Failure information
— Failure data
— FMECA

The preliminary hazards analysis is in the computer program arranged as a database with the following types of data:

— System element

— Subsystem
— Failure occurrence
— Influencing factors
— Consequences

It is important to uncover a picture of the most significant possible occurrences or conditions which influence system function and production availability. An assessment should include problems known through earlier experience with the system or similar conditions and work tasks which may have negative effects. Methods of elimination or control of these problems should also be registered.

The results from an analysis will not be better than the quality of the data and the information used in the analysis. These should therefore be given due consideration for assurance of quality and relevance. The difference between 'information' and 'data' as presented in this paper is that 'information' is mainly qualitative, static or verbal system information, while 'data' is quantitative, dynamic system information, such as failure data.

Failure Mode, Effects and Criticality Analysis (FMECA)

The last point in the failure investigation is to perform the Failure Mode, Effects and Criticality Analysis (FMECA), which shall be used as the basis for determining the relevant preventive actions.

The problems and failures which, through assessment and analysis, have been shown to be the most important for disturbance of system function, should be analysed in a FMECA to uncover the conditions and deterioration mechanisms which influence the life of the components.

One part of this FMECA is arranged to evaluate the criticality of each mode through an assessment of the probability of occurrence of the mode under investigation, and through an assessment of the severity of possible consequences. This is to be used as a basis for decision about the modes to be surveyed for preventive maintenance analysis. The valuation is performed through multiplication of quantified factors related to the two parameters.

The FMECA is in the computer program arranged as a database, to be sorted and rearranged as needed.

Analysis for Relevant, Efficient Maintenance

The last phase of the analysis is to decide on a balanced preventive maintenance programme to handle the failures and problems which threaten the objectives and demands defined beforehand. This is done by answering, for each mode given priority in the valuation of criticality, up to ten interrelated questions in a logical step analysis.

The following are the questions asked in the RCM sequence:

— Can function degradation or loss resulting from this failure mode be deferred by servicing?
— Is function degradation evident to the operator during routine operation?
— Is function failure evident to the operator during routine operation?
— Can the hidden function be verified during routine checking?
— Does the failure degrade safety significantly?
— Does the failure reduce availability below an acceptable level?
— Does the failure increase life cycle cost above the level necessary for prevention through maintenance?
— Does the failure rate increase substantially with operating or calendar time?
— Can the remaining safe, useful life be assessed?
— Is loss of function attributable to a limited life failure source?

The programme includes comments and ideas for every 'Yes' and 'No' answer, and the sequence systematically presents requirements and possible solutions for relevant maintenance actions. If no such action is found, one possible solution suggested is redesign, either to prevent the failure, or to adjust the preventive maintenance. Depending on the consequences of a possible failure, it may also be recommended that the mode be handled by corrective maintenance.

A printout gives the results of the question sequence arranged as a programme for preventive maintenance for the equipment.

CONCLUSION

This chapter has presented the outline of a computerized tool for maintenance management and planning. The tool has been designed for assistance in setting up efficient maintenance programmes aimed at handling technical problems and serving production equipment on the basis of their individual needs, position and criticality.

The professional basis for the tool is the following central criteria for efficient maintenance:

— Priorities and programmes in maintenance are results of a company structure of goals and strategies, where needs and demands in availability performance assurance form the basis for maintenance actions.
— No preventive maintenance action should be performed unless it causes an improvement in availability, safety or life cycle cost.
— The maintenance function of the plant should be dynamically adjusted for application of efficient preventive maintenance, including condition monitoring.
— Analysis and decision for efficient preventive maintenance should not be a one-off exercise for each piece of equipment, but ideally should be performed the first time under planning and preparation for production and repeated after some time when practical experience has been gained and relevant data about failure problems have been collected.

REFERENCES

Moss, M.A. (1985). *Designing for Minimal Maintenance Expense. The Practical Application of Reliability and Maintainability.* Marcel Dekker, New York.
Moubray, J. (1988). Maintenance management. The third generation. In *Euro Maintenance 88*, Helsinki, 24–27 May.
Østvik, R. & Thuestad, L. (1990). *Driftssikkerhetsstyrt Vedlikehold. Omtale av Analyseprogram* (Reliability Centred Maintenance. Description of Analysis Programme). SINTEF Report STF 20 A90003. (In Norwegian.)

4.2

Information Flow in a Decision Support System for Maintenance Planning

JETTE L. PAULSEN and KURT LAURIDSEN

Risø National Laboratory, DK-4000 Roskilde, Denmark

ABSTRACT

The concept of a reliability centred decision support system for maintenance planning is described. The concept is based on a set of reliability models of the plant in question, and the chapter describes the change and the details behind the change of reliability of a plant during its lifetime, and how to use this information in maintenance planning.

INTRODUCTION

In order to improve the maintenance planning of industrial plants it is necessary to increase the quality and quantity of information available to the planners. The present paper describes the information flow in a decision support system being designed under two projects in the Nordic Terotechnology Programme: 'A Technical/Economic System for Maintenance in Industrial Plants' and 'Exchange of Information between Designer and User of Industrial Plants'. The main idea behind these projects is to develop a software tool for improving the operation and maintenance planning by supervising the current reliability state of the plant and its components, and to use this information to set up a decision support system (DSS) for the maintenance planners. Furthermore, a differentiated user interface is going to serve several members of the organizational hierarchy, such as managers, operational staff, and maintenance workers with information and advice suited for their specific needs.

A number of different types of information are flowing in such a system:

— Measured values of parameters influencing component and plant reliability, e.g. vibrations, wear, excessive temperatures, power consumption, etc.
— Failure and repair reports input by the staff
— Results of statistical calculations
— Requests for calculations or other information
— Results of calculations with a reliability model of the plant
— Advice from the DSS
— Operational and maintenance strategies

The various types of information need different processing and presentation. Data measured in the plant most often will have to be preprocessed and evaluated before they can be used for assessing the change in reliability. It is envisaged that an 'expert system' will be utilized for this task. Most of the information types mentioned above will, however, involve communication with the human operator. Therefore, a key point in the project is the creation of interfaces which ensure an easy exchange of information.

A central element in the system is a 'Dynamic History Data Base' (DHDB) containing all information about the maintenance and operational history of the plant. Much of the information exchange between users and system as well as internally in the system happens via the DHDB.

Depending upon the flow routes the information can roughly be divided into three categories:

(1) Information input to the system
(2) Information output from the system
(3) Information flowing between parts of the system

The different categories of information will be described in further detail in the following sections. The system concept is shown in Fig. 1.

RELIABILITY MODELS

The most important element of the software system is the reliability models to which most of the input information is eventually directed. The system must contain several models, one for each event which is specified as 'critical'.

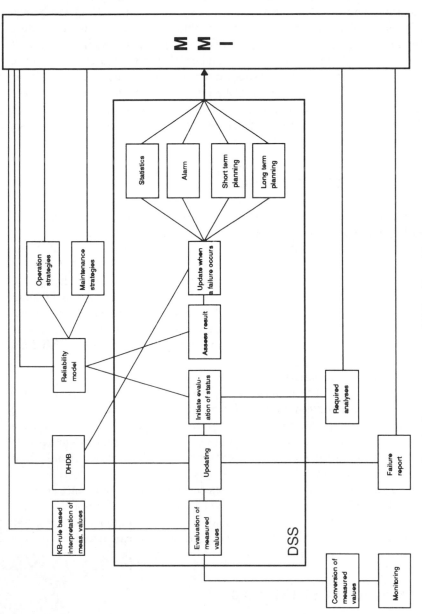

Fig. 1. System concept. MMI = Man–Machine Interface.

The reliability models can be generated automatically by a fault tree generator developed at Risø (Taylor, 1982). The output from the generator is a reliability model which is able to evaluate the up-to-date reliability of the plant, its components and subsystems. As input the fault tree model will need values of a number of parameters such as failure rates, repair times, test intervals, and restoration times. The model is plant and event specific and must be updated at any change of the plant or in case new 'critical' events are to be added to the system. Such changes may also give rise to a reassessment of the operational experience data collected in the data base (see later section in this chapter).

MAINTENANCE STRATEGIES

The maintenance plans and strategies are normally determined before the initial start-up of the plant. If a reliability analysis of the plant or the process is needed this is usually also required before the initial start-up. Maintenance plans are changed during the life of the plant due to different circumstances, such as breakdown of components, changes to new components, changes of plant configuration, lack of the relevant competence and skill at the scheduled time for maintenance of special components, etc., but the resulting change in reliability of the plant due to those changes is normally based on engineering judgement rather than on calculations.

Computer programs for maintenance planning are available on the software market. Such programs give assistance in the maintenance task scheduling, calculation of cost for maintenance operations, recording changes in the plant, generating reports, etc. As output from such a maintenance program the information on the scheduled changes in configuration of the plant can be extracted, which is an important input to the reliability model generator.

The system being developed enables checking the maintenance strategy from a reliability point of view, which could be of importance for operational safety. If there is a change in the maintenance plan, the resulting change in reliability of the plant can be calculated before the change is carried out.

OPERATIONAL STRATEGIES

Planning of operational strategies depends on the type of production. Some plants have plans for several years, and others only for one week at a time. Maintenance plans are dependent on the operational strategies. The influence of the operational strategies on the reliability model is the influence of changes to the maintenance plan due to changes of the planned configuration of the plant. Obviously, the possible change of, e.g., maintenance intervals will affect the reliability of components and systems.

FAILURE REPORTS

One of the most important inputs to the reliability models comes from the failure reports. For new process plants the reliability data for the components are in general drawn from data bases derived from operational experience or from test data describing the behaviour of the components given the operating conditions. In the case of older process plants the failure reports may form the basis for a calculation of the present reliability of the components and, consequently, the present reliability of the plant.

One application of data from the failure report is to reveal possible ageing of components. A plotting technique such as TTT (Total Time on Test) plots (Bergman & Klefsjö, 1984) is as useful as any other measuring equipment in the plant, because it readily shows ageing as a deviation from a straight line. A deviation from normal in the TTT-plot may have to be supplemented by further information in order to interpret the result, but it is a good indication of possible component ageing and thus can be used to estimate whether maintenance periods can be prolonged or should be shortened, seen from a reliability point of view. The final decision about the maintenance condition of the components needs some further information which can be extracted from the system.

The information about components as well as the failure reports is part of the system's DHDB, which will be described later. The remarks written in the failure reports by the staff are an indispensable part of them and an important contribution to a 'manual' decision about the state of the components.

CONDITION MONITORING

Another possible source of data for the reliability model is input from the condition monitoring systems. Condition monitoring is measurement of the condition rather than the function of the single components. A bad condition of a component does not necessarily influence the functioning of the component in the sort term, but may do so in the longer term. Condition monitoring of critical components (cf. this book, Chapter 3.2) is an intelligent and efficient maintenance methodology for prevention of equipment breakdown. Condition monitoring methods can be classified in at least three different categories:

— On-line monitoring
— Off-line monitoring
— Process data monitoring

On-line monitoring is continuous measurements of, e.g., vibrations, bearing temperatures, deformations, lubrication oil flow, and power consumptions of motors.

Off-line monitoring is periodic measurement of values such as wall thicknesses, leakages, temperatures in selected locations, and efficiency of heat exchangers. The results of off-line monitoring have to be entered into the system manually.

Process data monitoring can be used for specific components such as pumps, for example, where a comparison of rotation, flow, pressure and pump characteristics could give an indication of the condition of the

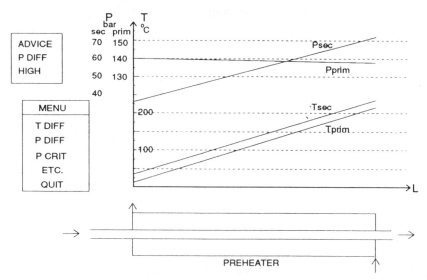

Fig. 2. Monitoring of temperatures and pressures in a preheater.

pump. In the case of heat exchangers a comparison between the calculated and the present mean temperature difference gives an indication of the efficiency of the heat exchanger, and this could contribute to the decision about when a cleaning of the heat transmission surfaces is necessary. Examples of such displays from process data monitoring are shown in Figs 2 and 3.

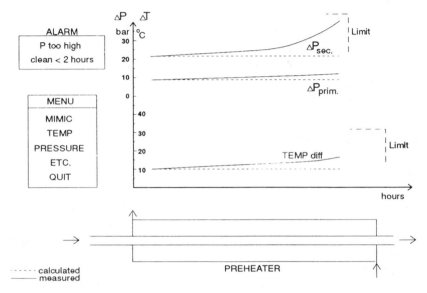

Fig. 3. Comparison of calculated and measured temperature and pressure differences in a preheater.

The link between an observed condition and the reliability of the component in question is not easy to establish and may in most cases be based on either recommendations from the supplier, general engineering judgement, or experience, if available. The area is not well developed for this purpose, because lifetime experiments are only possible for special components, e.g. electronic components, ball bearings and such types of spare parts which can be tested under laboratory conditions. It would be very useful for the reliability analysis if, for example, laboratory tests of bearings could result in criteria for the assessment of the residual lifetime of turbine bearings on the basis of vibration measurements on the turbine.

DATA BASE

The data base (Dynamic History Data Base) is one of the thoroughfares of all input and output of the system. The contents of the data base can be divided into several different 'areas' depending on the use of the data. The data base, for example, contains the following information:

— Technical information about each component
— Spare part information for each component
— Maintenance instructions
— Maintenance periods
— Various remarks about the components (from failure reports)
— Reliability data (initial and all updated data)
— Maintenance cost and time

RELIABILITY TEST FACILITY

One of the facilities of the dynamic reliability analysis is the possibility of testing operational and maintenance plans from the reliability point of view before they are carried out. This means that for every change in the plans the reliability can be assessed before the final decision about the change is taken. Another use of the dynamic reliability calculation is to optimize the system in case of changes of components or control equipment. Some components or controllers influence the reliability more than others, which is easy to check with the test facility. The facility could be useful in discussing the need to install redundant systems or not. The test facility may prevent investment in wrong components if there is a choice.

INTERFACE SYSTEMS

In this type of computer program, some things are specific for the single plant and some things are common to all plants. The primary intention of the program is to serve as a decision support system primarily for the staff involved in the maintenance plans and the operation plans, but it is also intended to give other members of the staff a better overview of the location of the critical areas of the plant, and this could contribute to a better understanding of the operation, and to a higher reliability of human actions.

In this system there are tree types of screen interfaces. The first type is mimic diagrams of systems and of single components, with the corresponding process data information shown as curves or columns or in another appropriate form of graphic presentation of the data and their corresponding limits.

The second screen type is the active input screen where failure reports, test systems and input of new data belong. For the main part of the input system, the displays are questionnaires to be filled in. It is important to design these questionnaires to be very easy to access and to have them tested by the people who are going to use them.

The third type of interface is the 'alarm system', the information system and the advice system. The 'alarm system' mainly gives information about exceeding the limits of different variables and advice about what to do. The information system will give a graphical or numerical, if appropriate, presentation of the variations in selected process parameters, such as, e.g. heat exchanger efficiency, as well as the results of statistical calculations. These curves and different types of calculations should serve as a support to the decision makers in making better decisions. The advice system should give advice about the need for changing the maintenance plans for the components in question. All these possibilities for alarms and advice should, eventually, result in a minimization of the operational and maintenance costs, which was the main aim of the project.

CONCLUSION

A concept for a reliabilty centred maintenance planning system has been described. The central idea in the concept is to base the maintenance on the actual reliability state of the plant in question and its components. This actual reliability state is calculated by means of a set of reliability models using measured data from the plant as input. The chapter has discussed the types of information which can be converted into input for the models. Furthermore, the interface to the users of the system has been touched upon.

During the development of the concept for a decision support system several interesting subjects for further work have arisen, for example

— What is the link between condition monitoring signals and reliability?
— How is information given to the staff in the right way?
— What is the system's requirements to the skills of the staff?

as well as many others.

It can be mentioned that a system using some of the same features as the concept described above is currently being installed in one of the nuclear power plants in Canada (King *et al.* 1990).

REFERENCES

Bergman, B. & Klefsjö, B. (1984). The total time on test concept and its use in reliability theory. *Operation Research*, **32**, 596–606.

King, F.K., Harvey, S.B. & Packer, C.E. (1990). An integrated program of risk assessment and operational reliability monitoring at Ontario Hydro. *Reliability Engineering and System Safety*, **27**, 231–40.

Taylor, J.R. (1982). An algorithm for fault tree construction. *IEEE Trans. on Reliability*, **R-26**, 2.

4.3

The Use of On-line Reliability Analysis for Maintenance Planning

PALLE CHRISTENSEN and HANS ERIK KONGSØ
Risø National Laboratory, DK-4000 Roskilde, Denmark

ABSTRACT

This chapter describes the outcome of a study of, and experiments with, the interaction between a reliability model and the strategies for operation and maintenance in a decision support system for maintenance planning. Models for operation and maintenance are normally verbal in nature, while reliability models are numerical, based on logic and statistics. In on-line reliability analysis the reliability model will work directly on component reliability data and data for operation and maintenance. The main object of the work reported is the creation of compatibility between models for operation and maintenance and reliability models.

INTRODUCTION

In maintenance planning in industrial plants, benefits can be derived from the use of a dynamic planning scheme where the actual reliability state of components and plant is taken into account in contrast to conventional maintenance planning on the basis of calendar time, operational time or number of demands.

Computer based maintenance planning and reliability analysis are two fairly well established disciplines. Computer based maintenance is described by Cawdery (1988), Petersen (1989), and Østvik in Chapter 4.1 of the present book. Traditional fault tree analysis is described in Platz and Olsen (1976) and Poucet (1985). The areas of overlap between mainten-

271

ance planning and reliability analysis are treated in Kirkeby and
McGlashan (1989), Petersen *et al.* (1989), and Johanson *et al.* (1990) and
by Paulsen and Lauridsen in Chapter 4.2 of the present book.

A deeper study of the interaction between the reliability model and the
strategies for operation and maintenance of a plant, as described in
Chapter 4.2, is treated here. As the domains of abstraction of reliability
models and those of common operation and strategies for maintenance
are not the same, consideration will be given to the translation of data
between those.

This chapter, as well as Chapter 4.2, reports on work done under the
projects 'A Technical/Economic System for Maintenance in Industrial
Plants' and 'Exchange of Information between Designer and User of
Industrial Plants' of the Nordic Terotechnology Programme.

The reliability model and the models for strategies of operation and
maintenance which will be described here are important parts of the
decision support system (DSS) for maintenance planning for industrial plants (Chapter 4.2) which is being developed by Risø National
Laboratory.

The decision support system will take input from a number of sources,
primarily

— measured values of parameters influencing component performance
  and reliability, e.g. vibrations, wear, excessive temperatures, power
  consumption, etc.;
— failure and repair reports input by staff;
— strategies for operation and maintenance.

The main target of the decision support is the plant maintenance planner,
though a dedicated user interface support information will also be
available to the plant operational staff, managers, and in fact the whole
organization.

The interface will give support by means of data derived from the
actual state of the system; output will be in the form of advice based on
results of calculations of system and subsystem reliability and statistics.

It is thus understood that the user interface is a very important part of
the system as it not only presents results, but also mediates interactively
the carrying out intermediate calculations for the production of end-
results.

The DSS is shown schematically in Fig. 1, where each box depicts a
separate function of the system software. The figure is slightly different
from Fig. 1 of Paulsen and Lauridsen in Chapter 4.2, in that some boxes

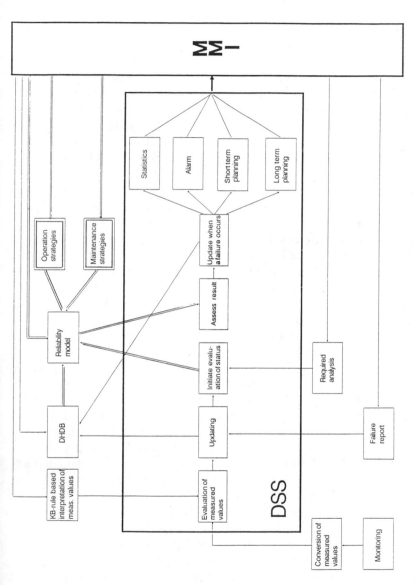

Fig. 1. Decision support system. Dual lines indicate areas of interest. MMI is the Man–Machine Interface.

and lines are double. The double line items refer to the parts under special consideration here.

RELIABILITY MODEL

The decision support system will supply the maintenance planner with a set of items of advice as an aid to his further decisions in both short and long term planning. The DSS will give advice on the basis of input from the plant condition monitoring system, the fault reports, and the reliability model for the plant. This model will have to describe the performance dynamically, i.e. always presenting up-to-date indicators. This means that plant configuration with subsystems and components as well as performance data for the latter should always be stored in an up-to-date state.

The input to the DSS from the reliability model will be a series of plant performance indicators such as plant availability, plant safety, and performance of essential subsystems of the plant.

The present work has been limited to the use of plant availability as a performance indicator. Conventional quantitative fault tree analysis has been used in the availability modelling. Based on plant strategy for operation it is decided which events are the top events. With failure mode and effect analysis the failures causing the top events can then be located and corresponding fault trees constructed with component and subsystem failures modelled as gates.

The fault tree analysis is carried out using two computer programs developed at Risø, i.e. FAUNET by Platz and Olsen (1976) and EM by Kongsø (1991). FAUNET and EM were originally made for DEC computers, but are now being transferred to PC. FAUNET will calculate the system unavailability as a function of time based on the fault tree topology and the corresponding reliability data. EM creates the user interface to FAUNET for input of fault tree topology and the reliability data, the latter comprising failure rate, average repair time, and fault type.

The reliability model applies data from models for strategies of operation and maintenance, as described below, as well as from the Dynamic History Data Base (DHDB) of the decision support system, where fault rates, experience gained from repair reports, information from component condition monitoring, etc., are stored.

On request the reliability model will present the momentary plant availability as a basis for identification of trends threatening the operation. The model can also be used for analysing the effects of proposed plant alterations.

The next two sections will describe in some detail the strategies for operation and maintenance, whereas the DHDB is described in Chapter 4.2. Operation and maintenance are described in terms well known to production and maintenance staff. The mapping of these terms on the reliability parameters will be discussed in some detail as there is no evident one-to-one correspondence between them, and an example will be given to visualize this matter.

STRATEGY FOR OPERATION

The strategy for operation of a plant will be a formalized part of the general technical description of the plant. The strategy will depend on the overall goals and strategies of the company, especially the type and volume of the product, where 'product' should be understood in a very broad sense as the output of a plant.

Overall goals and strategies are formulated by the company management in words, and from these the plant management formulate, also in words, the strategy for operation. For the model described here quantifiable parameters are needed. Østvik in Chapter 4.1 lists a number of such parameters, i.e.

— Production capacity
— Production regularity
— Production quality
— Technical safety
— Production availability, etc.

Such expressions are well known and partly overlapping, but they can all be reduced to the following set of parameters:

— Production capacity (under various time schedules)
— Availability
— Total production in plant lifetime
— Time schedule for the production
— Product quality
— Safety of equipment and personnel

Availability and capacity are very basic to the fulfilment of the higher strategy of producing a certain amount of goods in a certain time. The other factors are important, too, but availability and capacity most heavily influence plant maintenance requirements.

In this project the model for strategy of operation is very simple and easily explained as above, and all the data which are needed by the reliability model form a set of parameter values. These are kept in a file in the computer in the form of a table. From this table the reliability model can acquire values for its calculations. As mentioned earlier a certain amount of data adaptation will be needed before the reliability model can use the values of the operation strategy table.

STRATEGY FOR MAINTENANCE

The strategy for maintenance will reflect the strategy of operational requirements of the plant in order to create the possibility of fulfilling the latter. A maintenance plan will normally be defined during the latest part of the design phase for the plant. The maintenance programme will be based on more or less structured analysis methods and traditions in the company. Reliability Centred Maintenance (RCM) as mentioned in Chapter 4.1 is a method for optimizing the maintenance efforts. Changes of plant configuration and later introduction of new component types as substitutes for original ones, as well as reliability experience gained during operation, may change the original plans to a considerable degree.

Maybe the greatest advantage of the maintenance decision support system is the possibility of predicting changes to reliability and operational safety caused by proposed changes of plant. This can be done by running the reliability model with changed maintenance parameters in accordance with the properties of the proposed new equipment.

The main concepts of the maintenance strategy are the rules for

— preventive maintenance,
— distribution of the maintenance work within the staff, and
— information exchange between plant departments concerned.

Preventive maintenance may be based on the following:

— Calendar time
— Operation time
— Number of demands for operation
— Monitored conditions of the plant and equipment
— Premature maintenance during occasional downtime
— The dedicated plant maintenance staff
— Plant operators
— Hired staff from outside the plant

DERIVATION OF RELIABILITY MODEL PARAMETERS FROM OPERATIONAL AND MAINTENANCE DATA

As mentioned earlier the reliability model of the DSS receives input data from the DHDB and from the models for strategies of operation and maintenance.

Both in the plant design phase and in normal plant operation situations the maintenance strategy is derived from the plant availability requirement. It has been determined by experienced plant designers and plant managers by means of structured planning principles. There are two main tasks of the DSS to consider, i.e. the presentation of plant reliability changes if the reliability data in the DHDB change with unaltered maintenance strategy, and the opposite case in which the maintenance strategy is changing with unaltered DHDB values.

This paper focuses on the latter case where the DSS can help the user to find out if a proposed change in maintenance strategy will have an acceptable effect on plant reliability, before a decision on such a change is taken.

The two model parameters which can be influenced by change of maintenance strategy are the repair time and the test interval.

The repair time comprises the sum of the repair time itself and the time from detection until repair can start. Both of these time intervals will depend on which part of the staff takes care of the repair; all three groups may not be equally available, leading to different repair times. For some very special components the three groups cannot substitute for each other with the same quality of work. This fact could be treated in the reliability model by introducing a repair man ruining a sound component as a failure mode; the corresponding failure rate will be different for the different types of staff.

The test interval will be taken as the interval specified between times of preventive maintenance of components. The staff should be kept qualified to guarantee the maintenance intervals specified. In cases where this is not possible, the effect of prolonged test intervals can be found by means of the model, too.

EXAMPLE

This simple example will demonstrate the use of the model for estimation of the plant unavailability when maintenance factors influencing repair time are changed from the normal situation.

The example is a lubricating system for the main bearings of a power station turbine feed water pump. A pump driven by an electromotor is delivering oil from a reservoir, the oil being cleaned by a filter on its way. A piping diagram of the pumping system is shown in Fig. 2.

The main operational specifications are as follows:

Product: Lubrication oil supply
Capacity: 170 litre/s
Time schedule: Continuous for 1 year, then a few weeks revision, etc.
Quality: Particles in the oil <0·08 mm

Maintenance Specifications

Oil flow is monitored in the plant control room. Sudden total lack of flow will be caused by oil pump stop; this situation will cause turbine stop and require help from the plant maintenance staff. Decrease in oil flow may be caused by either loss of oil in the reservoir or by filter blocking. In both cases quick action from the operational staff will cure the fault and prevent turbine stop.

Reliability Model

The reliability model will be a fault tree where the top event is turbine stop because of no flow of oil to the feed water pump bearings. Figure 2 contains a table of failure modes of the components and the corresponding fault tree. The fault rates and average repair times are estimated with the plant maintenance staff and operators working as indicated above.

This example will consider the filter maintenance. Under normal conditions the filter will block the flow after 1000 hours of operation corresponding to a fault rate of 1000×10^{-6}/h. Normally flow will decrease slowly enough to allow operators to make a filter change without reaching a turbine stop. But it is anticipated that in one out of 20 cases blocking will happen too quickly; this means that filter blocking occurs $(1000 \times 10^{-6})/20$/h $= 50 \times 10^{-6}$/h. The filter change time is 1 hour for the operators.

This situation can be described by means of the fault tree, and the reliability data are shown in Fig. 3. The quantitative fault tree analysis can then be carried out in the mode with fault rates and repair times used as mean values in exponential distributions. The program is run with values from 0 to 8760 h (1 year) with results shown in steps of 730 h (1 month). The result of the analysis is shown in Fig. 3. Plant unavaila-

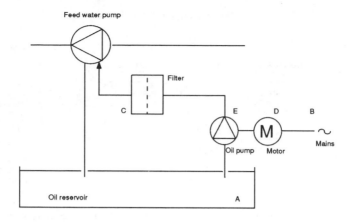

Label	Component	Failure mode	Fault rate x 10^{-6} h^{-1}	Mean repair time h
A	Oil reservoir	No oil	10	1
B	Power cable	Broken	10	2
C	Filter	Blocked	see examples	see examples
D	Motor	Broken	10	1
E	Oil pump	Broken	20	6

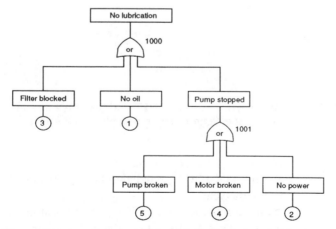

Fig. 2. Example piping diagram, table of failure modes, and fault tree for the top event.

TIME	UNAVAILABILITY		FAILURE INTENSITY	EXPECTED NO OF FAILURES
0.000	0.00000E+00	0.00000E+00	0.00000E+00	0.00000E+00
730.000	0.20997E-03	0.20997E-03	0.99979E-04	0.48656E-01
1460.000	0.20997E-03	0.20997E-03	0.99979E-04	0.12164E+00
2190.000	0.20997E-03	0.20997E-03	0.99979E-04	0.19463E+00
2920.000	0.20997E-03	0.20997E-03	0.99979E-04	0.26761E+00
3650.000	0.20997E-03	0.20997E-03	0.99979E-04	0.34060E+00
4380.000	0.20997E-03	0.20997E-03	0.99979E-04	0.41358E+00
5110.000	0.20997E-03	0.20997E-03	0.99979E-04	0.48656E+00
5840.000	0.20997E-03	0.20997E-03	0.99979E-04	0.55955E+00
6570.000	0.20997E-03	0.20997E-03	0.99979E-04	0.63253E+00
7300.000	0.20997E-03	0.20997E-03	0.99979E-04	0.70552E+00
8030.000	0.20997E-03	0.20997E-03	0.99979E-04	0.77850E+00
8760.000	0.20997E-03	0.20997E-03	0.99979E-04	0.85149E+00

TIME	UNAVAILABILITY		FAILURE INTENSITY	EXPECTED NO OF FAILURES
0.000	0.00000E+00	0.00000E+00	0.00000E+00	0.00000E+00
730.000	0.16498E-03	0.16498E-03	0.99984E-04	0.48659E-01
1460.000	0.16498E-03	0.16498E-03	0.99984E-04	0.12165E+00
2190.000	0.16498E-03	0.16498E-03	0.99984E-04	0.19463E+00
2920.000	0.16498E-03	0.16498E-03	0.99984E-04	0.26762E+00
3650.000	0.16498E-03	0.16498E-03	0.99984E-04	0.34061E+00
4380.000	0.16498E-03	0.16498E-03	0.99984E-04	0.41360E+00
5110.000	0.16498E-03	0.16498E-03	0.99984E-04	0.48659E+00
5840.000	0.16498E-03	0.16498E-03	0.99984E-04	0.55957E+00
6570.000	0.16498E-03	0.16498E-03	0.99984E-04	0.63256E+00
7300.000	0.16498E-03	0.16498E-03	0.99984E-04	0.70555E+00
8030.000	0.16498E-03	0.16498E-03	0.99984E-04	0.77854E+00
8760.000	0.16498E-03	0.16498E-03	0.99984E-04	0.85153E+00

TIME	UNAVAILABILITY		FAILURE INTENSITY	EXPECTED NO OF FAILURES
0.000	0.00000E+00	0.00000E+00	0.00000E+00	0.00000E+00
730.000	0.11588E-02	0.11588E-02	0.10488E-02	0.51041E+00
1460.000	0.11588E-02	0.11588E-02	0.10488E-02	0.12760E+01
2190.000	0.11588E-02	0.11588E-02	0.10488E-02	0.20416E+01
2920.000	0.11588E-02	0.11588E-02	0.10488E-02	0.28072E+01
3650.000	0.11588E-02	0.11588E-02	0.10488E-02	0.35729E+01
4380.000	0.11588E-02	0.11588E-02	0.10488E-02	0.43385E+01
5110.000	0.11588E-02	0.11588E-02	0.10488E-02	0.51041E+01
5840.000	0.11588E-02	0.11588E-02	0.10488E-02	0.58697E+01
6570.000	0.11588E-02	0.11588E-02	0.10488E-02	0.66353E+01
7300.000	0.11588E-02	0.11588E-02	0.10488E-02	0.74009E+01
8030.000	0.11588E-02	0.11588E-02	0.10488E-02	0.81665E+01
8760.000	0.11588E-02	0.11588E-02	0.10488E-02	0.89321E+01

Fig. 3. Results of analysis with FAUNET for the three instances of the example in the same order as described in the text.

bility, i.e. the probability at a moment that the plant is down, is 0·000 21 over the whole period, and the expected number of turbine shutdowns (top event) is 0.85 for the year.

By training the operators, both in identifying the beginning of the filter blocking and also in changing the filter, the repair time used in the reliability model was reduced to 0·1 h. A new computation gives an unavailability of 0·000 16 and an expected number of failures in one year of 0·85. The results are shown in Fig. 3.

In order to demonstrate the capability of the model to indicate a dramatic change in plant behaviour, it is anticipated that filter change is no longer done by operators, but by a busy maintenance staff with such a delay after detection of the flow decrease and call for maintenance that all filter blockings cause a top event; this leads to a fault rate of 1000×10^{-6}/h, and the mean repair time can be set to 1 hour.

A new run of the model gives an unavailability of 0·0012; the total number of expected failures for 1 year is 8·9. The results are shown in Fig. 3.

These figures show quite clearly that the 'performance' of the plant compared with the first instance of the example will be only moderately improved by operator training, i.e. the unavailability will decrease from 0·000 21 to 0·000 16, with 0·85 expected turbine stops caused by lack of oil in both cases. Using the busy maintenance staff to change filters decreases plant performance strongly; unavailability will be more than 10 times higher and the expected number of stops in one year will be 8·9.

CONCLUSION

It has been demonstrated that it is possible to build an on-line reliability plant model taking its input from models of strategies for operation and maintenance. At the stage when operation and maintenance data are fed into the reliability model, interactive support from the analyst will be needed. The feasibility has been further proved by an example executed using existing programs. The work with the example has shown that the conversion of operation and maintenance data into input data for a reliability model is even more difficult than initially anticipated. The user interaction may be substituted with a small expert system; this will necessitate that operation and maintenance strategies be formulated in standardized rules. Eventually a strictly defined practice for using these data could also be useful for plant managements. A further integration into a full decision support system thus seems very promising.

REFERENCES

Cawdery, P.R. (1988). Computer aided maintenance management—without the paperwork. In *Euro Maintenance 88*, Helsinki, 24–27 May.

Johanson, G., Holmberg, J., Laakso, K., Lehtinen, E. & Björe, S. (1990). *International Survey of Living—PSA and Safety Indicators*, Internal Draft Report NKS/SIK-1 (90) 10, Chapter 4.

Kirkeby, S.P. & McGlashan, R.S. (1989). Reliability engineering and life cycle costing in the Troll Phase 1 Gas Project. In *Reliability Achievement*, ed. T. Aven, Elsevier Applied Science, London, pp. 1–11.

Kongsø, H.E. *Event Modelling Program*. Risø National Laboratory. To be published.

Petersen, K.E. (1989). Reliability based maintenance systems; a knowledge based approach. In *2nd Scandinavian Artificial Intelligence Symposium*, Tampere, Finland.

Petersen, K.E., Rasmussen, B. & Jensen, P.H. (1989). Reliability analysis in life cycle cost estimation for small windturbines. In *SRE Symposium*, Stavanger, Norway.

Platz, O. & Olsen, J.V. (1976). *FAUNET: A Program Package for Evaluation of Fault Trees and Network*. Risø Report No. 348.

Poucet, A. (1985). CAFTS: Computer aided fault tree analysis. In *Proc. ANS/ENS Int. Topical Meeting on Probabilistic Safety Methods and Applications*, San Francisco.

APPENDIX. LIST OF ABBREVIATIONS

DHDB	Dynamic History Data Base
EM	Event Modelling (program)
FAUNET	Fault Trees and Network (program)
DSS	Decision Support System
MMI	Man–machine Interface
PC	Personal Computer
RCM	Reliability Centred Maintenance

4.4

Maintenance Management Profiles for Industrial Systems

UFFE THORSTEINSSON and CHRISTIAN HAGE

The Technical University of Denmark, Institute of Production Management and Industrial Engineering, DK-2800 Lyngby, Denmark

ABSTRACT

This chapter presents an analytical tool to be used by companies who require a visual presentation of the managerial efforts concerning maintenance. The tool can be used (1) to increase awareness of how the organization handles the managerial maintenance tasks, and (2) as a preliminary means of analysis before the company designs a new maintenance strategy. The chapter includes examples of maintenance management profiles for some different industrial companies. The examples illustrate how pitfalls in the management of the maintenance tasks can be detected.

INTRODUCTION

Through the 1970s and 1980s there have been rapid technological changes in industrial companies. The extension of automation and the complexity of the production systems have increased rapidly. These developments have been made possible by the use of information technology in combination with new designs in production technology.

The changes in design of production systems have been followed by a change in cost structure: labour costs have become less important and fixed costs more important. Logically this should also be followed by a change in care for the production factors, focusing more on the care and maintenance of the production systems.

Care for the production systems has played a major part in production management in the process oriented industries for a number of years, but for the more conventional industries maintenance has been a subject of only minor interest. With the new types of production systems, this picture has changed. Maintenance has become a subject of major interest for not only the process oriented industries. These other types of industries have had to increase the level of maintenance efforts, as shown in Fig. 1.

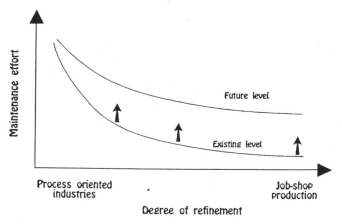

Fig. 1. The level of maintenance effort has to be increased in conventional industries due to the change in technology and the design of process oriented solutions for the production system concept.

Due to increased competition, efforts are being made to cut down both the delivery time and the inventories as well as to increase the delivery precision. An increasing maintenance effort might be the solution to this.

Another group of companies are facing a number of problems in relation to the risk of damaging the environment. This group also has to develop its maintenance activities.

Against this background we conclude that a number of companies are being forced—for different reasons—to look at their maintenance function from a new point of view and to increase their managerial efforts in the maintenance direction. They have to plan new strategies for maintenance. As a first step in this direction, it will be necessary to draw a picture of the present situation of their maintenance activities.

Based on this we set up our goal for the project VEDSTYR:

• To develop an analytical tool to be used by industrial companies to 'measure' or draw an X-ray picture or radar diagram of the managerial effort concerning maintenance.

The analysis should ask where and how we have to develop the maintenance management, if we want to reach a specified level.

A similar analytical tool has been developed to draw profiles of the project management efforts and to draw profiles of the capabilities of project management software. The two types of profiles have then been used in software selection for project management (Thorsteinsson *et al.*, 1986, 1987).

The experiences from this field show that a major feature of this 'X-ray' picture or radar diagram was the ability to answer the following question: Where do we actually allocate our managerial effort—and where should it be? The picture makes it clear to management where they do manage and *where they don't*. But the pictures have also been used to suggest a change in management structure to the organization.

The tool will be useful for two groups of companies:

- Companies who want to analyse the maintenance function. In this group we have
  — companies with their own maintenance function
  — companies who buy the maintenance services from a number of vendors
- Companies selling maintenance service

The purpose of the analytical tool is to:

- Improve the maintenance management by
  — clarifying the weak points in the actual maintenance management
  — follow-up former decisions about improvement of maintenance management: is the improvement implemented?
- Evaluate vendors of maintenance service, or present the 'maintenance service products' of a company
- Document the extension or quality of the maintenance management
- Compare maintenance management
  — between companies
  — for different parts of production systems in a company, with the aim of identifying differences
  — for different types of craftsman work

In an extended future version it is planned that the tool will be able to:

- Specify the requirements for facilities in maintenance management programmes

- Choose maintenance management programmes
- Analyse the extension of the use of an existing maintenance management programme.

THE CONCEPT OF THE ANALYSIS

Our main model for the maintenance function is a model with the maintenance as a controlled system as shown in Fig. 2. This will be used to illustrate how the analytical tool is designed.

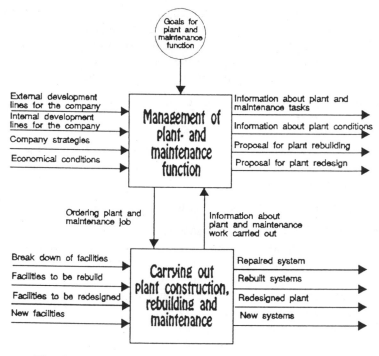

Fig. 2. The maintenance function as a controlled system.

Before that we must look at Fig. 3 which illustrates a control loop including the following phases:

- Formulation of goals and strategies
- Specifying and planning

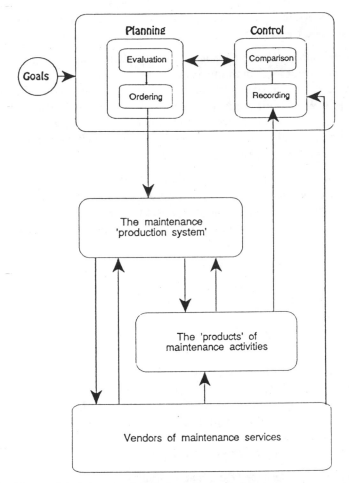

Fig. 3. The traditional control cycle in a controlled maintenance management system.

- Ordering or conducting the work
- Recording/supervision/control
- Analysis/evaluation

The phases represent different degrees of managerial effort. The sequence of the phases is logical and theoretical. In practical work we operate in a different way. When we have to do a specified task, we can decide to do it with more or less managerial effort, before we start the task.

Therefore we have designed a scale to 'measure the managerial efforts' or to describe the level of managerial efforts.

Managerial effort level 1: Conducting the work, making the activities
This is the lowest level of managerial effort. At this level we order the job without any further specification, planning and thoughts about how to do the job. We do not make any reflection about how to do the job, the working methods, the purpose, the time and resources required, the relation between different jobs, etc. Our managerial effort is limited to the short term handling of the job activities.

Managerial effort level 2: Specifying and planning
At this level we decide to make specifications and plans for how to do the jobs. The specification concerns jobs, tasks, activities and sequence of activities (paper flows, calculations, etc.) and a scheduling of the activities, etc.

Managerial effort level 3: Recording, control, checking, supervision
At this level we also record task progress, quality in relation to the specifications, the consumption of resources, etc. Besides this we also have active evaluation, deviations to specifications and plans. These activities may include simple calculations of deviations, which may result in decisions to put the activities on the right direction again.

Managerial effort level 4: Analysis
If we have deviations, we have to make decisions to correct activities. We may need to analyse different possible solutions and consider technical, economic, human and environmental aspects. A number of problems cross the 12 main maintenance managerial fields (see Fig. 4) and the analysing level therefore crosses these fields.

Managerial effort level 5: Goals and strategies
Here we have recognized the demand for a specified goal as a basis for the total work and the perception of different strategies for doing the jobs. Both goals and strategies are related to the general goals and strategies in the company.

This scale is the first fundamental part of our analytical tool. The next part is the definition of 12 main fields for managing the maintenance. These main fields are specified in Fig. 4. They are divided into three groups. The first six are related to the 'technical part' of the maintenance, the next group is related to the 'human part' of the maintenance and the last part to the economic conditions and consequences of the maintenance.

The maintenance 'products'
Specification of the different types of service and 'products' from the maintenance function. Specification in relation to each plant system.

Quality of the maintenance 'products'
Specification of quality of the maintenance jobs. Quality reports, certification documents, decision about maintenance standards etc.

Maintenance working methods
Specification of working methods, time standards, relation between maintenance jobs etc.

Maintenance resources
Equipment for maintenance, buying maintenance services, information about new equipment, capacity of equipment, usage control etc.

Maintenance materials
Inventory planning (spare parts etc), warehousing, relation to vendors etc.

Controlling maintenance activities
Scheduling of maintenance jobs, progress in work, manpower planning etc.

Internal relations in maintenance function
Relation to other department, corporation and coordination especially to production.

External relation for the maintenance function
Relation to external parties, especially related to environment and safety. Contact local authorities, press, labour organization, customer, vendors, neighbours etc.

Organization of the maintenance function
Design of the organization, selection of people, relation between groups of skills, responsibility and authority.

Structure of maintenance
Work break down of maintenance, responsibility for work packages, area structure, relation to accounting system, specification base (drawings, documentation) etc.

Maintenance economy
Economic control of maintenance: Cost estimates, budgets, cash flow, accounting for the maintenance function. Plant investment and financing.

Production economy
Production economy versus maintenance economy, cost benefit of maintenance.

Fig. 4. The 12 main maintenance management fields.

Based on these two dimensions—the 12 main fields and the five managerial effort levels—we design our fundamental structure of our analytical grid with 60 check points. (The frame is designed in analogy with a similar frame used to describe and identify the task for the management of production systems.)

Each of the 12 main fields is divided into a number of 'control areas in focus'. Figure 5 shows examples of focus areas for two of the 12 main fields of maintenance. For each focus area there are a number of check questions related to the five levels of managerial effort.

Maintenance working methods
- Standardization of working methods
- Choosing of working methods (development)
- Base of time standards for working methods
- Administration routines for maintenance

Maintenance resources
- Resource consumption
- Choice of the type of resources
- Buying of resources (equipment etc.)
- Vendors
- Buying of maintenance services

Fig. 5. Examples of focus areas.

Next we used our analytical grid to describe the management activities in the plant and maintenance function. Figure 6 illustrates how the analytical frame is used to elucidate the function. The five circles represent the five levels of managerial effort. We use the model as a communication medium for our maintenance management profiles. This increases the value of the information collected in the checklists. It is possible to show three dimensions in the radar diagrams:

(1) Number of sectors (our 12 maintenance management fields)
(2) Number of sector levels (our five managerial effort levels)
(3) Sector width as a percent of total possible sector width (in our case this is used to represent the extension of managerial effort at the actual level)

A managerial effort in a management field results in a scattered area in the relevant sector and level. The width of the scattering indicates the extension of the managerial effort.

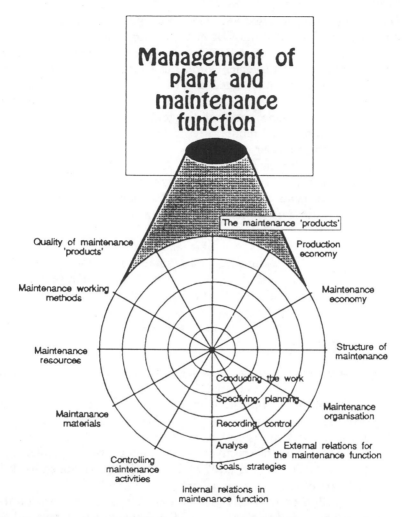

Fig. 6. The analytical tool includes a network which is used as background for drawing the maintenance management profile. The five circles represent the five steps in the managerial effort scale. The network has 60 check points.

The diagram has a built-in psychological feature based on the fact that a part-sector area is not proportional to the actual level. A part-sector representing level 4 (analysis level) will appear more dominant than a part-sector representing level 2 (specifying and planning level). This has the effect that the managerial levels with high scores appear more dominant and demand attention. This effect is very useful in the communication process, but it must be handled with care.

The managerial effort depends upon a number of factors. When we draw a maintenance management profile it is also necessary to describe both the system to be maintained as well as the goals to be achieved. Therefore we shall use the 12 main fields for maintenance to describe both the total maintenance task and the goals to be achieved.

This results in our final model (Fig. 7), based on the model shown in Fig. 2 and the three former models.

The assumptions for the radar analysis are that the production system is fixed and that there is a maintenance task. The radar analysis will be able to give statements about how the maintenance managerial task is solved. These statements are related to the degree of formalization of the management task.

Based on the picture of the maintenance management profile in the radar diagram it is possible to draw some conclusions. The radar diagrams are 'still pictures'—if we draw a new picture half a year later, it might be quite different due to the fact that the management has developed in some way.

The logical test of the shape of the profile in the radar diagram has two elements (Leisner, 1990):

- A test based on the variance inside the sectors representing the main maintenance fields, for example:
  — IF the efforts on the specifying and planning levels are smaller than that on the carrying-out level THEN there might be carried out some work not specified or planned;
  — IF the efforts on the specifying and planning level are greater than that on the conducting level THEN specified or planned work is not carried out;
  — IF the effort on the analysis level is greater than the efforts on the recording and controlling levels THEN analyses are attempted on missing data.

- Statements based on the extension of managerial efforts in different main fields:
  — IF the managerial efforts in controlling maintenance activities are greater than the managerial efforts in maintenance work methods THEN there might be insufficient time standards for the working methods.

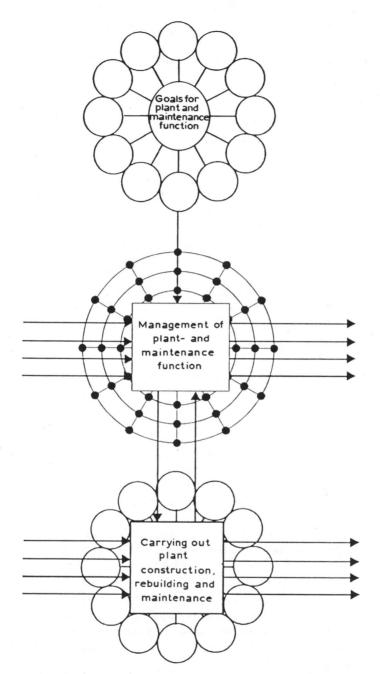

Fig. 7.

HOW TO USE THE TOOL—WITH OR WITHOUT
THE COMPUTER PROGRAM

The maintenance management profile and the radar diagrams are designed to be used either manually with a number of checklists or by a PC
computer program. The use of the tool depends on the purpose of the
analysis.

The phases in the analysis are as follows:

(1) Recording the existing maintenance managerial effort (radar diagram:
maintenance management profile). This is based on a systematic
recording of the maintenance management activities (checklists).

(2) Describing the system to be maintained and the 'degree of difficulty'
in the total maintenance task. The 'degree of difficulty' can be expressed by a number of factors:
— number of main systems
— number of subsystems
— number of connections between systems
— total plant investment
— total geographical plant area
— number of maintenance jobs per time unit
— number of plant specifications
— number of work specifications
— number of checkpoints
— number of plant redesigns per time unit
— number of maintenance service vendors
— number of inventory spare parts
— number of labour unions
— number of shifts and working hours in the system to be maintained
— number of workers in the maintenance function
— number of possible points where environmental problems exist,
etc.

(3) Describing the goals for the maintenance function. Which of these
goals determine the success of the maintenance function?
— The total maintenance cost is below X.
— The total cost of breakdown in the production system is below Y.
— The maintenance function is prepared to repair all main systems
within Z hours.

(4) Analysing the managerial effort based on (a) the goals, (b) the task,
and (c) the shape of the maintenance management profile. The

analysis focuses first on the coherence in the maintenance management profile and next on the evaluation of the shape of the profile in relation to the task and the goals.

(5) Development of a new maintenance management profile and, if necessary, new goals and strategies for the maintenance function.

(6) Supervision of the change.

In the development phase we have tested the concept for the analysis by making analyses based on checklists in a number of companies. Based on this we have had some experiences with the checklists and the diagramming technique. On this basis we have redesigned checklists, etc., and have developed a prototype of the PC program. At the moment this is under further development. As soon as we have a running version we are going to test this in cooperation with a number of companies. Figures 8–11 illustrate screens from the program.

Figure 8 shows three pop-up windows. The first is related to the main menu subject, 'Description'. From this it is possible to set up the data for the different parts of the analysis. Calling subject C, 'Data input form for radardiagrams, company', will give a new window showing the 12 maintenance management fields to which the checklists are related.

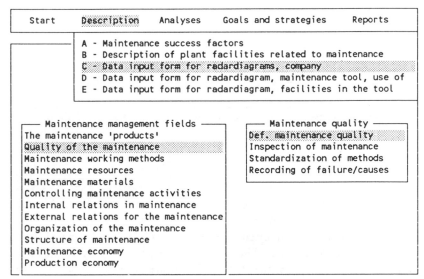

Fig. 8. Three-window screen for sequentially selecting the input form for checklist questions.

Choosing 'Quality of the maintenance' calls the next window with the four focus areas under the quality heading. Calling 'Def. maintenance quality' will give a new screen, shown in Fig. 9. This is the data input form for answering the checklist questions. The questions are answered with an estimated percentage for the extension of actual points. The program has default value 1 for the weight of the factors, but this can be changed by the user. The user can also write comments to the answers to an editor. These comments will be used in a report.

```
Quality of the maintenance:
Def. of maintenance quality

                                                          Weight Rank
1 Common understanding of quality for maintenance jobs       1     100
2 Quality specifications                                     1      0
3 Recording of failure and causes in maintenance            1      0
4 Analyzing quality parameters                              1      0
------------------------------ Editor -----------------------------
Line 1      Col 1         Indent  Insert
The maintenance workers have a common understanding of the quality level
which must be achieved for maintenance jobs.




Arrows:Move. F1:Help. F2:Editor F5:How F9:Screen to file. Esc,F10:Close.
```

Fig. 9. Two-window screen for answering the checklist questions about definition of maintenance quality.

Figure 10 shows a two-window screen for selecting the input form for describing the plant characteristics affecting the need for maintenance or factors which make the maintenance task difficult. Selecting menu B and the first management area, 'The maintenance products', calls the input form shown in Fig. 11. A number of factors are shown in Fig. 11. Rank percent is estimated based on the information available from the help function.

The next main menu, shown in Fig. 12, covers different types of

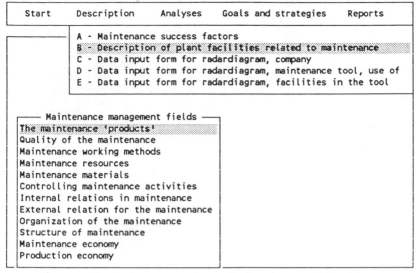

```
    Start      Description      Analyses   Goals and strategies   Reports

            A - Maintenance success factors
            B - Description of plant facilities related to maintenance
            C - Data input form for radardiagram, company
            D - Data input form for radardiagram, maintenance tool, use of
            E - Data input form for radardiagram, facilities in the tool


        ── Maintenance management fields ──┐
       │The maintenance 'products'
       │Quality of the maintenance
       │Maintenance working methods
       │Maintenance resources
       │Maintenance materials
       │Controlling maintenance activities
       │Internal relations in maintenance
       │External relation for the maintenance
       │Organization of the maintenance
       │Structure of maintenance
       │Maintenance economy
       │Production economy
```

Enter - Please choose menu. Esc - Closing the menu. F1 - Help.

Fig. 10. Two-window screen for selecting the input form for describing the plant characteristics influencing the extension of the maintenance tasks.

```
    Factors affecting the need for maintenance and management of maintenance:
    The maintenance 'products'

                                              Weight   Rank percent
    Average age of production system             1         20
    Number of construction redesigns             1         100
    Company culture for maintenance              1         100
    Number of maintenance types                  1         20
    Number of equipment drawings                 1         20
    Number of maintenance specifications         1         10
```

Arrows:Move. F1:Help. F2:Editor F5:How F9:Screen to file. Esc,F10:Close.

Fig. 11. Input form for describing plant characteristics related to the maintenance 'products'.

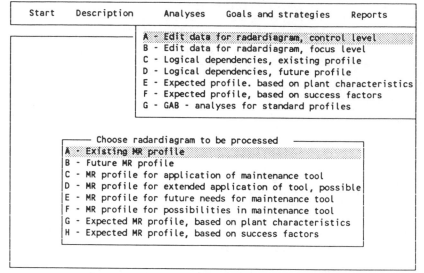

Fig. 12. Two-window screen for review of input information at different
levels.

activities—editing and analysis. Choosing A and A calls screen table 1
(Fig. 13) showing the calculated values for the managerial effort in the
different areas. Choosing C and A, as shown in Fig. 14, results in a logical
test of the radardiagram and messages about the consistency of the
managerial efforts, based on tests of the 12 main areas and between the
areas (Fig. 15).

From the main menu report it is possible to view the results on a
colour screen and in the form of printed reports. It is possible to make
comparisons between existing and future situations, and to print diagrams based on success factors or plant characteristics, etc. Figure 16
illustrates a plot where the factors making the maintenance task difficult
are aggregated (outer small circles) and shown together with the maintenance management profile (sectors in the inner circles). The picture
gives a visual indication that there are probably too few management
resources being devoted to the fields of (1) maintenance 'products', (2)
maintenance quality, (3) controlling the maintenance activities, and (4)
maintenance structure.

Company: GRAND & Co. Ltd.						
	1	2	3	4	5	G
1. The maintenance 'products'	93	50	3	5	0	30
2. Quality of maintenance	87	25	12	6	0	26
3. Maintenance working methods	80	12	0	0	0	18
4. Maintenance resources	50	35	32	0	8	25
5. Maintenance materials	83	3	0	0	21	21
6. Controlling maintenance activit.	66	25	0	0	0	18
7. Internal relations	100	8	0	0	0	21
8. External relations	35	30	25	0	0	18

Arrows:Move Enter:Checklists F1:Help F2:Editor F9:Screen to file Esc,F10:Close

Fig. 13. Screen table 1 for review of calculated values for managerial effort on the five levels.

Start	Description	Analyses	Goals and strategies	Reports

```
                              A - Edit data for radardiagram, control level
                              B - Edit data for radardiagram, focus level
                              C - Logical dependencies, existing profile
                              D - Logical dependencies, future profile
                              E - Expected profile, based on plant characteristics
                              F - Expected profile, based on success factors
                              G - GAB - analyses for standard profiles


             ──────── Analyses of expected profile ────────
             A - Evaluation of management efforts
             B - Calculation of expected profile
             C - Logical dependencies, expected profile
             D - GAB-analyses: existing - expected profile
             E - GAB-analyses: future - expected profile
```

Enter - Please choose menu. Esc - Closing the menu. F1 - Help.

Fig. 14. Two-window screen for selecting type of analysis.

```
┌─────────────────────────────────────────────────────────────────────┐
│  Start     Description     Analyses   Goals and strategies   Reports  │
│                         ┌───────────────────────────────────────────┐ │
│                         │ A - Draw radardiagrams                    │ │
│                         │ B - Compare radardiagrams, draw           │ │
│  ┌──────────────────────┤ C - Draw 2 radardiagrams                  │ │
│  │                      │ D - Draw radardiagram based on plant information │
│  │                      │ E - Draw radardiagram based on success factors   │
│  │                      │ F - Print checklist                       │ │
│  │                      │ G - Print explanation til answers to questions │
│  │                      │ H - Setup for printing to printer/file/screen  │
│  │                      │ I - Progress report                       │ │
│  │                      │ J - Print explanation to plant characteristics │
│  │                      │ K - Print explanation to success factors  │ │
│  │                      └───────────────────────────────────────────┘ │
│  │                                                                    │
│  │                                                                    │
│  │                                                                    │
│  │                                                                    │
│  └────────────────────────────────────────────────────────────────   │
└─────────────────────────────────────────────────────────────────────┘
```

Enter-Please choose menu. Esc-Close menu. F1-Help. F3-Editor

Fig. 15. Menu for selection of reports.

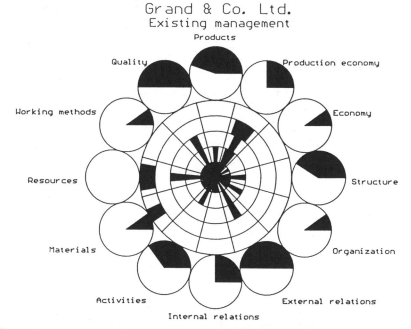

Fig. 16. Plant factors (outer, small circles) influencing the maintenance tasks related to the managerial efforts.

From our tests of the analytical tool we have some examples of maintenance management profiles from different companies.

One test was from a steelworks, where we analysed the maintenance of the bar mill. A number of persons in the organization were interviewed, based on the checklists, profiles were drawn for different maintenance functions (electrical wiring, mechanical maintenance, spare part warehousing, purchasing, etc.) and comparison were made. Figure 17 illustrates a profile from this study.

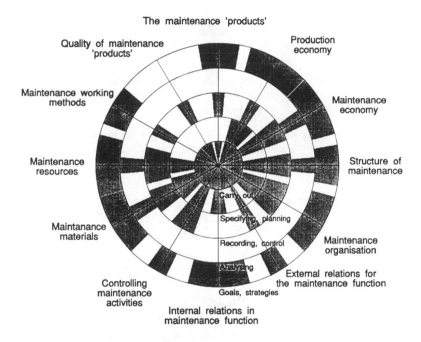

Fig. 17. Examples of maintenance management profile from a bar mill.

Another test was made in a company producing electrical lamps. The maintenance management profile from this study is shown in Fig. 18. A third test concerned a company selling industrial control systems and maintenance services for these systems; see Fig. 19.

Based on the shape of the profile it is possible to draw some conclusions about the quality of the management. This information is essential for formulation of new maintenance strategies.

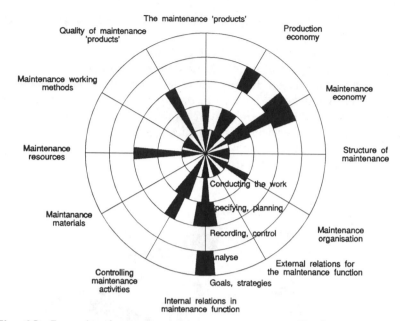

Fig. 18. Example of a maintenance management profile from a company producing electrical lamps.

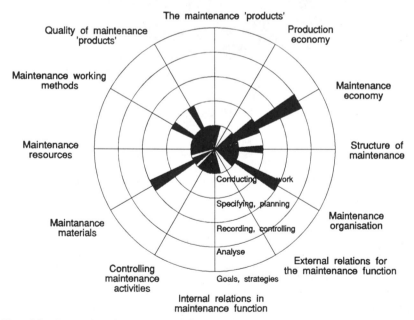

Fig. 19. Example of a maintenance management profile from a company selling industrial control systems and maintenance services for these systems.

REFERENCES

Leisner, J. (1990). *Vurdering af den logiske struktur i radar-diagrammer.* Student work. Driftsteknisk Institut, Højskole. (In Danish.)

Thorsteinsson, U. (1990). *Styringskoncept for vedligehold.* Driftsteknisk Institut, Danmarks Tekniske, Højskole. (In Danish.)

Thorsteinsson, U. & Godfredsen, M.L. (1990). *Beskrivelser af nøgleord.* Driftsteknisk Institut, Danmarks Tekniske, Højskole. (In Danish.)

Thorsteinsson, U., Riis, J.O. & Mikkelsen, H. (1986). (1) *Mikrodatamat projektstyring;* (2) *Afprøvning af software til projektstyring på mikrodatamater.* Driftsteknisk Institut, Danmarks Tekniske, Højskole. (In Danish.)

Thorsteinsson, U., Riis, J.O. & Mikkelsen, H. (1987). Project management aided by microcomputer. *Int. J. Project Management,* **5**(2), 91–6.

4.5

Marine Maintenance—The Development of a Computer Graphics Program for Modelling and Operation of Complex Systems

Nils Gjersøe Fog and Christian Aage

The Technical University of Denmark, Department of Ocean Engineering, DK-2800 Lyngby, Denmark

ABSTRACT

Ships and offshore structures are characterized by operating in a hazardous environment, the use of low manning rates, and high down-time costs. These factors, which demand a high degree of safety and reliability, put special emphasis on maintenance. A brief review of research areas relevant to marine maintenance is given. The use of modern high-speed computers in maintenance related engineering is discussed. Examples of computer applications in operation and maintenance management of large technical systems are given. The need for development of new computer based methods for visual definition and modelling of complex marine installations as a tool for obtaining a better overview and understanding during operation and maintenance activities is stated. The basics of a new and simple computer graphics approach for interactive creation and modification of physically oriented system models is presented. The method applies interactive definition of plane system figures situated in general planes in three-dimensional space. Two- and three-dimensional viewing, zooming and panning are used. A concept for hierarchical and parallel system figure definition by use of an absolute or a relative definition mode is described. The method will act as a low cost alternative or supplement to large scale CAD models—primarily suitable for the needs of operation and maintenance. Examples of practical applications of the modelling technique are shown. The possibilities of using the described method in combination with computerized maintenance management systems, reliability calculations and other engineering applications are discussed.

INTRODUCTION

Complex technical systems, such as ships and offshore structures, require a large flow of information to be handled by few people, often under stressful conditions, in order to operate efficiently. This emphasizes the need for effective tools in the field of information processing.

Marine engineering systems are composed of a variety of mechanical, electrical and chemical process machinery. Furthermore, a number of separate or linked computer systems are used for monitoring, data collection, process control, bridge control, traffic control, navigation, alarms, etc.

Effective and safe operation and maintenance of such complex systems require tools that can give the operator a clear understanding of part and overall system configurations and system data at all levels. Also in relation to overall design strategies a clear representation of complex system architecture is important.

There is an increasing demand for tools that can be used by non-expert and non-specialist decision-makers to comprehend, visualize and overview complex systems and their functionality.

An outline of a computer-based visual modelling system for this purpose has earlier been presented by the authors (Fog & Aage, 1990). In the present paper a more detailed description of the program is given together with some application examples related to ships and offshore structures.

MAINTENANCE RESEARCH

The most important research areas related to marine maintenance are shown in Fig. 1. A first distinction is made between research on the *component* level and that on the *systems* level. Most engineering research on the component level is carried out towards quantitative goals. On the systems level there is a need for development of qualitative methods, for example in the area of *functional visual models*. Other important areas are *administration* and *calculation*.

A second distinction can be made between condition-based and time-based preventive maintenance. The necessary data can be collected on an individual basis by condition monitoring, or on a statistical basis in the form of component life test data. General methods have been described by Bayliss *et al.* (1988), Durant *et al.* (1988), Gaushell and Darlington

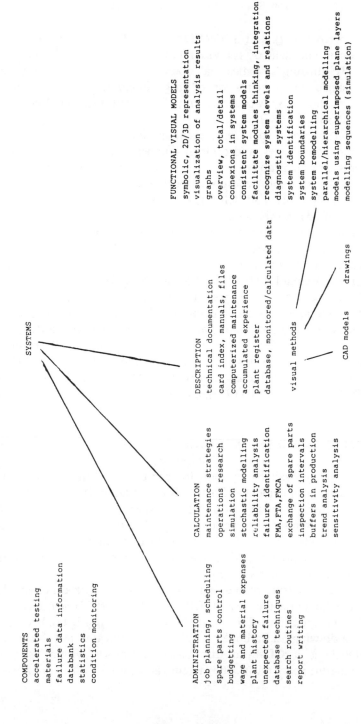

Fig. 1. Keywords in maintenance research.

(1987), Pomeroy (1987), and in OREDA (1984). Promising development is going on in the field of systems reliability estimation by stochastic methods. By utilizing statistics and operations analysis, reliability and safety of single compoments or of large integrated systems can be estimated, as shown by Madsen *et al.* (1986, 1989), Frankel (1988), and Solberg and Solem (1987).

Inspection intervals, spare part exchange intervals, use of buffers in stock or production lines, and optimal number of stand-by machines or components, are all problem areas where a computerized maintenance system can give valuable decision support to the operator. Lyytikäinen *et al.* (1988), Rumble and Chu (1987), and PROBAN (1987) have presented methods in this field.

Other important methods related to reliability of complex systems are the use of fault tree analysis (FTA), failure mode effect analysis (FMEA) and failure mode effect and criticality analysis (FMECA); see Ulerich and Powers (1988), Reinholds (1987), and McKelvey (1988).

Possible new areas include topics like visualization of analysis results, diagnostic techniques, systems definition by components and parts, systems functional flow, internal relations in systems, and methods for the consistent definition of system and subsystem boundaries. Research in man–machine relations is a related important aspect. Examples of references in these fields are Inagaki and Ikebe (1988), Lee *et al.* (1988), Sylla *et al.* (1988), Tamassia *et al.* (1988), and Yoon and Hammer (1988).

COMPUTERS AND MAINTENANCE

The commercially available systems for computerized maintenance and operation have been dedicated first of all to the administrative functions like job planning, budgeting, bookkeeping, spare parts handling, etc. In general, these systems do not yet comprise calculation modules based on stochastic methods or analysis of data obtained by condition monitoring.

In *Survey of Maintenance Management* (1987) a comprehensive survey is given of maintenance management programs.

In the area of marine maintenance several computerized systems for operation and maintenance exist. PRINS (1988) is a PC-based document system for the operation of offshore platforms and rigs. It holds data in the form of drawings, data books, catalogues, certificates, test sheets, etc. ILS (1988*a,b*) is a CD-Rom disc based inventory system used for localizing marine spare parts. The system can be used with PC-databases and carries information on 22 million spare parts worldwide. ISMIS (1988) is an integrated information system to be carried on board ships performing tasks in navigation, alarm logging, trim and stability, cargo and engine, information, voyage report, crew list, payroll, spare parts information, ship's account, planned maintenance, stock control, purchasing of parts, stores and provisions. Blanke and Tvedt (1989) describe an integrated ship control system developed in response to a demand for reduced ship manning. Enhanced surveillance, one-man-operated bridge, automated report writing, machine and equipment diagnostics to avoid accelerated wear and breakdown are some of the keywords in this system. AMOS-D (1988) is a PC-based maintenance system for ships and offshore installations. It has a plant register and supplies information on spare parts, job specifications, suppliers, planned maintenance, job orders, purchasing of specific parts, reporting and control. Some statistical and expense calculation is included. IPMS (1988) is a computerized management system developed for operation of subsea pipelines. The system is described by Svensson et al. (1988).

References to other computerized maintenance systems are MOSES (1988), a computerized bar chart, MCSI (1988) and MPMS (1988), maintenance control systems, and TEROMAN (1988), a computer aided maintenance management system.

THE HUMAN FACTOR

The human factor is a key element in maintenance management as in all management of large complex systems. It is a fact that even the most experienced and responsible operators can make serious mistakes, often without explicable reason. Most accidents with ships, aeroplanes, trains and cars are due to human and not technical errors. Three examples will illustrate the problem:

(1) In a paper factory the lubrication of all roller bearings in a new production line was put in the hands of one trusted worker. Unfortunately, the man consistently ignored one particular bearing for two years, resulting in a very costly repair and production stop.

(2) On a passenger aeroplane, loss of lubrication oil pressure was observed in flight on all three engines nearly simultaneously. The reason was that magnetic plugs for collection of wear particles had been changed on all three engines by one mechanic, who had failed to install the necessary rubber seals on all plugs.

(3) The Piper Alpha disaster in July 1988 was allegedly caused by a stream of hydrocarbon condensate being sent through a production line where a safety valve had been removed for scheduled maintenance and repair. The whole platform and 167 lives were lost.

In all three cases the human factor was the direct cause of serious failure in well-designed systems. In all cases it was the systematic maintenance itself that paradoxically led to the failure.

Effective measures against the problems of human failure include spreading out the maintenance jobs over time and personnel, making back-up systems really independent, also in terms of maintenance, and securing optimum system state information and overview for the operator.

The traditional text messages and numbers on paper or screen are not well suited for these purposes. Interactive, simple but realistic computerized graphical displays seem to be the most effective tools available today.

SYSTEMS MODELS AND COMPUTER GRAPHICS IN DESIGN, OPERATION AND MAINTENANCE

The increasing complexity displayed in modern ship and offshore technology emphasizes the need for good tools to help understand system functionality and architecture. Modern computer methods combined with the use of computer graphics possess a large potential for development of new engineering tools in this modelling area.

Technical systems are traditionally described by the use of drawings, card indexes, files, books and text manuals. CAD definition is a recent development as a method to model complex systems. Database and CD-Rom disc storage technology as well as interactive video are new information processing techniques which are able to capture and keep track of large amounts of information. A typical CAD model of offshore process equipment is shown in Fig. 2.

The intention of such a model is often to create a physical resemblance between the system object and the system model. The main use is in design and manufacturing, giving physical visualization and keeping track of pieces and geometries. The physical model is furthermore a foundation for automated manufacturing techniques (CAM and CIM). For operation and maintenance applications CAD models are often too detailed and complicated and other types of models must be considered.

Fig. 2. A typical CAD model of offshore process equipment.

Other computerized models are presently being developed in the area of functional visual models (see Fig. 2). The development is primarily related to control room management of process equipment and is based on displaying diagrams and drawings by computer graphics techniques. The use of colour display will aid the operator during plant and process operation. An example of this type of graphics software is SCREEN-WARE (1988) which is a PC-based computer screen animator primarily intended for use in the process industry, Fig. 3.

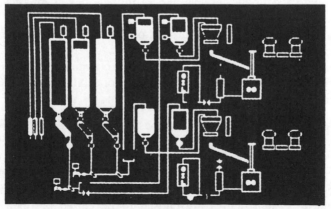

Fig. 3. Computerized process diagram as a system model.

Automation systems designed for use in the offshore industry typically use CAD techniques or computerized diagrams to display system architecture. An example is McDermott (1989).

MODSY: A COMPUTER GRAPHICS PROGRAM FOR COMPLEX SYSTEMS

The development of a computer graphics program for the modelling of complex technical systems is going on at the Department of Ocean Engineering, The Technical University of Denmark. The program uses interactive computer graphics and is characterized by the following qualities:

- Sketch-like geometrical visual modelling of complex systems.
- Easy build-up of system models, alternative to CAD modelling.
- Structure, consistency, breakdown of system hierarchy into details.
- Full three-dimensional definition of system models by use of plane system figures.
- Parallel/hierarchical representation of system architecture using absolute/relative definition mode.
- Three-dimensional visualization including plane projections, perspective, zoom and pan.
- Easy visual modification of system models by use of system blocks. Fast processing and presentation of the modified model.
- Use for obtaining overview, understanding of system functionality and architecture.
- Building of symbolic models and of models having physical resemblance to the real system.
- Use also by non-experts for design, operation and maintenance.
- Possible future use in combination with calculation modules.
- Interactive program control by keyboard command and mouse.
- Storage of data in Unix-files space. Use of relational databases as a future possibility.

A system part is modelled by the basic geometrical element which is called a *system figure*. System figures are general plane figures defined on the screen by mouse digitizing. The definition is always carried out in a chosen plane projection. Normally, a plane parallel to one of the three major coordinate planes is chosen, but a completely general plane could be specified. System figures are chosen to be closed or open lines or curves. A full three-dimensional geometrical definition of the figures is used. Each system figure is characterized by:

— name
— supername
— colour
— closed/open figure
— curvetype
— starting point
— definition point coordinates

A *name* is assigned to each system figure when defined. Two modes of definition are possible:

— absolute definition mode
— relative definition mode

Whether the absolute or relative mode is applied is determined by the *supername* also assigned to each system figure. If *supername* is entered as *global*, a system figure is defined in absolute mode. If *supername* is chosen to be a previously defined system name, this will cause the system to belong to this superior system and it is said to be defined in relative mode.

By use of system figures, the system parts, subsystems or components are modelled. Normally, closed lines or curves are preferred for this purpose, but open system lines could be chosen, for example if only a connection between two system figures is modelled. In Fig. 4 some possible system figures are shown.

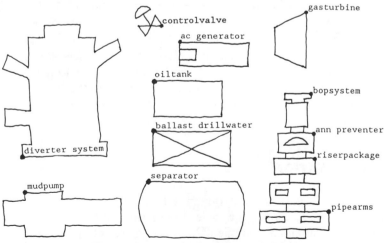

Fig. 4. Some possible system figures.

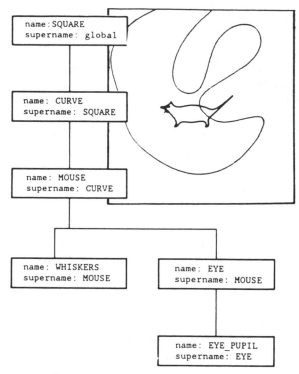

Fig. 5. System figures and hierarchy.

By using the relative definition mode it is possible to create system blocks, Fig. 5. By use of a single command it is possible to move the whole system block in three-dimensional space: only a new position for the starting point of the top system is digitized in a chosen plane and all lower level system figures in this system hierarchy will automatically be moved to have the same relative position in relation to the top system. A new *supername* for the top system could be specified in this process. Figures 5 and 6 illustrate how a system block can be moved.

IMPLEMENTATION

The program is implemented on an HP 9000 computer and mainly programmed in C. Some lower level Fortran routines are included. HP-Starbase graphics are applied. A colour subset of approximately 50

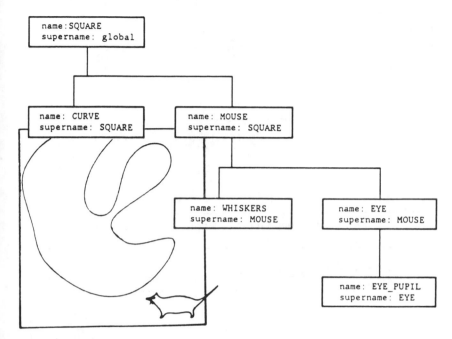

Fig. 6. System figures and hierarchy after the figure 'mouse' has been moved.

colours is used. All system data are stored on a system data stack. System parts are recognized only by their 'name' and the stack is fully updated each time a change has been made. The data are stored in Unix-files. Data for a single system element are shown in Fig. 7.

Only a set of two-dimensional coordinates for each defined system object is stored on the system coordinate stack. In addition, a set of coordinates defining the system definition plane and the name of the first superior system (*supername*) are stored. This representation will make no distinction between relatively and absolutely defined system figures.

In the present prototype version of the program only 100 system figure elements can be processed as one structure. Several parallel system structures can be defined and loaded by a single command. A keyboard driven command module is used for interactive communication with the program.

An extract of the manual sheet showing some of the implemented commands is shown in Fig. 8.

A basis for the modelling concept is the use of geometrical calculations.

```
Data for system no.      3
-----------------------------------------------------------
system.name.................:pip2
supername...................:zeebrugge
definition.plane.coor.index.:      3
definition.plane.coordinate.:+0.000000E+00
text.size.factor............:+5.757422E-03
pitch.out.of.def.plane......:+0.000000E+00

system contour
number.of.defining.points...:      23
line/curve.as.contour(2,4)..:      4
color.of.contour............:      12

contour definition points, pairs of coordinates:

+2.313487E+02 -6.230713E+02 +2.313665E+02 -6.234518E+02 +2.313665E+02 -6.234518E+02
+2.313665E+02 -6.234518E+02 +2.317054E+02 -6.239869E+02 +2.317054E+02 -6.239869E+02
+2.317054E+02 -6.239869E+02 +2.314141E+02 -6.241832E+02 +2.314141E+02 -6.241832E+02
+2.314141E+02 -6.241832E+02 +2.313665E+02 -6.242188E+02 +2.313130E+02 -6.243674E+02
+2.314141E+02 -6.245161E+02 +2.314973E+02 -6.245637E+02 +2.314973E+02 -6.245637E+02
+2.314973E+02 -6.245637E+02 +2.362658E+02 -6.281252E+02 +2.362658E+02 -6.281252E+02
+2.362658E+02 -6.281252E+02 +2.359269E+02 -6.287435E+02 +2.359269E+02 -6.287435E+02
+2.359328E+02 -6.287435E+02 +2.357723E+02 -6.294154E+02
```

Fig. 7. Unix-file data for a single system element.

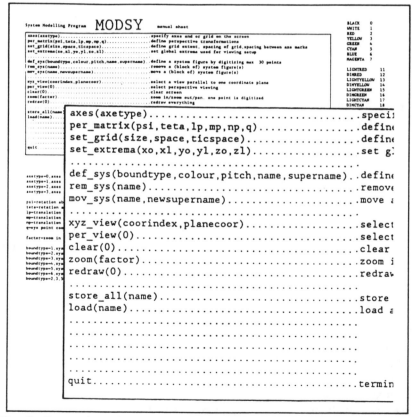

Fig. 8. Extract from the manual sheet showing typical program commands.

Definition of system figures is carried out interactively on the screen using the mouse. System figures are generated as B-spline curves. Depending on the chosen mode of definition, it is simple to generate combinations of smooth curves and polygon lines. B-spline representation is chosen for its ability to easily represent complicated shapes and for the sake of obtaining simple mathematical consistency.

Sub-programs for rendering and visualization have been developed. They perform coordinate transformations using homogeneous coordinates, visualization by plane projections to the three coordinate planes, or perspective projection, zooming and panning.

EXAMPLES

The following examples are included to illustrate possible modelling principles. The have not been modelled in detail, but will give an idea of the concept. Only black-and-white reproductions of the computer screen colour images are shown. The original screen images display up to 50 different colours, also using variable colour and light intensity.

North Sea Pipelines and a Harbour

Figure 9 shows in principle how a model of the North Sea could be created. The model, which is primarily a plane model, includes most of

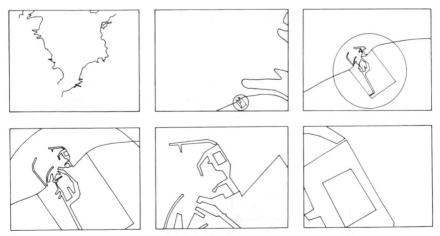

Fig. 9. Basis for a North Sea model. Black and white reproduction from computer colour display.

the North Sea and its coastlines. A model of a single harbour (Zeebrügge) is included. The model unit has been chosen as 1 km.

Representation of sizes down to 0.1 m is possible without round-off errors. This model could act as a superior framework where oilfield locations, major pipeline routings, etc., are mapped. The name of an oilfield could be a model name itself, where platform locations, pipelines and subsea installations are modelled within.

Platform

A possible principle for the modelling of a single offshore platform installation is shown in Fig. 10. The modelling is done in a semi-physical way. Other more abstract, symbolic diagrammatic modelling concepts could also be applied and perhaps serve well for operation and maintenance purposes. The model could incorporate the modelling of platforms,

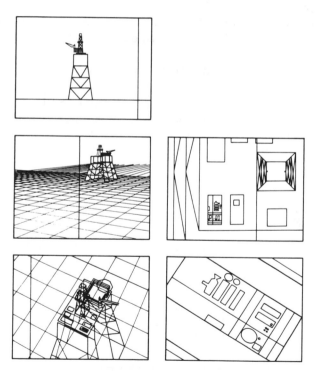

Fig. 10. Simple model of an offshore platform.

topside installations, riser and pipeline configurations. Further detailing than displayed in the model could perhaps preferably be modelled in separate lower level system models to avoid confusion of lines in the three-dimensional visualization. These lower level systems could apply the same units and the same coordinate system. The loading of a lower level model is carried out by typing a single command, see Fig. 8.

FURTHER DEVELOPMENT

A natural further development of the described modelling concept and computer program would be the integration with a relational database, or the use of the program as an application model in a computerized maintenance management system. Visualization of process simulation and system states are obvious possibilities. Visualization of diagnostic techniques, search procedures, results obtained by reliability analyses as well as the use for operator training and education represent other possibilities.

In Fig. 11 examples are shown of complex technical installations that would seem obvious to model. They include a process facility and a fleet of ships. Here the ship colours could be shown in one main definition plane as illustrated in Fig. 11. System blocks and figures for the detailed modelling of each ship could be defined in parallel definition planes, thereby creating a three-dimensional model.

CONCLUSIONS

Typical research areas relevant to maintenance are discussed. Examples of the use of computers in relation to marine operation and maintenance are given.

Visual systems modelling by modern computer graphics techniques is discussed. It is stated that there is a growing need for the development of new tools for representation, definition and modelling of complex technical systems. The capacity of modern computers to store, process and display information gives good prospects for matching this need.

A simple concept for geometrical visual systems modelling using computer graphics is proposed. The concept has been implemented in a prototype computer program. Examples which have been modelled by use of the program are given.

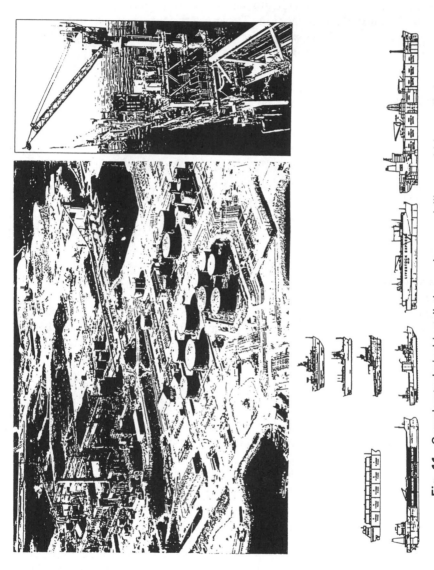

Fig. 11. Complex technical installations where modelling could be applied.

ACKNOWLEDGEMENTS

This work was carried out as part of the Nordic Research Programme on Terotechnology, sponsored by the Nordic Industrial Fund and the Danish Technical Research Council.
The command module used for interactive program control is based on ideas developed in Navco Aps by Otto Jacobsen and Jan Hee. Hugo Heinicke has given valuable assistance with the illustrations and Marianne Bonde typed the manuscript.

REFERENCES

AMOS-D (1988). Maintenance Systems, Spectec Consult AS, Kongensgt. 6, 0253 Oslo 1, Norway.

Bayliss, M., Short, D. & Bax, M. (1988). *Underwater Inspection*. E. & F.N. Spon, London.

Blanke, M. & Tvedt, E.I. (1989). Tomorrow's ship automation systems. *Schiff & Hafen*, **41**(8), 42–5.

Durant, W.S., Lux, C.R. & Galloway, W.D. (1988). Data bank for probabilistic risk-assessment of nuclear-fuel reprocessing plants. *IEEE Trans. Reliability*, **37**(2), 138–43.

Fog, N.G. & Aage, C. (1990). A concept for computerized modelling of complex systems as a tool for marine maintenance, *Proc. Ninth Int. Conf. on Offshore Mechanics and Arctic Engineering, OMAE'90*, ASME, Houston, TX, pp. 525–32.

Frankel, E.G. (1988). *Systems Reliability and Risk Analysis*, 2nd edition. Kluwer Academic Publishers, Dordrecht, The Netherlands.

Gaushell, D.J. & Darlington, H.T. (1987). Supervisory control and data acquisition. *Proc. IEEE*, **75**(12), 1645–58.

ILS (1988*a*). Design data detailed. *The Motor Ship*, **68**, No. 811, 44–5.

ILS (1988*b*). *Inventory Locater Service*, 3781 Premier Cove, Memphis, TN 38118.

Inagaki, T. & Ikebe, Y. (1988). A mathematical analysis of human–machine interface configurations for a safety monitoring system. *IEEE Trans. Reliability*, **37**(1), 35–40

IPMS (1988). Integrated Pipeline Management System for Marine Pipelines and Risers, DHI/R&H Pipedata, Teknikerbyen 38, DK-2830 Virum, Denmark.

ISMIS (1988). *Integrated Ship Management Information System*. Data-Ship (UK) Ltd, 215 Vauxhall Bridge Road, London SW1V 1EJ.

Lee, K.W., Tillman, F.A. & Higgins, J.J. (1988). A literature survey of the human reliability component in a man–machine system. *IEEE Trans. Reliability*, **37**(1), 24–34.

Lyytikäinen, A., Viitasaari, O., Päivinen, R. & Ristikankare, T. (1988). Improved management of electric switching stations by using a computerized RAM-data system module. In *Proc. EuReData Symp.*, September 1988, Stockholm. 11 pp.

Madsen, H.O., Krenk, S. & Lind, N.C. (1986). *Methods of Structural Safety*. Prentice-Hall, Englewood Cliffs, NJ.

Madsen, H.O., Sørensen, J.D. & Olesen, R. (1989). Optimal planning for fatigue damage of offshore structures. *Proc. ICOSSAR'89, 5th Int. Conf. on Structural Safety and Reliability*, San Francisco. ASCE, New York, pp. 2099–106.

McDermott (1989). *The McDermott International Offshore Automation Package*. McDermott Offshore Automation, PO Box 36100 Houston, TX 77236.

McKelvey, T.C. (1988). How to improve the effectiveness of hazard and operability analysis. *IEEE Trans. Reliability*, 37(2), 167–70.

MCSI (1988). Maintenance Control Systems Inc., 7350 S. Gallup St., Littleton, CI 80120.

MOSES (1988). *Efficient Workshop Scheduling. A Computer Bar Chart for Better Workshop Control*. National Engineering Laboratory, East Kilbride, Glasgow G75 0QA.

MPMS (1988). *Maintenance Engineering Systems*. Microsystems Technology Ltd, Old Council Offices, Toft Road, Knutsford, Cheshire WA16 6YA, UK.

OREDA (1984). *Offshore Reliability Data Handbook*, 1st edition. Veritec and Penwell, Høvik, Norway.

Pomeroy, R.V. (1987). The generation and use of reliability data for marine engineering systems. *Proc. ICMES'87, Fourth Int. Symp. on Marine Engineering Systems*, September 1987, Malmö, Sweden, pp. 48–66.

PRINS (1988). *Document Information System*. EB Industry and Offshore, Solaveien 3, PO Box 3860, N-5033 Fyllingsdalen, Norway.

PROBAN (1987). *Examples Manual for PROBAN: Probabilistic Analysis Program*. A.S. Veritas Research Report No. 86-2038, July 1987, Høvik, Norway, 71 pp.

Reinholds, E. (1987). Fault tree analysis as a tool of safety analysis of submarine systems. *Proc. ICMES'87, Fourth Int. Symp. on Marine Engineering Systems*, Malmö, Sweden, pp. 88–104.

Rumble, E.T. & Chu, B.B. (1987). An approach for integrating plant operations and maintenance information with system reliability analysis. *Nucl. Techn.*, 79, 7–19.

SCREENWARE (1988). *Controls for Industry*. Starkstrom, Beith Road, Johnstone PA10 2NS, Strathclyde, UK.

Solberg, D.M. & Solem, R.R. (1987). Safety and reliability—a methodological and systematical approach. *Proc. ICMES'87, Fourth Int. Symp. on Marine Engineering Systems*, Malmö, Sweden, pp. 67–75.

Survey of Maintenance Management (1987). Conference Communication, Monks Hill, Tilford, Farnharn, Surrey GU10 2HJ, UK, 12 pp.

Svensson, T., Larsen, L.C., Hinstrup, P.I. & Nielsen, J.A. (1988). Development of an integrated pipeline management system (IPMS). *Proc. Third Hydrocarbon Symp.*, Luxembourg. 16 pp.

Sylla, C., Drury, C.G. & Babu, A.J.G. (1988). A human factors design investigation of a computerized lay-out system of text-graphic technical materials. *Human Factors*, 30(3), 347–58.

Tamassia, R., Di Battista, G. & Batini, C. (1988). Automatic graph drawing and reliability of diagrams. *IEEE Trans. Systems, Man, and Cybernetics*, 18(1), 61–79.

TEROMAN (1988). Computer Aided Maintenance Management. Scicon Ltd, Wavendon Tower, Wavendon, Milton Keynes MK17 8LX, UK.

Ulerich, N.H. & Powers, G.J. (1988). On-line hazard aversion and fault diagnosis in chemical processes: the diagraph + fault-tree method. *IEEE Trans. Reliability*, **37**(2), 171–7.

Yoon, W.C. & Hammer, J.M. (1988). Aiding the operator during novel fault diagnosis. *IEEE Trans. Systems, Man, and Cybernetics*, **18**(1), 142–7.

Index